WRITING WITH AUTHORITY

A Guide to the Research Process

WRITING WITH AUTHORITY

A Guide to the Research Process

DELIJA J. VALIUKENAS
Bridgewater State College

Random House
New York

First Edition
987654321

Published in the United States by Random House, Inc., and simultaneously in Canada by Random House of Canada Limited, Toronto.

Library of Congress Cataloging-in-Publication Data

Valiukenas, Delija J.
Writing with authority.

Bibliography: p.
Includes index.
1. Report writing. 2. English language—Composition and exercises. 3. Library orientation.
I. Title.
LB2369.V25 1986 808'.042 86-27968
ISBN 0-394-36334-5

Cover design by Katherine Von Urban
Design and composition by Arkotype Inc., New York, NY

Manufactured in the United States of America

Acknowledgments

Basic Books From THE GAY WORLD by Martin Hoffman, copyright © 1968 by Basic Books, Inc., Publishers.

R. R. Bowker Company From THE SUBJECT GUIDE TO BOOKS IN PRINT, 3, 1982–83, page 5969.

Delacorte Press/Seymour Lawrence Excerpted from the book HOW CHILDREN FAIL Revised Edition by John Holt. Copyright © 1964, 1982 by John Holt. Reprinted by permission of Delacorte Press/Seymour Lawrence.

Encyclopaedia Britannica "Bowerbird" from ENCYCLOPAEDIA BRITANNICA, 14th Edition (1972), 4:32; from "Courtship, Animal," 6:669–671; from "Khyber Pass," 13:337–338, in ENCYCLOPAEDIA BRITANNICA, 14th Edition (1972).

Esquire THE BLACK AND WHITE TRUTH ABOUT BASKETBALL: A SKIN-DEEP THEORY OF STYLE by Jeff Greenfield. Reprinted with permission from *Esquire* (October 1975). Copyright © 1975 by Esquire Associates.

Grolier The following excerpts from THE ENCYCLOPEDIA AMERICANA, 1986 edition: from "Baths and Bathing," 12:363; "Comics," 7:370; "Geisha," 12:363; "Graffiti," 13:142; "Japan," 15:712; "Judas Iscariot," 16:205; "Hansel and Gretel," 13:779; "Everglades," 10:724, 725–726; "Marriage," 18:345, 346–347; and "Clothing," 10:103–104. Reprinted with permission of *The Encyclopedia Americana,* © 1986 by Grolier, Inc.

Harper & Row From STRONG POISON by Dorothy Sayers, © 1930, reprinted by permission of Harper & Row, Publishers, Inc., David Higham Associates, and Victor Golancz, Ltd. From THE ART OF LOVING by Erich Fromm, specified excerpt on pages 18–21. Copyright © 1956 by Erich Fromm. Reprinted by permission of Harper & Row, Publishers, Inc.

Harvard Business Review Excerpt from THE WORK ALIBI: WHEN IT'S HARDER TO GO HOME by Fernando Bartolomé (March–April 1983). Copyright © 1983 by the President and Fellows of Harvard College; all rights reserved. Reprinted by permission of Harvard Business Review.

Harvard Medical School Health Letter From A LEISURELY LOOK AT STRESS. Excerpted from the October 1979 issue of *The Harvard Medical School Health Letter* © 1979 President and Fellows of Harvard College.

Alfred A. Knopf From WORD PLAY by Peter Farb. Copyright © 1973 by Peter Farb. Reprinted by permission of Alfred A. Knopf, Inc.

Macmillan From THE WORLD OF WINES, Revised Edition, by Creighton Churchill. Copyright © Creighton Churchill 1963, 1964, 1974. Reprinted with permission of Macmillan Publishing Company.

The National Observer From HOW THE SCANDALS OF HISTORY LEFT . . . MUD ON THE WHITE HOUSE STEPS by James R. Dickenson. Reprinted by permission of *The National Observer* © Dow Jones & Company, Inc., 1973. All rights reserved.

Nation's Business A FRONTIER FOR U.S. BUSINESS by Henry Altman. Reprinted by permission from *Nation's Business,* December, 1985. Copyright 1985, U.S. Chamber of Commerce.

Newsweek "A Blossoming in China Trade" by Merrill Sheils, 22 September 1980; "Reagan's War on Drugs" by Mark Starr, 9 August 1982; "What TV Does to Kids" by Harry F. Waters, 21 February 1977. Copyright 1980, 1982, 1977, by Newsweek, Inc. All rights reserved. Reprinted by permission.

The New York Times "American wines are . . ." by Terry Robards Wine Talk, 1/21/81; "Progressive educators are keenly aware . . ." by Amitai Etzioni, 9/26/76; New York Times Index–Wine, 1978; New York Times Index page 1495, 1979; New York Times Index, 1981 (Wine); New York Times Index July–Sept. 1982 (Wine). © 1976/78/79/81/82 by The New York Times Company. Reprinted by permission.

The New Yorker From: A CONCRETE LOOK AT NATURE, CENTRAL PARK (AND OTHER) GLIMPSES (Quadrangle). © 1974 Eugene Kinkead. Originally in The New Yorker.

Random House From WITHOUT FEATHERS by Woody Allen. © 1975 by Random House, Inc.

Science 83 From "Godliness and Work" by Lionel Casson; "Horse of a Different Culture" by David Monagan; "Science Takes the Stand"; and "Roots of Madness" by Joann Ellison Rodgers. Excerpted by permission of *Science 83 Magazine,* copyright the American Association for the Advancement of Science.

Time From "The Mind in the Machine" by Roger Rosenblatt, 3 May 1982. Copyright 1982 Time Inc. All rights reserved. Reprinted by permission from *Time.*

The Wharton Magazine Reprinted with permission from "The Office of Yesterday," by Donald Sutherland, *The Wharton Magazine,* Vol. 6, No. 2, copyright © 1981 by The Trustees of the University of Pennsylvania.

The H. W. Wilson Company From *Readers' Guide to Periodical Literature,* Copyright © 1978, 1979, 1980, 1981 by The H. W. Wilson Company. *Bibliographic Index* Copyright © 1982 by The H. W. Wilson Company. Material reproduced by permission of the publisher.

To My Mother
and
the Memory of My Father

Preface

The following approach to composition and the research paper was a course before I conceived of its possibilities as a book. Hence the assumptions basic to the course are also basic to the text:

1. English composition should be taught systematically; in one- or two-semester composition courses random writing assignments are demonstrably ineffective.

2. While composition cannot be reduced simply to a rational process, at the freshman level a structured approach, accompanied by prose models, seems to produce more measurable results in the short run than writing activities of the "personal growth and awareness" variety.

3. A research paper should not be taught in a vacuum. Integrating what is taught in the "rhetoric" half of a course with the "research paper" half makes sense for several reasons: it more accurately represents the way a writer actually works, since rhetorical acts do not, as a rule, appear separately; it takes some of the novelty out of the writing of a research paper; and it provides continuity between assignments.

4. The evils of plagiarism and of "cut and paste" are not a simple matter of dishonesty, laziness, or ignorance of the principles of documentation. Both often derive from an inadequate assimilation of material, resulting in a paralyzing overdependence on notes. Both can be minimized by methodically requiring students to flesh out and develop on their own various ideas relevant to their subject.

Therefore, this alternative—strictly utilitarian—method shifts the focus from the current emphasis on mechanical library skills to a treatment of the research paper as a logical extension of rhetorical modes. It addresses the concerns both of research texts (choice of subject, use of library, documentation) and of basic composition (organization, paragraphing, thesis statements, topic sentences, rhetorical strategies). It promotes the "argumentative" research paper that writes to a thesis rather than the informational paper or report that is frequently fostered in secondary schools. In short, it takes as its goal the teaching of the research essay through concentration on content and process, no less than on format.

The text includes the following features:

1. *"Miniature" Research Essays.* Using articles as "secondary sources" in Chapter 2, students are first taught to draw inferences from data and are then assigned to write several brief essays using the data from the articles to support the inferences in their essays. By asking students to begin with the simpler wholes of the research miniatures, the assignment initiates students into the larger, more complicated structure of the research paper. They are asked to write two miniatures under the assumption that such duplication is "progressive" in teaching the essentials of the research essay: focus, coherence, and the synthetic interplay between documented (though documentation as such is not required in the exercise) and undocumented material.

A note about the selection of articles in Chapter 2: I chose them for their imitable style—clear, correct, and aimed at a general audience; but more importantly, for a feature that was relatively difficult to find, given the foregoing requirements, namely, their density of factual but not highly specialized information. Since the exercise requires students to reorganize selected data, it was paramount that the articles contain enough data to be selected and reorganized.

2. *Prewriting.* Chapters 8 through 12 constitute the core of the program. Students draft five independently conceived but ultimately related segments of a research paper, basing the segments on five of the traditional modes of development (example, classification, definition, causal analysis, comparison); they then integrate the seemingly discrete parts into a unified whole. Student as well as professional models of the rhetorical modes are provided.

Such prewriting activity offers students an alternative to the usual method of processing and organizing information through the arrangement and rearrangement of note cards (Chapter 7). Nor are they locked into the five sections that they do prewrite. Should any of the segments resist integration into the final paper, students are free either to revise it or find a place for it in a content note.

3. *Use of the Library.* Chapters 3 through 6 on the technicalities of library research cover the same matters that are found in standard texts but focus on the processing of ideas as the essential component of note taking and organizing information. Chapters 13 and 14 on documentation and research paper format follow the revised specifications for documentary references recommended by the Modern Language Association in 1984 and the American Psychological Association in 1983. Footnote/endnote reference style is also described.

4. *Two Sample Research Papers.* The two essays differ in length and style, though like the research paper topics suggested in Chapter 3, they address a general audience. For this reason, I've omitted literary topics, although another reason also comes to mind: they rely on skills in the analysis of literature that freshman students have not yet been taught at the college level. As for length, the approach used here works as well with the five- to seven-page essay as it does with those essays that run fifteen pages and up. The student models supplied in Chapters 8 through 12 have been drawn from the sample research papers at the end of the text.

Finally, a word about the demands such a program makes on the instructor. It involves reading eight pieces of student prose (seven short and narrowly focused; one long), thus consuming roughly two-thirds of a semester. For the instructor, however, who has less than two-thirds of a semester to devote to the research paper, or who intends to assign a particularly short paper, the program can be compressed to eliminate several, or even all but one, of the modes and thus weeks of instruction. In such a case, I offer the following suggestions. For the instructor interested in teaching the mode that would best serve as an organizing principle for the entire essay, then either causal analysis or division would seem to be the most suitable choice (with the former requiring closer monitoring of the topic for appropriateness to the mode). In terms of student appeal, however, as well as easy integration into the research essay, example and definition work well. If time permits the use of two or three modes, then a combination of the foregoing sets of choices is a suitable compromise: division, to bring order to the subject; example, to introduce specificity to student prose and encourage the use of personal experience and undocumented detail; definition, to elicit independent thinking and here, too, to free the student briefly of sources.

Either compressed or full-length, the process-oriented system should be helpful in demystifying the research paper for students while sharpening both their cognitive and writing skills in general.

For useful criticisms and suggestions, I am grateful to the reviewers of the manuscript in its early stages, especially Steven Robins; William Connelly, Middle Tennessee State University; Mary Jane Dickerson, University of Vermont; James Ford, University of Nebraska; Roy Fox, Boise State University; Michael Ketcham, Texas A & M University. Many thanks also to the librarians, especially Joyce Leung and Susan Pfister, and to Richard Neubauer, at the Clement C. Maxwell Library, for generously sharing their expertise, time, and resources; to Roberta Bena, Bridgewater State College, for photocopies of library materials; to Kate Williams, of Grolier, for furnishing the tear sheets from *The Encyclopedia Americana*; and finally to the editors at Random House, particularly Steven Pensinger, Cynthia Ward, and Elisa Turner, for providing ideas and a mood for accomplishment.

D.J.V.

Contents

1 Introduction to the Research Paper

Most of what you know about the research paper is probably a misconception: it does not have to be long; it is not a report to be copied out of an encyclopedia with quotations thrown in for good measure; it is not a project whose only rationale is to teach you the use of the library; it is not a "mechanical" exercise on a "dry" subject with a lot of "dull" facts; and it is not any more difficult to write than any other essay.

Quite the opposite! A research paper is really nothing more than an essay but with a shift in emphasis: In the "research essay" you are using facts, quotations, and the opinions of specialists *primarily* instead of your own impressions, feelings, thoughts, and experiences to explain, support, and authenticate the point that your essay is making. The essay can be on any subject; it can be as short as three typewritten pages or as long as your subject allows. Quotations should not dominate the paper. In fact, too many (more than 10 percent of the essay) signal trouble. And while you will be using other people's ideas *primarily,* you are not expected to put your own thinking on "hold" in the process. Finally, doing research on a subject of interest to you and writing an essay based on the results of it should be a stimulating experience. If you're not enjoying it, you're doing something wrong.

Because there is so much unwarranted dread attached to the writing of a research paper, and because it's billed in students' minds as a special form of writing like nothing else they have done before, and because so many research papers do come out as just a summary of what a student has read, you are about to undertake an *alternative* approach to the one that is traditionally used in teaching the research paper: (1) You will be taught various writing strategies, which you will use to *prewrite* five segments of your research essay before completing the research paper itself; (2) you will have an opportunity to rewrite these five installments before incorporating them into the research paper; (3) therefore, you will get the opportunity to *practice* the various research skills before *using* them in the final version of your research paper.

Purpose of a Research Paper

There is more than one reason for learning to write a research paper. First, of course, there is the pragmatic reason; it's a service to you in preparation for the research papers you will be asked to write in your college courses. But that is probably the weakest reason of all since it's no secret that some students manage to slip through college without ever writing a research paper (other than in Freshman Composition). So there has to be some other justification for it. And there is. In fact, several justifications: one, because of what it teaches you about college; and, two, because of what it teaches you about writing.

Needless to say, college is for learning; learning is an act of discovery, of asking questions and seeking answers; and doing research on a subject is one way in which this act of discovery takes place. What is more, higher education values *independence* in the learning process: thinking on your own; taking the initiative to pursue information for the sheer pleasure of knowing—not merely on the instructions of an instructor or in anticipation of an exam; pulling books off library shelves because they're intriguing; making it a habit to spend an hour browsing through the latest journals. If there's an essential difference between high school and college, it's in what makes a student a student. In high school it's the classes attended, the material memorized, and the exams taken. In college you do that too, but you are expected to do *more:* you are expected to *like* ideas, enjoy having them take hold of your mind, fire your imagination, dominate your life, interrupt your sleep; college is for toying with ideas, for getting them to click and fall into place, for getting a charge out of the connection that you make—on your own—between what you heard here and what you read there; it's discovering how putting words on paper generates ideas—literally out of the blue. And if that is what you are expected to do in college, it is also what you are expected to do in a research paper.

The second justification for undertaking the research paper is more practical in nature; it deals with learning how to write. You could say that the research paper is the ultimate writing project at this stage: If you think you've mastered the basic writing skills, it will test you in them; if you haven't, it will teach them. Assuming that you're having no serious grammatical difficulties, you have only three basic areas of composition to master: having a point that you want to make; developing the point; sticking to the point.

What follows, therefore, is a writing project that provides you with ideas on which to draw, concentrates your energies on the *basics* of composition, establishes continuity between assignments, gives you sufficient direction to keep you from feeling lost on your own, and allows you the satisfaction of getting it together in a final performance called the "research paper."

Role of Personal Experience

What should make writing a research paper particularly enjoyable and challenging is the very fact that it is not just a dry report on what you read. Your own thoughts based on your own experiences should play a role in the research process. You should use your own thinking to elaborate on other people's ideas, to explain concepts, supply examples, perceive contrasts (or similarities), raise questions, and so on.

Let's say you were researching Yemeni wedding ceremonies. Here's how your thinking might proceed. For a while you would simply read about their customs. Unsurprisingly, you would find them strange. "How odd their customs are," you might muse aloud, thus launching a train of thought entirely your own. Your past experience with wedding ceremonies in America would enable you to reflect on the differences between Western and Middle Eastern marriage rites. But then somewhere further down the line in your reading, your attention might be arrested once again—this time perhaps by the similarities. The author's description of the Yemeni bride as "happy and excited" might lead you into another train of thought: "Just like any other bride. The groom is probably nervous. And the married women, no doubt, look on nostalgically as they reminisce. . . ."

What you have, in fact, been doing is engaging in mental activities that transcend mere recording of information; you have been generating ideas, thinking on your own. What is more, the differences and similarities you've perceived may very well be material you can use in a paper on Yemeni weddings. Somewhere in the course of such an essay, showing the differences or pointing to the similarities between the two cultures may be just the thing to highlight a point, arouse interest, create vividness. Here's a brief example of what the results might be like. Notice how the paragraphs blend what you've read with what you've thought (the latter underlined for emphasis).

Yemeni wedding ceremonies do not seem to have much in common with the marriage rites of Western nations. The Yemeni bride sits on a homemade throne and merely observes the festivities in her honor. She is not expected to say much and does not get to dance with her husband, since the only dancing done is by the men outside in front of the groom's family home.

But since people are often more alike than different, the emotions at a wedding, whether Yemeni or American, are likely to be the same. The Yemeni bride may not say much, but, as Mandaville points out, the eyes and smiles reveal how "happy and excited" she is. The

```
groom is probably nervous and the ladies in the room look on either
nostalgically, if they're already married, or wistfully in anticipa-
tion of their own wedding day.
```

Similarly, your own research essay should be a synthesis of factual data, borrowed opinions, inferences, and personal observations.

Consideration of Audience

Anytime you write, you usually have a reader in mind: your mother, for example, when you tack a message to the refrigerator door or an administrator for the college application you submitted. Accordingly, you adjust your English: informal and personal to your Mom; formal and official to the college dean.

But formal/informal are not the only distinctions to be made between writing styles. Frequently, you have to adjust your style for explicitness or technicality of diction. It is all a question of audience. How much you say will depend on how much your audience already knows about your topic; how technical your vocabulary is will depend on how initiated your audience is in the language of your subject. A pediatrician addressing a convention of specialists like himself can toss out terms like *macrocytic anemia* and expect to be understood; the same pediatrician addressing parents at a local PTA meeting could not. He would have to eliminate the word *macrocytic* or explain it.

In short, you are expected to consider audience when you write your research paper, too. Your immediate reader, of course, is your instructor; however, because of his or her qualifications and characteristics, he or she also represents a larger type of audience: adult, educated, and impersonal. In terms of topic and style, therefore, your research paper should be equally adult, intelligent, impersonal, general, and formal rather than casual, but without ever getting stuffy or bogged down in technical terminology (jargon).

Overview

The order and the rationale behind the setup of the text is as follows:

1. *"Research Miniatures"* (Chapter 2). To take the mystery out of the composition of a research paper, you will begin with a series of brief and similar writing assignments; in certain key features they're research papers in miniature. Compared to a full-fledged essay, they will take less time and less effort to write and yet will introduce you to the essentials. Thus you will have a better sense of just what "research" involves, and by the time you actually sit down to write your final paper, you will be able to draw on the experience of having written something like it already.

2. *Library Research* (Chapters 3 through 6). Since most of your research will be in the library, you will be using it in three stages: first, to find a subject; second, to locate information on it; third, to transcribe the information into your notes.

3. *Using the Notes Taken* (Chapter 7). Since the notes will provide the basis for the paper you write, you will have to learn to incorporate them properly into the body of your own writing.

4. *"Prewriting"* (Chapters 8 through 12). The next stage will not be to write the research paper since it is precisely at this stage of the research process that serious problems begin to appear. Therefore, you will be instructed to undertake a series of writing assignments designed to short-circuit some of the avoidable difficulties.

The point is that before a good research essay can be written, the material that is being written about has to be digested. In order to digest it, you must *think* about it, be able to discuss it *without* depending on your notes for every single word and piece of information you have read, and derive some ideas of your own from it. Therefore, you will be asked to prewrite five separate segments of your research paper, sections that you will later be able to *incorporate* into it. You will, of course, use your notes, but you will find that they are inadequate to what you're being asked to write. And so you will be forced to think some ideas through on your own!

As you can see, the advantages of such prewriting activity are several: You will have given yourself a number of opportunities (five, to be exact) to digest your subject progressively in stages well *before* you have to write your final paper; you will have detached yourself from your notes, thus escaping the evils of plagiarism and the "cut-and-paste" method (to be discussed later); you will have worked most of the bugs out of your subject *before* the final writing stage; and, what may be best of all, you will have chunks of your essay written ahead of schedule.

Apart from the benefits to your research project, prewriting also enhances your writing skills. Chapters 8 through 12 are lessons in five of the basic strategies that the human mind and, therefore, writers use for developing and organizing ideas. Thus as you prewrite segments of your research paper, you are also getting practice in basic composition.

5. *Final Technicalities of the Research Paper* (Chapters 13 and 14). The most tedious and technical aspects of the research paper have been left for last. Most of your effort will have gone—where it belongs—into the content of your paper. But obviously you can't claim credit for the whole of it. Whatever ideas or words weren't yours to begin with must be acknowledged—it's a matter of honesty. Documentation (in the form of footnotes and bibliography) is to your paper what credits are to a film—hardly the most exciting part of the performance but not one to be overlooked either. The technicalities regarding the format of your paper are also treated in Chapter 13.

6. *Sample Research Papers* (Chapter 15). Two research essays written by students are provided as models.

2
Writing a Research Paper in Miniature

As you have already learned, a research paper is essentially an essay. The way in which it differs from an essay (see Chapter 1) does not in any way change the basic elements that the research paper has in common with it: Both are written to make a point, and both must in some way develop and explain it. In short, everything that they have to say must in one fashion or another revolve around a central point. Therefore, before you can write a good research paper, you must develop the very same compositional skills it takes to write an essay.

Basic Skills

These skills require the introduction and definition of some terms that are basic to composition. What has up until now been referred to as the **point** of an essay will be called the **thesis**. The thesis is the unifying or controlling idea of an essay and hence a research paper. Because it is an idea, it must always be written as a sentence, *never* a phrase; hence it is often referred to as a **thesis sentence** or **thesis statement**. "Graffiti as art" is *not* a sentence; therefore, it does *not* express an idea; therefore, it could *not* serve as a thesis. "Graffiti is art" *is* a sentence; it *does* express an idea; therefore, it could serve as a thesis.

Just as an essay must have a unifying idea to keep it flowing in a single direction rather than (to continue the metaphor) puddling up and going any which way, so, too, each paragraph in the essay must have direction. It must be controlled by its own unifying thought, called the **topic sentence** (or **topic idea** if it's merely implied rather than expressly stated). In other words, a paragraph is a self-contained unit of prose within an essay that also revolves around a single idea. In fact, a topic sentence is to a paragraph what a thesis is to an essay:

$$\frac{\text{Topic sentence}}{\text{Paragraph}} = \frac{\text{Thesis}}{\text{Essay}}$$

Needless to say, topic sentences have to relate to the thesis statement. They're the smaller components of the larger concept, called the thesis. Together they form the basic organizational structure of an essay. Everything else is **development**, a very broad term to cover all the devices the writer uses to *elaborate* on the topic ideas of the paragraphs, thus, in turn, elaborating on the thesis of the essay.

Paragraph development comes in a variety of forms, and no one form is any better than any other form. Writers make use of as many as they need to build the strongest possible case for each topic idea. They quote authorities, use their opinions, borrow their ideas, supply substantiating facts, data, and information, define terms, classify and compare subjects, illustrate, narrate, and describe, as well as show cause and effect, and even resort to analogies.

Consider the following piece of prose about the entertainer Dick Gregory, which the student writer thought was an essay. However, it isn't. An essay, as you've learned above, has *three* basic essentials: thesis, topic ideas, development. The prose below has only *two* of these: thesis and topic sentences. No development. Therefore, it's only the **skeleton** of an essay.

Dick Gregory's reputation as a sixties comedian has been replaced by a more impressive reputation as a political activist and respected authority on health and nutrition. In the beginning Dick Gregory was just another black comedian making it big on the night club circuit. But as time passed, he became more and more interested in politics. He became aware of the world hunger situation, so he directed his energies toward that. As a result, he learned a great deal about nutrition and health and has written some books on the subject.

The first sentence is the thesis; the rest are topic sentences. All the sentences are related to the thesis but need development. The basic structure of a fine research paper is there, as you can see for yourself.

A
Thesis Dick Gregory's reputation as a sixties comedian has been re-
B
placed by a more impressive reputation as a political activist and
C
respected authority on health and nutrition.

Topic sentence keyed to part A of the thesis. In the beginning Dick Gregory was just another black comedian making it big on the night club circuit.

Topic sentence keyed to part B of the thesis. But as time passed, he became more and more interested in politics.

Topic sentence keyed to parts B and C of the thesis. He became aware of the world hunger situation, so he directed his energies toward that.

Topic sentence keyed to part C of the thesis. As a result, he learned a great deal about nutrition and health and has written some books on the subject.

Obviously, this is a very simply structured essay; nevertheless, the structure is sound and does exactly what the structure of even the most complex essay must do: state the thesis, isolate its component (topic) ideas, and arrange them in a logical order. When this "essay" was sent back to the student for development, he or she wasn't expected to add any new ideas onto the end of what was written; the student was expected to develop the topic sentences already written.

As you can see, writing an essay is *composing*. As in photography, for example, it's imposing order on the parts. In fact, it's no accident that the word *composition* is used by writers and photographers alike. A photographer composes the shot; a writer, the essay. Both use their respective mediums to make a statement. Both speak of "focusing" their compositions to give them unity and exclude irrelevant detail.

Research Miniature

Before you actually choose a subject on which to write your research paper, you will be asked to undertake a writing exercise that is based on the reading of several news articles. It involves two separate but similar writing assignments designed to give you practice in precisely those *three* skills that are crucial to the writing of a successful research paper, indeed any essay: formulation of a thesis; construction of topic sentences to fortify the thesis; development of topic sentences. By training yourself, first, to recognize this tripod of thesis, topic sentences, and development in your reading and then to observe it in your own writing, you will have mastered one of the most demanding aspects of composition: organization. You will also find research papers—and essay exams—considerably easier to write.

In each of the two assignments you will actually compose a miniresearch paper using one or more news articles as a source of information. In other words, you will be doing in miniature what you'll be doing later on a larger scale: taking the central idea of the essay you plan to write; breaking it down into its component ideas; examining works written by other people for the purpose of finding evidence to substantiate these ideas; and, as a result, supporting your thesis.

Obviously, the two "research miniatures" you're about to write would not do for a "real" research paper because you will be relying on too few sources (which creates the problem of excessive borrowing of the language of the original article) and because you will not be asked to document what you borrow from the news articles. To be sure, responsible research requires acknowledging other people's words and ideas even in the shortest piece of writing; but, in this case, since the assignments are *primarily exercises* in organization and the source of your borrowings will be known to your reader (the instructor), the possibility of deception is ruled out. Therefore, in this one set of exercises, you won't be asked to document what you take from *Newsweek* and *Nation's Business* to develop your topic ideas.

In the case of each assignment, your *objectives* are the following:

1. To study the selected news article for its thesis, topic sentences/ideas, and development.
2. To formulate a thesis for your miniature essay (in the first assignment, just to get you started, the thesis will be formulated for you).
3. To formulate the topic sentences that correspond to the thesis.
4. To gather the data from the original article that supports your topic sentences.
5. To write your miniature.

Sample Article

The following article, "A Blossoming in China Trade," and the student miniature essay based on it are provided as models of the two assignments found in this chapter.

First, notice how the reading half of the assignment has been handled. The *Newsweek* essay has been analyzed for the three basic elements of composition by:

1. the underlining of the *thesis* statement with *two* lines;
2. the underlining of each *topic* sentence with a *single* line, if it's stated in the paragraph, or writing out the topic sentence in the margin, if it's merely implied;
3. the numbering of the *data* that support the topic idea in each paragraph;
4. the lettering of any *examples* that are used to illustrate the data.

A BLOSSOMING IN CHINA TRADE

For much of this month the lobby of the Peking Hotel has seemed very much like an American colonial outpost. Texas oilmen on a mission to inspect offshore oil fields drawled enthusiastically over cocktails about the deal they hoped to clinch. Tired U.S. Government officials hovered nearby, waiting to initial the first Sino-American civil-aviation agreement, and a contingent from the Pentagon added a flash of medals and braid as they swept back and forth from talks on military-equipment sales. Outside Peking, the first group of U.S. soybean growers to visit China was exploring the Chinese fields where soybeans were first produced, on the lookout for disease-resistant strains that might be useful to the United States. And meanwhile, back in San Francisco, Chinese representatives in dark Mao jackets were putting the finishing touches on a historic exhibition—the first official trade show China has ever staged in America.

It isn't evolving quite as either side had anticipated, but trade between China and the United States is finally beginning to take off. This week in Washington, government representatives from the two countries will sign several formal agreements covering bilateral relationships in such areas as textiles and shipping. Total business between the two nations is expected to reach $4 billion in 1980—almost twice last year's level—making China the biggest American trading partner in the Communist world. And by 1985, the Commerce Department predicts, Sino-American trade will hit $10 billion. Much of the improvement is due to steady progress in the normalization of relations. Last January, Congress approved most-favored-nation status for China, and recently Jimmy Carter authorized the Export-Import Bank to extend credit to give the China trade a fresh boost. At the same time China itself is taking steps to reform tax laws and other internal regulations that have impeded foreign investments. "Once the new laws are adopted," says Rong Yiren, head of the China International Trust and Investment Co., "all the problems are solved."

Well, not quite. Many serious barriers to a full-scale trade boom still remain, and most American businessmen agree that while growth will be steady, it will also be slow. Each side, for example, is still struggling for a firm fix on just what the other wants. American businessmen feel stymied by the formidable Chinese bureaucracy, and Chinese importers are severely hampered by their country's chronic shortage of hard currency to pay the bill for foreign goods. Last year China's money problems forced Peking to slash its ambitious modernization program, canceling plans for 120 major capital projects. "The Chinese realized that they wouldn't be able to pay for the projects," says Ken Morse, president of Chase Pacific Trade Advisers, an arm of Chase Manhattan Bank, "and they prudently put on the brakes."

No Milk

With the brakes on, American shipments to China have settled into four main categories. Grain and foodstuffs—especially corn, soybeans and wheat—lead the U.S. export list, followed by cotton and polyester fibers, oil-drilling and mining equipment, and trucks, automobile parts and special vehicles such as tractors. American consumer products, from soft drinks to cosmetics, crowd the hotel shops. But for the Chinese masses such products are largely curiosities since few ordinary people can afford a 60-cent Coke—and the American businessman's dream of treating 1 billion headaches with aspirin and spraying 2 billion armpits with deodorant has failed to materialize. "You have to remember that the Chinese are not a throwaway society," says A. Jackson Rich, a China specialist at the Commerce Department. "But many times American companies fail to realize basic things. They tried to sell China dietary supplements that required milk, for instance, even though the Chinese don't drink milk and never have."

For their part, the Chinese turn much of their American cotton and polyester into clothing for women and infants, which they then ship back to the United States as their single biggest trade item. In addition, the Chinese ship fireworks, antiques, handicrafts and, increasingly, cheap labor. But perhaps most important, China is a potentially huge exporter of crude oil. And the Chinese themselves see oil exports as one of the best means for attracting the foreign cash they so desperately need for development.

Red Tape

Although American businessmen are eager to expand the China trade, many of them have grown disenchanted since Richard Nixon's visit in 1972. One big reason is China's incredible tangle of red tape. Potential exporters must walk through a maze of trade organizations, sometimes wasting months in negotiations only to learn that they have been dealing with the wrong bureaucrats. Lower-ranking officials often delay decisions for fear of being overruled. It took one foreign businessman eight cajoling letters and eleven months just to persuade a beer factory to send him a sample bottle label. "It's terribly frustrating," says an official of Intercontinental Hotels Corp., which has scrapped plans to build five or six hotels in China and has been negotiating for two years over terms for building just one. "They're nice people, but many of them have never been out of China. How the hell do they know what a modern hotel needs?"

The foreign-exchange problem is even more frustrating. Without cash on hand the Chinese cannot afford the equipment they need to develop the industries that provide their own exports. As a result, China has resorted to "compensation trade," convincing foreign companies to accept Chinese products as payment for the technology and equipment they supply. In past years, for example, Fiat accepted hams, Volvo took tea and Toyota got rugs as partial payment for their goods. But American companies often balk at similar arrangements. "I don't think anybody who sells heavy equipment can afford that," says William Cherones, vice president of Harnischfeger Corp., a Milwaukee manufacturer of construction and mining equipment.

Cashing In

Still, most businessmen will accept compensation-trade deals if necessary. And at least one American firm is capitalizing on the situation. The Noble Trading Co., of Alexandria, Va., acts as middleman for U.S. companies, negotiating with the Chinese for marketable products and then selling them in the United States. China gets the equipment, the American exporter gets cash instead of hams, tea or carpets and Noble gets a share of the profits.

Meanwhile, China has hit on a new way to attract American dollars. Last weekend its first official trade exhibition opened in San Francisco—a dazzling display of Chinese merchandise that will later travel to Chicago and to New York. At a cost of about $6 million, $4 million from the Chinese government and nearly $2 million from the China Exhibition Corp., the U.S. sponsor, the exhibit includes everything from "jellies" (transparent, rubbery shoes) to petroleum products, linens to electronics, antiquities to canned samples of roasted moose snout. At least 200,000 San Franciscans are expected to visit the display, ogling the wares and watching Chinese craftsmen—including glass blowers, paper cutters and three of Peking's finest chefs—perform their magic.

And upstairs, in eighteen curtained booths, the Chinese will be ready for business. They hope to sell department-store buyers, manufacturers and other American importers at least $300 million in goods in the first sixteen days alone. "This is the opening gun in their effort to sell to the United States," says Gilbert A. Robinson, head of the exhibition corporation, "so they can earn dollars they can spend to buy goods from the United States."

"Old Friends"

They already have some takers. Starting next week all fourteen stores in the Bloomingdale's chain will participate in an exhibit that is being billed as the biggest promotion of Chinese goods in U.S. history. Buyers for the chain spent two years and $10 million preparing the show and took more than 130 trips to China to select products. Among their choices: down jackets, cashmere sweaters, rattan furniture—even Chinese chocolate. Bloomingdale's chairman, Marvin Traub, signed an agreement with

Chinese officials that designates his store their main American outlet for 1980—and Traub insists the relationship will last. "The Chinese put a great deal of emphasis on dealing with old friends," he says. "We are now old friends."

That, in fact, may be the key to successful trade with the Chinese—the patience to become tested and trusted partners like the Japanese and European firms that have long done business in China. "It will be the tortoise and the hare," says Chase's Morse. "Those companies going for the quick hit will flame out early." But those with staying power may reap the bonanza China's huge market has always promised. In the years ahead the Chinese will need more grain, more equipment to develop their oil potential and more advanced technical assistance for building other industries. For the United States, with all its agricultural and technological riches, the China trade is a challenge difficult to resist.

Merrill Sheils with Pamela Lynn Abraham in New York, Jerry Buckley in Washington, Melinda Liu in Peking, Michael Reese in San Francisco and bureau reports. *Newsweek,* September 22, 1980

Analyzing the Article

You will have noticed in reading the article on Sino-American trade that the authors have observed all the principles of a well-organized essay: **unifying idea** (although trade between China and the United States is finally beginning to take off, many serious barriers to a full-scale trade boom still remain); **subordinate ideas** (if you read off the underlined topic sentences, you'll get a complete picture of the ideas that are being used to authenticate the thesis); and **discussion** of these ideas (everything else in the article that is not underlined). What is more, you'll also notice a certain structural pattern in the essay:

1. The complete thesis appears early in the essay.
2. The topic sentences usually appear at the beginnings of paragraphs.
3. Development consists of facts, figures, examples, descriptions, and quotations.
4. Wherever developmental data (numbered material) is of a general nature, examples (lettered material) are used to illustrate it.

Nevertheless, you must also have noticed that the authors take liberties with the rules as you've been taught them: The thesis isn't stated as a single sentence but as two sentences expressing the main idea; several times it also takes the writers two (even three) sentences to express the unifying idea of a paragraph; and two of the topic sentences also serve as the thesis statement of the essay.

There is obviously nothing wrong with this kind of loose interpretation of the "rules"—provided you know what you're doing. In short, if you find yourself struggling with these assignments, don't deviate but follow the basics religiously:

1. State the thesis at the very beginning of the essay.
2. State each topic idea explicitly as the first sentence of the paragraph.
3. Discuss the topic sentences with data and ideas drawn from the reading.

Following the basics will help you organize your material and produce an essay that is, at least, coherent and unified, even if not particularly inspired at this point. Later as your experience and self-confidence increase, you can take liberties with the rules.

Sample Student "Miniature"

The next step of the assignment is to write the miniresearch essay based on "research" of the *Newsweek* article. Read the sample essay below in which the student has formulated the following thesis: "Trade between the United States and China has not been an immediate success."

BARRIERS TO SINO-AMERICAN TRADE

Jeff Gordon

Trade between the United States and China has not been an immediate success. It has been hindered by (1) China's lack of cash to pay for American products, (2) its bureaucracy and red tape, and (3) unfamiliarity of both countries with each other's needs and tastes.

China's lack of cash is a major obstacle, which has made it difficult for China to purchase technology and

2

equipment. (1) It has had to rely on "compensation trade"-which is nothing other than bartering on an international scale. (a) For example, such countries as France and Japan have exchanged automobiles for foodstuffs. (2) But American companies are reluctant to exchange their products for hams, tea, or rugs. (a) So if a company like Harnischfeger, for instance, which manufactures construction equipment, refuses to barter, China is forced to cancel building projects.

Another obstacle to the smooth flow of trade has been China's bureaucratic structure and red tape. (1) Its tax laws and regulations are archaic and in need of reform. (2) Its various levels of management often confuse foreign exporters, who find themselves getting nowhere by "dealing with the wrong bureaucrats." (3) Finally, simple ignorance of Western ways of doing business is also obstructing trade. (a) For example, a Chinese beer factory refused to send an interested importer just "a sample bottle label" for nearly a year. (b) In another instance, Chinese refusal to let Intercontinental Hotels Corp. build "five or six hotels in China" without interference from the Chinese, which according to one foreign spokesman, do not know "what a modern hotel needs," caused Intercontinental to cancel most of its projects in China.

Finally, there is the problem of mutual unfamiliarity with the other culture. (1) As a result, both countries have exported consumer products that the

3

other side does not use. (a) The deodorants, cosmetics, milk products, and aspirins that Americans exported did not sell. (b) Similarly, "roasted moose snout" and "transparent, rubbery shoes" on display at the San Francisco trade show could not have been very hot items with Americans. (2) (a) What's more, even if the Chinese wanted to drink Coke, another exported item, the average person in China couldn't afford the 60-cent bottle.

In other words, the potential for trade may be enormous. A billion people is a dazzlingly huge market for American goods. But the obstacles are there, and it's obvious that no unprecedented profits for American companies nor instant entrance into the twenty-first (or even twentieth) century for the Chinese is going to happen overnight.

Analyzing the Student Miniature

Notice the following:

1. The student essay is *not* a summary of the *Newsweek* article. Even its thesis, which is going to be similar to that of the "parent" article, has a different focus: the student essay discusses only the barriers to Sino-American trade; it does *not* follow the order in which the information is presented in the article; it pulls data from various sections of the article without any regard for where the information appears in the parent essay; it arranges its paragraphs and organizes its information according to its own thesis and topic sentences; it does *not* use the conclusion of the article for its own conclusion because the two essays have different focuses; and perhaps most significantly, it does *not* use the language of the *Newsweek* essay. See page 109 for a discussion of how to paraphrase correctly.

2. The student has marked the essay in the same way in which the article was marked; the thesis is underlined with a double line, the topic sentences with a single line, the data in support of the topic sentences are numbered, and the examples that illustrate the data are lettered.

ASSIGNMENT 1

Writing the Miniature

Write an organized, well-developed miniresearch paper (500 words) using the same *Newsweek* article, "A Blossoming in China Trade," as your source of information and the following statement as your thesis:

Trade between the United States and China is not free of obstacles, but both countries are taking steps to overcome them.

Review the discussion of the sample student essay for key points to remember when writing your own. Furthermore, keep in mind the following advice:

1. Examine your thesis, notice its component parts ("obstacles" and "steps"), determine which component is being emphasized, and arrange the order of discussion accordingly.
2. Avoid the inclination to begin each paragraph with data. Begin instead with a topic sentence.
3. Be sure that your topic sentences cover all the information you provide in the paragraph and that none of the paragraphs carries information that is irrelevant to your topic sentence.
4. Be sure to keep your data as specific as they are in the parent essay; don't dull or generalize data by removing the detail; use statistics, names, places, and so forth whenever possible.
5. In order to avoid heavy quoting and the tendency to lift whole sentences and paragraphs from the article, write the first draft of your essay *from memory* and turn to the article afterwards only for additional facts or a correction of the facts as you remembered them; when you do use the exact words of the *Newsweek* article (even if they're only two significant words in the same order as found in the article), be sure to supply quotation marks.
6. When you're finished writing, be sure to underline your thesis and topic sentences and number and letter the development of your ideas. If you find your paragraphs lacking in numbered or lettered items, add them.

ASSIGNMENT 2

Read "A Frontier for U.S. Business," which has been taken from *Nation's Business* magazine and brings you up to date on the very subject you have just been writing on (U.S. trade with China).

A FRONTIER FOR U.S. BUSINESS

Stand in the broad plaza before the Hall of Preserving Harmony in Beijing, capital of the People's Republic of China, and you get a glimpse of three Chinas.

You are inside the Forbidden City, home and workplace of the Ming and Qing emperors (1368–1644 and 1644–1911), so you see structures and statuary that are evidence of the awesome past of man's oldest continuous major civilization.

The plaza teems with representatives of present-day China—eager sightseers. These drably garbed thousands are only a smidgen of the world's largest population, which has more than doubled since the Communists took over the country in 1949. The birth rate is now down, because of a government campaign that began in the '70s to limit children to one per family. But the population rose an estimated 11 million—to 1,036 billion—in 1984 alone. The rise was more than the population of New York City.

On the horizon, you see evidence of a future China. Look east, west, north or south—everywhere, high-rises are under construction, festooned with giant cranes.

China, long a slumbering giant economically—the late dictator Mao Zedong (Tse-tung) gave it several sleeping pills, culminating with his anarchic Cultural Revolution—appears to be awakening. That can mean giant opportunity for American business people.

American technology is already in demand. And, says one member of the U.S. business community in Beijing, "What a market this could be someday, as living standards rise and the economy grows! Many of us want to get in on the ground floor."

So do business people from Japan, China's No. 1 trading partner, where there is new emphasis in the schools on teaching Mandarin, the Chinese national language. Hong Kong ranks second in trade with China, and the United States, third. The U.S.-Chinese total is expected to hit $7 billion this year [1985], up from the $2.3 billion of 1979, the year that followed establishment of diplomatic relations between the two countries.

Americans and others think not only in terms of selling in China, but also of taking advantage of low labor costs by buying or joining in manufacturing in China and selling abroad. The climate for that is a lot better than it used to be.

A giant photo of Mao still looks out on Beijing's 98-acre Tiananmen (Gate of Heavenly Peace) Square, not far from the Forbidden City. But portraits of Marx, Engels, Lenin and Stalin that also hung there were removed five years ago, and the 10-year Cultural Revolution—with its anti-Western, Communist fanaticism, its killings, persecutions and shippings off to the countryside—is only a bitter memory. It ended after Mao's death in 1976.

Under China's present supreme leader, diminutive Deng Xiaoping, there has been increasing experimentation with economic autonomy, competition and incentives. Productive factory workers and managers can get bonuses. Farmers—80 percent of China's population is rural, though only 11 percent of its land is arable—give collectives much of their output but can keep the rest and sell it for profit. Millions of individually owned small businesses have been started. And there has been a strong push for foreign trade and foreign investment, primarily for joint ventures with enterprises from abroad.

Incomes and consumption have jumped. Walk through a shopping area any morning in Beijing, or Shanghai or Hangzhou, and it is like the last shopping day before Christmas in Atlanta, or Chicago or Denver. There are hordes of people in every store of every nature—clothes, tools, musical instruments, food, sporting supplies, you name it. And the shelves and display cases hold many things to buy.

China seems to have gone from Cultural Revolution to Consumption Revolution.

Frank L. Morsani, chairman of the U.S. Chamber of Commerce, is among U.S. business leaders who have witnessed the phenomenon of today's China. Morsani led a Chamber delegation to China in October at the invitation of the All-China Federation of Industry and Commerce, a 500,000-member organization of Chinese with business experience. (Many characterize themselves as having been "capitalists" before the 1949 "liberation" from the Nationalists, whose government was recognized by the United States as China's through 1978.) The ACFIC's object is to promote business both within China and between China and other countries.

In addition to talking with the ACFIC, Morsani and his delegation conferred with Chinese government leaders and toured production facilities.

Says Morsani, a Tampa businessman: "Investment opportunities in China are probably as great as any in the world today. There are three basic requirements for financial flows—a good labor market, a good return on investment and a stable government. China obviously has the first and offers the possibility of the second. It appears to have the third, as well." He pledged efforts to facilitate economic interaction between China and the United States.

Charles H. Smith, a former U.S. Chamber chairman who was in the Morsani delegation, notes that the consequences of China's increased economic vigor can include competition for foreign business, along with opportunity. Smith, chairman of Cleveland's SIFCO Industries, a maker of forgings —high-strength parts used in equipment—says: "It appears that China will be a very important factor in labor-intensive industries. If you think we have competition now, watch!"

A recent World Bank study says China has a good chance of reaching a targeted \$800-per-capita national income by the turn of the century, up from less than \$300 in 1980. That would hardly put the Chinese in the same income category as rich nations' citizens—the comparable U.S. figure in 1984 was \$12,500—but they would be in the middle-income bracket.

Beyond that, who knows? China, the third largest nation in area—after the Soviet Union and Canada—has metal and mineral resources that are largely unexplored. Its coal reserves are exceeded only by those of the United States and the Soviet Union. It has the world's greatest hydroelectric potential, an irony when you consider that electricity brownouts are frequent in cities like Shanghai.

As for human resources, the Communists have drastically cut China's once-rampant illiteracy, though only 65 percent of Chinese youngsters finish primary school, and less than 1 percent of college-agers get into college. And as the defeated Nationalists in their island bastion of Taiwan, the Hong Kong Chinese and "overseas" Chinese in Singapore and elsewhere have dramatically shown, a flair for business is characteristic of their ethnic group. A young American stationed in Beijing by IBM, which has opened a Chinese sales office, delights in initiating trainees into the mysteries of the private enterprise system. "When I show them the stock tables and what the figures represent—how you can make money in the market—their eyes light up," he says.

But today's China is still far from being a market economy. Individually owned businesses, which typically have no more than a handful of employees, if any, possess only a tiny slice of the pie. Collectives have a bigger slice, but they are government-controlled to a large degree. And the government owns outright a still larger slice. Virtually all jobs are assigned, not found.

Communist Party leaders late last year released a reform blueprint that called for a "socialist commodity economy with Chinese characteristics."

Says a U.S. government analysis: "Simply put, 'socialist' means that the state will remain the most important economic actor, controlling a large share of the production and distribution of key industrial and agricultural products. Its relative importance will shrink, however, and its means of control will shift to more reliance on economic levers such as prices, taxes and credit, rather than administrative fiat. 'Commodity' means that the allocation of an increasing number of goods will be determined according to market forces—that is, they will be treated as commodities."

One commodity in short supply is management expertise. Enterprises stagnated during the Cultural Revolution. Also, its witch-hunts against accused "capitalist roaders" plunged higher education into chaos, shutting many colleges and universities for years. Young people who might have gotten management training did not.

So China is seeking joint ventures with foreign business not just to get capital and technology, but also to get managerial expertise. The need for such expertise is often obvious to Westerners.

On the 11th floor of the main building of Shanghai's Jin Jiang Hotel—which overlooks a street painted red during the Cultural Revolution by Red Guards trying to demonstrate devotion to communism—seven musicians play American big band-era music nightly. (Until recently, rock music was terra incognita in China. A young Ministry of Foreign Economic Relations and Trade researcher, assigned as an interpreter to the U.S. Chamber delegation, had never heard of the Beatles.) Nowhere in the hotel—certainly not in the elevators as would be the case in the States—is there an obvious notice calling attention to the musicians. They play to a nearly empty room.

Present-day China's first piece of commercial legislation was promulgated in July, 1979—the Law on Joint Ventures Using Chinese and Foreign Investment. Since then there has been a series of laws and regulations involving the investor from abroad. In 1984, according to a Chinese report, 700 equity joint ventures with foreign partners were formed—more than the total launched in the preceding five years. Tax breaks sweeten the pot for the foreigners.

U.S. equity in joint ventures with the Chinese exceeds $150 million, the State Department says—much less than the $600 million-plus that U.S. companies have put into offshore oil exploration in China but, judging by a swelling stream of business visitors to China, only the beginning.

Most of the ventures involve manufacturing. Products range from electronic instruments to razor blades, from canned food to pharmaceuticals, from elevators to Jeeps. American Motors and the Beijing Automobile Works signed a 20-year contract in 1983, with the U.S. firm acquiring a 31.4 percent interest in a $51 million venture.

The path is not necessarily smooth for the U.S. partner in a joint venture. China, desperate for foreign exchange to finance purchase of needed equipment, limits American or other foreign partners' take-home profits to amounts the venture earns abroad. That makes for difficulties, obviously, if the venture's only market is Chinese.

Frank W. Considine, chairman of Chicago-based National Can Corporation, was also a member of the U.S. Chamber delegation that visited China in October. Considine, a Chamber regional vice chairman, says: "The potential is enormous for American investment, but the key problem for U.S. businesses is to create foreign exchange in order to repatriate funds. Creative approaches will have to be found."

One such approach was found for the 3M Company. It saw an opportunity to make electrical tape in China for Chinese customers, though it could not see a market for the tape elsewhere. It rejected a joint venture arrangement. Chinese authorities eventually allowed it to launch a wholly owned operation, which now has 20 employees. "We received a dispensation," says 3M China Affairs Director John Marshall. The company will buy products in China that it thinks can be sold abroad. When it sells them there, it will supply the Chinese with foreign exchange to offset profits it can then take home.

Americans in China to do business face personal difficulties, too. There is an acute shortage of suitable living quarters, and when found, they do not come cheap. A Chinese executive—a factory manager, say—may be paid less than the equivalent of $100 a month, and his workers, half that. Housing for the Chinese is subsidized, but the resident American will pay thousands monthly in rent.

An American lawyer pays $2,000 a month for a small apartment in the China International Trust and Investment Corporation's 31-story headquarters. CITIC, founded in 1979, has pieces of numerous joint ventures with foreign companies as well as all-Chinese ventures. It rents most of its building—which has separate wings for living quarters and offices—to foreigners, for a reported total of $36 million a year. There is so much foreign business activity in Beijing that CITIC has bids out for construction of a second, 50-story, building.

Another American, a businessman, reports the only suitable apartment he could find was in a hotel. His monthly rent for 900 square feet: $6,000.

Americans with children can send them to an English-language school in Beijing, where the resident U.S. community at last count totaled 700, compared with 120 in Shanghai. But classes extend only through primary grades.

Single? "The authorities frown on nonbusiness friendships with foreigners," says a bachelor American executive who lives in Shanghai. "Until a couple of years ago, they were actually forbidden."

Golf? In all of China's 3.7 million square miles, there is just one course—in Guangzhou, the southern metropolis that used to be known as Canton. Beijing is building one.

In addition, there are the obvious language difficulties. Many Chinese in mover-and-shaker circles can carry on conversations in English, but others have no such capability. Available interpreters' knowledge of wording is sometimes questionable.

Some conversations that would be private in this country are not so in China. An American tells of being surprised by an interruption from the operator during a phone call. The Chinese complained the conversation was too fast, making it hard to understand.

An unprepared American visitor to China is apt to have many surprises. For one thing, not all successful business people fled the country or were imprisoned or executed after the Communists' 1949 victory. Many, surrendering their properties, were put in charge of their businesses again after an interim in which the government learned that Communist cadres do not necessarily make factory managers.

Such business people later lay low or were persecuted when the Cultural Revolution's "roughies," as one MIT-educated Chinese calls them, were running wild. But today they talk of adequate compensation for property that the government seized, of restoration of the trappings of wealth and of being able to pass on wealth to their children.

Gu Gengyu had a 500-employee animal byproducts company in Sichuan Province before 1949. He had a U.S. office in New York and was known, he says, as "the pig bristle king" (the bristles are used in shaving brushes). Under the Communists, he says, he ran a 500,000-employee enterprise—all animal byproducts operations, including leather, were centralized. Now 80, Gu no longer runs that business, but he is still active. He is a vice chairman of Incomic Development Corporation, an ACFIC affiliate that acts as a consultant for foreign enterprises in China.

Another surprise is apt to be the extent of American ties of prominent Chinese. Xu Qi-Chao, vice governor of Zhejiang Province, graduated from Arizona State University and got American air force training during World War II. Xu, who greeted the U.S. Chamber delegation in Hangzhou, his province's largest city, was greeting another visitor at the same time. An American-citizen brother was leading touring motorcyclists across China.

Gu Gengyu has two sons and two daughters in the United States. One son, working toward a Ph.D., is among 15,000 students from the People's Republic now in this country. Another such student, also seeking a Ph.D., is a son of Deng Xiaoping himself.

Even Chinese who appear to know no English sometimes produce surprises. At a typical Chinese banquet for the Chamber delegation—15 courses, endless bottoms-up toasts of sweet wine and a 120-proof, clear sorghum liquor called *maotai*—one host suggested a song. He burst into "Stormy Weather," which he had obviously learned phonetically decades earlier.

The biggest surprise of all may be the Chinese people. You see so many of them, all apparently well-fed. (Beggars? Not a one.) Phalanxes of bicycles transport thousands and thousands. On broad boulevards there are special lanes for bikes, but on narrower streets, autos and standing-room-only buses thread their ways through silent cyclists in a manner that can make an American gasp. Staggered workdays for many mean that there is always an anthill-like crowd during shopping or tourist hours. And added income from private enterprise—portions of crops sold independently in the city—means that many farmers now have the wherewithal for bus tours to the Great Wall, the Forbidden City or the sights of Shanghai and Hangzhou.

Private enterprise has also increased incomes in urban areas, where entrepreneurs are in assorted retailing and manufacturing ventures.

Communists often talk about private owners exploiting workers. Do such entrepreneurs consider themselves exploiters?

No, says Liu Guogiang, 26, whose furniture-making enterprise has seven employees. Under his guidance, he explains, workers can increase skills and get better jobs.

That kind of answer would once have been very much out of place in what, after all, is still Communist China.

Americans who live in the country say that there is obviously less repression than there used to be, but that in no way can China be considered a democracy in the Western sense. Will there be more political freedom, will the Communist Party's dominance end? A Chinese "former capitalist" says no and quickly changes the subject.

Deng Xiaoping is 81. Will China turn from its present economic path when he leaves the stage? No, says the "former capitalist." He adds: "China is the world's largest developing country. The United States has the world's largest developed economy. We can do a lot of things together."

Henry Altman, *Nation's Business,* December 1985

Writing the Miniature

This time in writing your miniresearch paper, you will be asked to devise your own thesis. Perhaps the most natural question that would arise as a result of reading two articles written five years apart on the same subject of China trade is whether the trade relationship has improved or deteriorated. Have the "old" obstacles been surmounted? Have "new" ones materialized? In other words, what has happened in U.S.–Chinese relations in the intervening five years?

Formulate a thesis which addresses the extent to which the U.S. trade policy with China has worked out or not. Then by using *both* articles, write an organized essay (500–600 words) developing your thesis. Do not allow the amount of material in the two articles to overwhelm you. You have no obligation to "cover everything." Limit your thesis to only those points of discussion that can be developed *thoroughly* in a 500- to 600-word essay.

A few additional guidelines:

1. Review your instructor's corrections and criticism of your essay on China trade. Avoid repeating the same mistakes.
2. Be sure that your thesis and your development are in perfect agreement, that what you promise to discuss you actually discuss.
3. Be thorough and exhaustive. Remember you have to validate (prove) your thesis, not merely illustrate what you mean by it. Therefore, the more evidence you provide for your thesis, the better.

3
Using the Library

Selecting a Topic, Restricting It, and Formulating a Preliminary Thesis

What the experience of writing a research paper is going to be like will depend a lot on your subject and your thesis. If you invest time and effort in preliminary research at the very beginning for the purpose of finding a good topic and manageable thesis, you will be setting the foundation for a pleasurable and stimulating experience.

Selecting a Topic

First of all, there's the topic to be selected. Understandably, you want to find a subject you're interested in and can stand to live with in the coming weeks. If you already have a fascination with something, by all means, pursue it. If you breathe, eat, and sleep, say, tennis, do take your obsession one step further and research it. But if—as you read this sentence—no particular topic comes to mind, then think "adventure." Don't be reluctant to spend time just browsing through subjects to find something "different" to write about.

There's no question that some subjects command more immediate interest than do others. Some topics, dreams, for example, are compelling because they reveal people to themselves; others, like Satanism, appeal to people's natural fascination with the bizarre; still others, like cocaine, subliminal advertising, and teen-age suicides, arouse interest because they're relevant to the contemporary scene. To be sure, they're all solid, workable subjects. But, unfortunately, many students don't try to get beyond their natural inclinations to look further afield for subjects that don't suggest themselves quite as readily as the ones above and yet might be just as interesting, if students only gave themselves a chance to discover them.

Take the following topic, for example: violins made by the Guarneri and Stradivari families during the seventeenth and eighteenth centuries. You can hardly imagine a less compelling interest for anyone of the pop culture generation. And yet consider this fact about the violins: Despite the latest advances in sound reproduction and compact-disc technology, which have given us Bach on a laser beam, no one has yet been able to figure out the secret behind the totally unique and magnificent sound of these violins—much less been able to reproduce it. Surely, the very thought that an age without electronic wizardry could surpass us in anything is astonishing and worth pursuing.

The point is that you should, of course, settle on a topic that you like, *but* do it only after you have given a couple of other topics a chance to catch your eye.

When you do finally decide on a topic, it will either be one that you know something about already or one that you don't. Rest assured that if you have no previous knowledge of your subject you are not at any particular disadvantage as compared with the student who is familiar with the subject; both types of topics have their advantages and pitfalls; neither type of topic is "easier" than the other.

The Familiar Subject

If you're writing on a subject that you know something about, you will most likely have opinions on it already. Say you have a personal interest in nursing homes because you work in one or you know about the Mt. St. Helens eruption because you live in the area or you have some expertise on the subject of boxing because you read *Sports Illustrated* and attend the fights. However, there is a hazard associated with topics in which you're well versed: namely, the understandable inclination to rely on your own knowledge *primarily* and add footnotes only for cosmetic reasons. But if you were to do that, you would not be writing a research paper. In a research paper, you have to do research to corroborate your point of view and your information with outside data and the opinions of authorities. Remember that despite what you know about your subject, you haven't studied it *systematically.* For example, as someone who has worked summers with mildly retarded children, you may have concluded that they are not as handicapped as people assume. In fact, it seems to you that as you play with them, read to them, and teach them things, they respond and learn and grow much like other kids. Such has been your *impression.* But in a research paper, you are not supposed to rely solely on your impressions; you are expected to find support for such impressions in the expert judgments of authorities and the data they've compiled in books and other library materials.

But what if you're doing a paper on boxing, you ask, and have all the *Sports Illustrated (SI)* magazines you need at home. You've been reading them for years and already have quite a command of the subject. Can't you use just *SI* for corroboration? Or what if you're doing a paper on nuclear power plants and have some inside knowledge because your father works in one. Couldn't you just rely on your father for information—his own as well as brochures, pamphlets, and other printed studies he can get at work? The answer, of course, to both questions is "no." You can use *SI and* the information put out by the nuclear power plant itself, but your research would not be objective if you relied *solely* on the point of view of one magazine or one sportswriter or one industry or one person in the industry. You must rely on a *range* of authorities.

In short, that part of your thinking that is based on your previous knowledge, reading, and experiences *will* inevitably play a role in your paper. So will the thinking you do in the course of your research. (See "Role of Personal Experience" in Chapter 1.) But it should complement your research, *not* replace it.

The Unfamiliar Subject

There are also advantages and pitfalls—though different ones—when you're writing on a subject in which you're interested but ignorant. Because you're not writing about what you know, you don't have to worry about relying strictly on your own opinions or some narrow source of information that you already have a corner on. But you will have to resist the opposite temptation: to be so dependent on your sources that you fail to think on your own at all. You will have to resist the even greater temptation to summarize just *one* source, a book or article that you think says it all for you. For example, in a paper on dreams you'd be writing a book report not a research paper if you merely reshuffled the information you found in Sandra Shulman's *The Interpretation of Dreams and Nightmares* and didn't use any other sources. In other words, if you rely merely on Shulman, you are not doing research; you're doing a book report. Therefore, your goal is to read a number of sources, then digest and absorb them thoroughly *before* writing. You should become as comfortable with your subject as is the student who is writing on a familiar subject.

Restricting the Topic and Formulating a Preliminary Thesis

Once you choose your subject, fully aware of the different demands of each kind, the next step is to narrow it down to manageable size. First, remember that a research paper is intended to be an investigation of some *aspect* of a subject, not of the subject itself. If you want to write on a subject as broad as "the Vikings," for instance, plan on writing a book; something like "the Viking voyages to the Massachusetts coast" would be more suitable for a research paper. Some students deliberately resist narrowing their subject for fear that they won't have enough to say unless they can find stacks of books and articles on precisely the same subject as that of their thesis. Such fear is groundless. Regardless of how narrow your subject (and the narrower the better), you *will* have plenty to say. You'll be instructed in how to develop ideas on your own, so that you won't need to rely on sources for *every* sentence of your essay.

Second, remember that the aspect you plan to write on should require *library* research. Take, for example, "the expense of dirt bike racing" as a topic. It may require research, but what kind of research? Wouldn't an independent survey of price tags, equipment, and other relevant expenses be enough to provide you with all the information you need to write this paper? Therefore, you'd have to restrict the topic of dirt bike racing differently.

In the process of restricting your subject, you will also be formulating a thesis. The two are more or less simultaneous procedures. You can think of the thesis as a **hypothesis**, an "educated guess," to be either verified or disproved not by a series of experiments but by the reliable opinions of authorities and their data. Or you can think of it as a "hunch" that needs proving one way or the other. In short, you will use the library not the lab to verify or cast doubt on the fact that ravens, to give an example, are one of the most intelligent species of birds. Ideally, you will find the opinions and data of experts to corroborate it; but you are not to think you've wasted any effort should your research lead you to the opposite conclusion—

Contrary to the opinion of some ornithologists, ravens are not as intelligent as formerly assumed.

or to a modification of your statement—

While ravens are certainly intelligent birds, they do not possess the kind of intelligence that would rank them as the most artistic of the bird species.

Notice that a thesis is never self-explanatory. In none of the statements on ravens above do you know exactly what the author means. Intelligent birds? What is intelligence in a bird? How is a raven any different from other birds? In short, you'd have to read the essay to understand the thesis fully.

A **thesis**, then, is (a) an expression of an arguable or debatable point of view; (2) is always stated as a sentence; and (3) needs further elaboration because it is not self-explanatory.

Notice how the following *two* statements fail to meet any of the specifications of a good thesis:

1. "Walt Disney's cartoon film *Fantasia* was followed by *The Reluctant Dragoon, Dumbo,* and *Bambi*." It's not a thesis because it's not a hunch, educated guess, or opinion. It's a statement of fact. It doesn't need elaborating. It's self-explanatory; it means what it says – no more. There's nothing to research and nowhere to go from it. And if it has its facts wrong, the disagreement is still over a fact and not over an opinion – to be resolved easily enough with a couple of dates – not a whole research essay.

2. "Incest is a subject of growing concern." While this statement *is* an opinion, it is also a very obvious one – so obvious in fact that no one is likely to disagree with it. What's more, such a broad statement of the obvious will force you into a *survey* of the subject, which is *not* the proper concern of a research paper.

Preliminary Research

The question then is: (1) *how* to narrow a topic and (2) *how* to formulate a thesis, which at this stage will be merely tentative. The preliminary thesis is not meant to be chiseled in stone. Use it primarily to give direction to your search and, *if* necessary, *modify* it as you go along.

One of the best ways to accomplish both (1) and (2) is to engage in some *preliminary* research in reference works, that is, in encyclopedias, biographical dictionaries, almanacs, atlases, gazetteers, as well as book jackets, prefaces, and introductions to books on your subject. The purpose of preliminary research is to get an overview and discover the different angles that can be explored profitably within the scope of a research paper. Furthermore, if you do your preliminary research thoughtfully, you might be able to find just the sentence that can be used as a preliminary thesis statement.

The following list presents the five types of general reference works that are most useful to you in doing preliminary research. Look for the most recent edition. Remember, you do *not* rely on encyclopedias, dictionaries, almanacs, yearbooks, atlases, or gazetteers to develop your thesis. You rely on them, primarily, to find a thesis and perhaps later, when you're doing the actual research, to find quick answers to specific questions: You might turn to the dictionary, for example, for the oldest meaning of a particular word; to biographical dictionaries for data about an individual's, say, nationality; to almanacs and yearbooks for some statistical information on schools; to atlases and gazetteers for information on population movements, for example, or war campaigns of fifteenth-century Europe. In short, these reference works are to be used now to suggest ideas for topics and thesis statements and later for discovering other pertinent facts. But under no circumstances should your actual research, once you've found a thesis, consist of copying articles out of reference books.

GENERAL ENCYCLOPEDIAS
Collier's Encyclopedia
The Encyclopedia Americana

New Columbia Encyclopedia
The New Encyclopaedia Britannica
Great Soviet Encyclopedia
New Catholic Encyclopedia
Encyclopaedia Judaica
Encyclopaedia of Islam

BIOGRAPHICAL DICTIONARIES

AMERICAN—CONTEMPORARY

Who's Who in America, 1899– .

Notable American Women: The Modern Period, 1951–1975.

Who's Who Among Black Americans, 1978.

American Men and Women of Science, 1976.

AMERICAN—DECEASED

Dictionary of American Biography, 1928–1937; Supplements 1–6, 1944–1980.

Notable American Women, 1607–1950.

BRITISH—CONTEMPORARY/DECEASED

Who's Who, 1849– .

Dictionary of National Biography, 1885–1901; Supplements 2–7, 1912–1971.

INTERNATIONAL—CONTEMPORARY

New York Times Biographical Service, 1970– . Concentrates on biographies of persons who are "newsmakers."

Current Biography, 1940– .

Contemporary Authors, 1962– .

INTERNATIONAL—CONTEMPORARY/DECEASED

Chambers's Biographical Dictionary, 1969.

Kunitz, Stanley, and V. Colby. *European Authors 1000–1925,* 1967.

ALMANACS AND YEARBOOKS

Annual Register of World Events, 1758– . Particularly strong on English affairs.

Facts on File Yearbook, 1940– . A digest of the significant news of the day compiled from a number of metropolitan daily newspapers.

The World Almanac and Book of Facts, 1868– . Miscellaneous information includes statistics on a variety of subjects: government, religion, schools, and so on.

Information Please Almanac, 1947– . Supplements the *World Almanac* without duplicating it.

Statesman's Yearbook: Statistical and Historical, 1864– . Valuable information on the world's governments.

Editorials on File, 1970– . Reprints of editorials on major controversial issues drawn from American and Canadian newspapers.

U.S. Bureau of the Census, 1878– . Statistical information on population, immigration, commerce, and so on.

ATLASES AND GAZETTEERS

Columbia Lippincott Gazetteer of the World, 1962. Geographical dictionary of place names and geographical features with additional information on population, industry, and so on.

The Times Atlas of the World, Comprehensive ed., 1975. Includes political maps and space exploration.

The Times Index Gazetteer of the World, 1965. Indexes about 345,000 geographical places and shows the location of 198,000.

Shepherd, William R. *Historical Atlas,* 1973. Covers the period from 1450 B.C. to the present day and includes maps of war campaigns, treaties, commerce, and so on.

Rand McNally Commercial Atlas, 1976. Particularly detailed treatment of U.S. states and territories.

The National Atlas of the United States of America, 1970. Features, in addition to geography, the political, social, economic, agricultural, and historical state of the country.

Paullin, Charles O., and J. K. Wright. *Atlas of the Historical Geography of the U.S.,* 1932. Reprinted 1975. Includes old maps and maps on explorations, settlements, early cities, and so on.

DICTIONARIES

UNABRIDGED DICTIONARIES

The Oxford English Dictionary (OED), 1888–1933; Supplement, 1976. Has as its purpose the history of every word in use since A.D. 1150, supported by numerous quotations.

Craigie, Sir William, and James R. Hulbert. *A Dictionary of American English on Historical Principles,* 1936–1944. Continues where the *OED* leaves off with the history of English words in the American colonies and the United States.

Random House Dictionary of the English Language, 1966.

Webster's New International Dictionary of the English Language, 1960.

SPECIALIZED DICTIONARIES

Partridge, Eric. *Dictionary of Slang and Unconventional English,* 1970.

Wentworth, Harold, and Stuart B. Flexner. *Dictionary of American Slang,* 1975.

Oxford Dictionary of Quotations, 1953.

Oxford Dictionary of English Proverbs, 1970.

Roget's International Thesaurus, 1962. A dictionary of synonyms.

Acronyms, Initialisms and Abbreviations Dictionary, 1976.

Sheffield City Libraries. *'Isms,* 1972. A dictionary of words ending in -ism, -ology, -phobia, and so on, listed by subject, thus enabling a reader to find a word he or she can't think of.

Using Reference Works to Select a Topic and Preliminary Thesis

The following section presents excerpts from various reference works on randomly selected topics. The brief discussion that accompanies each passage should give you an idea of how articles in encyclopedias and other general reference books can be used to explore a subject for angles and a possible thesis.

The General Topic

KHYBER PASS

Khyber Pass, the most important of the passes which lead from Afghanistan into West Pakistan, lies about 10½ mi. W. of Peshawar. It is threaded by a good metaled road, a caravan track and in greater part by rail. It is a narrow defile winding between cliffs of shale and limestone, 600 to 1,000 ft. high, stretching up to more lofty mountains behind. No other pass in the world has had such strategic importance or so many historic associations. Through it have passed the legions of Persians, Greeks, Tatars, Moguls and Afghans and in more modern times it was a key point in British control of the Afghan border and of the warlike tribes inhabiting the surrounding country.

from *Encyclopaedia Britannica,* 1972

Even though this is just the first paragraph of the article, it already suggests both a restriction of the topic and a thesis. Notice that the paragraph has only one sentence (possibly two) that is a statement of opinion rather than a specific fact: namely, that "No other pass in the world has had such strategic importance or so many historic associations." (The other possible opinion is that "in modern times it was a key point in British control of the Afghan border. . . .") Everything else in the paragraph is a fact. Consequently, since a fact can't be elaborated on, it can't serve as a thesis. But the general statements of opinion can be used as thesis statements. In other words, if you had chosen the Khyber Pass as a topic, a good thesis is the following: "The Khyber Pass has been of great strategic and historic importance."

GEISHA

Geisha, gā-shä, the traditional professional hostess in Japan. The term means "artistic or accomplished person." The geisha were usually the daughters of established hostesses or were poor peasants' daughters who were bonded to the owners of geisha houses. The girls began training when they were 6 or 7 and became full-fledged geisha at about 16. From the houses where they lived under professional female supervision they were engaged to perform elsewhere.

Most geisha were mature women. Usually they were hired at high
fees to attend all-male gatherings at which they displayed their skills in
song, dance, and poetry recitation. But their forte was light conversation and banter. Though they might grant some men their personal
1A favors, geisha were not considered prostitutes. Their great hope was to
meet a wealthy merchant or political figure who would set them up as
mistresses or marry them.

2A The geisha still exist, and in some parts of Japan they have been
unionized. Since World War II, however, the call for geisha entertainment has declined greatly.

Hyman Kublin, *Brooklyn College, The City University of New York*

Japan: 4. Sports . . . song, and social conversation. Her dance,
though coquettish, follows disciplined Japanese form and is performed
in a full, many-layered costume. It is never forthrightly sensuous, nor
is the geisha's performance a prelude to sexual encounter, despite the
1B misapprehension of many foreigners and notwithstanding the fact that
each geisha usually has an arrangement with a wealthy patron. Some
girls, however, use the geisha role as a screen for sexual invitations, and
2B they ask high prices, for the geisha tradition evolved as elite entertainment. But without an introduction and ample funds, a true geisha cannot be hired. Geisha entertaining at present seems to be at the edge of
extinction, unable to adapt to new tastes and compete with less expensive diversions.

from *The Encyclopedia Americana,* 1986

These two brief entries on the geisha are even richer than the paragraph on the Khyber Pass in suggesting several directions a research paper on the subject might take:

1A–B. It might correct the "misapprehension of many foreigners," who have usually considered the geisha a prostitute. Preliminary thesis: "Despite what foreigners might think, the geisha are not considered prostitutes."

1A–B. It might examine what "new tastes" and "less expensive diversions" are causing the geisha tradition to decline. Preliminary thesis: "Unable to compete with the new tastes and less expensive diversions, the geisha tradition is declining."

BATHS AND BATHING

Baths and Bathing. Baths are the receptacles, rooms, or buildings designed for bathing, the process of washing or soaking oneself. Throughout history baths have varied in size and elaborateness, from

the private tub to the public swimming pool, according to the purpose
1A of the bather. Three different purposes, discernible at an early stage
of history, remain today. These are general well-being, ceremonial purification, and cleanliness.

The idea of bathing for general well-being was known to the ancient Greeks of Homer's time. In Greece and Rome, warm baths were extensively used for relaxation and pleasure. Among the Romans, and later the Turks, bathing places became social and recreational centers. Bathing was also favored as a means for treating diseases. The modern custom of "taking a cure" at a spa can be traced back to an early belief in the medicinal qualities of mineral springs.

Bathing for ceremonial purification is also an ancient custom. Very early records of such ceremonial cleansing came from Egypt, where bathing was regarded as primarily a religious rite. The Mosaic code of the Hebrews required ritual washing, and this code influenced the Muslims. Among the Hindus, bathing has always been looked on as an essentially religious duty. The Hindus bathed for ritual purposes whereas the Greeks bathed for comfort.

Some authorities have speculated that the use of water for ritual purification grew out of the custom of washing for simple cleanliness, but it is difficult to determine which custom came first. It may be noted that at various times in history people have washed for ceremonial purposes or bathed for social and curative reasons even though they had very little concern for hygiene. In fact, the idea of washing to remove harmful bacteria from the skin could not have been conceived until after
1B the germ theory of disease had been accepted. Not until modern times
did cleanliness, for the sake of hygiene and appearance, become the unquestionably primary motive for bathing.

Ancient Civilizations

The public baths of Mohenjo-Daro, in the Indus Valley, and the palace baths at Knossos, on Crete, are the earliest known to man.

Built by a highly civilized people, Mohenjo-Daro is estimated to be
about 5,000 years old. One of its greatest features was a public bath about
2 24 by 40 feet (7.3 by 12.2 meters). In addition, an elaborate drainage
system enabled most houses to have at least one bathroom, with horizontal drains usually of brick, and terra cotta pipes fitted with spigot and faucet joints and protected by brickwork or by the walls.

The Minoan palace at Knossos included a sophisticated drainage plan with bathrooms, foot baths, and tubs, believed to date from between 2000 and 1800 B.C. The drains were made of stone, and vertical pipes, interlocked and cemented at the joints, may have been used for an upward

> flow of water. A modern looking bathtub (dating from between 1700 and 1400 B.C.) found in the queen's apartments is evidence that the structure of the tub, deriving as it does from its function, has remained relatively constant through history. There are, in fact, almost no examples in history of a "primitive" tub.
>
> from *The Encyclopedia Americana,* 1986

Don't be afraid of looking up topics that seem exceptionally broad, like bathing. Encyclopedia articles are rich in providing a range of angles when the subject is vast, because, as an overview, they're bound to section off the subject into subtopics.

The first seven paragraphs of this article on baths and bathing just begin to touch on the many fascinating possibilities for narrowing the topic.

1. The first idea grows out of the discussion of the three different purposes that bathing had throughout history: to produce "general well-being, ceremonial purification, and cleanliness" (1A). There is a thesis here. But the sentence marked 1B makes an even better one since it puts the focus on the most interesting fact of the thesis: "Not until modern times did cleanliness, for the sake of hygiene and appearance, become the unquestionably primary motive for bathing." Though essentially there is no difference between "bathing had three different purposes throughout history" and "Not until modern times did cleanliness . . . ," 1A sounds dull and vaguely factual, compared to 1B, which shifts the focus to modern times, expressing the opinion that only modern man bathes in order to be clean. As you can see, phrasing becomes very important. It changes the thesis above from a *list* of purposes (1A) to a *contrast* between purposes (1B).

2. The second possible angle appears in the section entitled "Ancient Civilizations." Notice that it gives you a whole series of remarkable facts. And while there is no explicit sentence that can be used as a thesis, the collection of facts implies a thesis that you merely need to frame into words. That is to say, it's remarkable that 5000 years ago a civilization had elaborate drainage systems, bathrooms, spigots, faucets, paraphernalia that we'd like to think of as "modern," but which obviously aren't. What thesis does all of this add up to? How about this: "Five thousand years ago the Minoan civilization had public and palace baths that had all the technology and fixtures that are normally thought of as 'modern.' "

The rest of the article goes on to discuss other aspects of bathing that make equally feasible and fascinating topics: (1) how the Romans in their love of luxury and pleasure raised bathing to a social art form; (2) how the advent of Christianity introduced a puritanical attitude to bathing; (3) how Islam had an impact on it; (4) how the Europeans introduced perfume and cosmetics as a substitute for bathing; (5) how Ben Franklin became a pioneer of American bathing; (6) how the bathroom evolved as a separate unit only in the Victorian era.

TOMATO

Tomato, an herbaceous plant and its succulent, acid fruit, of the family Solanaceae. All cultivated forms of tomato belong to the species *Lycopersicon esculentum* except the tiny currant tomato (*L. pimpinellifolium*).

History

The wild species originated in the Peru-Ecuador-Bolivia area of South America. Cultivated forms were developed before Columbus in Mexico and possibly in Central and South America. Definite records are lacking but evidence indicates that the tomato reached Europe from
1 Mexico. The first definite description, in Italy in 1554, carried the
common name *pomi d'oro*, or apple of gold. Thus the first form known to Europeans was yellow. Before the end of the 16th century the tomato, in both yellow and scarlet forms, was known in the gardens of England,
2A Spain, Italy, France, and mid-Europe chiefly as a curiosity called
3 "love apple" (*pomme d'amour*), probably because of its supposed
aphrodisiacal properties.

2B Although there was some resistance to its use as food, by the
mid-1700s the tomato was consumed in several European countries. There is no record of its culture in the U.S. until Thomas Jefferson grew it in 1781. It was used for food in Louisiana as early as 1812 but not in the northeastern states until about 1835. Until nearly 1900 many still believed it to be poisonous, possibly because some members of the family Solanaceae are poisonous. The genus name, *Lycopersicon,* meaning "wolf peach," is probably in allusion to that once held belief.

from *Encyclopaedia Britannica,* 1972

Another approach you can take in your search for a workable thesis is to look for unexplained statements that suggest the question *why.*

1. Why was the tomato called "apple of gold" in 1554? Was the label merely a reference to its color (according to the explanation that follows) or is there a more tantalizing explanation?

2A–B. Why was the tomato "chiefly a curiosity" and why the "resistance to its use as food"?

3. Why was it called a "love apple"? How did it get its reputation as an aphrodisiac?

Framing a thesis when you have only a question is obviously going to be riskier than using an existing statement because it means playing a hunch, and you could be wrong. But being wrong isn't fatal; it's part of research. Once you discover the extent of your "mistake," just modify the thesis—or leave a blank in the thesis sentence until you've done enough preliminary research to complete it.

Here are some sample thesis statements that have been formulated on the basis of the foregoing questions.

1. "The tomato was once called 'apple of gold' because of characteristics that were considered exotic among medieval vegetables."
2. "Prior to the 1700s, Europeans resisted eating the tomato because of various medical superstitions."
3. "The tomato had acquired its reputation as an aphrodisiac by the sixteenth century because ________________."

BOWERBIRD

Bowerbird, the name applied to birds of the family Ptilonorhynchidae, containing about 17 species like stout thrushes, 8 to 14 in. long. Although the females are usually dull, the males often sport brilliant plumage approaching that of their close relatives, the birds of paradise (*q.v.*), though without decorative plumes. Ten species occur in New Guinea, others in eastern Australia. In jungle or brush they construct courtship bowers or "runs" of sticks, decorating floor or entrance with small bones, shells and brightly coloured berries, flowers or feathers. Both sexes use bowers as a playground, and males fight, display or "dance" for the females.

The satin bowerbird (*Ptilonorhynchus violaceus*), abundant in the wooded mountains of southeastern Queensland, eastern New South Wales and Victoria, builds a walled corridor usually facing north and south though often hidden in the jungle. The "blue" males—lustrous bluish or purplish black—prefer lavish decorations of blue bits of glass or blue flowers, the greenish females and young males prefer green to decorate the bower entrance. Two blotched eggs are laid in a bulky nest 6 to 40 ft. up in bush or tree that may be some distance away from the bower.

The regent bowerbird (*Sericulus chrysocephalus*) is the most brilliantly plumaged bird in Australia, gorgeous in black and orange-yellow. Common in the McPherson ranges, Queensland, it rarely constructs a bower. Some species build no bower at all; one surfaces a bare spot with leaves to form a "circus ring." The gardener bowerbird (*Amblyornis inornatus*) of New Guinea builds a roofed bower, three feet wide, of orchid stems near the foot of a small tree, and covers the floor and entrance with moss, ornamented with fresh flowers and berries, which are replaced by fresh ones as they fade. *See* also COURTSHIP OF ANIMALS: BIRD. (G. F. Ss.)

from *Encyclopaedia Britannica*, 1972

At other times your preliminary research will force you to explore related topics and read several encyclopedia articles for a suitably narrow angle. Say your topic is the bowerbird, an incredible creature that landscapes, paints, and decorates its nest. The description that you find of it under "Bowerbird" is too factual. You can't simply describe the construction of the "courtship bowers" or its lavish decorations. That would be straight summary. But you notice that at the end of the entry, you are referred to two other topics, "Courtship of Animals" and "Bird," for further information.

COURTSHIP OF ANIMALS

Courtship, Animal. A peacock spreading his beautiful train to the full, and occasionally vibrating the quills to produce a rustling sound, turning from side to side before his mate, or a barn-door cock with drooped wing and special call circling close round a hen—these are familiar examples of animal courtship.

1 Courtship is a feature of sexual behaviour. It may be defined as any action executed by members of one sex to stimulate members of the other sex to sexual activity. Such actions include the display of bright colours or of adornments such as crests; special tactile contacts; dances or other antics; pursuit; music, vocal or instrumental; the discharge of scents and perfumes; and the presentation of prey or of inedible but otherwise stimulating objects. Primarily, courtship leads up to the sex act, which in many animals may be the only association between the mates. Many vertebrate animals, however, especially birds, but also some fish and mammals, develop longer associations between mates, who cooperate to care for their young just as humans do. Then courtship is associated with mate selection, with greeting after separation, and with choosing a nest site or spawning place, as well as with the sex act. The activities most immediately preceding the sex act and the sex act itself as it applies to vertebrates are discussed in detail in the article Sexual Behaviour.

Birds

It is among birds that courtship is most universal and striking. This is partly because birds are extremely visually and vocally oriented, and their displays are more conspicuous to us than are, for example, the scent displays of mammals. Bird reproductive habits, however, are such as to put a high premium upon cooperation and timing. The young are helpless and must be supplied with food, which is often very seasonal. Well-timed mating may assure the best of the food supply and sometimes make possible the rearing of an extra brood. Much bird courtship is therefore concerned with overcoming behavioural barriers to mating and with promoting physiological adjustments between the mates. All birds lay eggs, usually in a prepared nest. But females cannot retain fully developed eggs for long, nor can they store sperm. Hence, it is important that mating and egg laying should both occur at about the time that the nest is completed.

2 The "marriage systems" of birds vary from permanent monogamy (parrots, ravens) through monogamy for one season (most monogamous birds) or one brood (some wrens) to polygamy of the "small harem" type (jungle fowl, many pheasants) or of the promiscuous type (ruff, blackcock, peacock, probably some birds of paradise). Many monogamous birds maintain breeding territories and defend them against other males (or pairs) of the same species, thus often ensuring a private food supply for the young. All monogamous males (and a few polygamous ones too) assist with feeding the young and sometimes with incubation. Drakes mount guard while ducks incubate. The males of promiscuous species only play no part in rearing the young.

Courtship reaches its greatest elaboration in some of the promiscuous birds, especially those in which males gather for mating.

from *Encyclopaedia Britannica,* 1972

Unlike the short entry on bowerbird, the much longer discussion of courtship among birds is filled with possible topics, some requiring that you switch from just "bowerbird" to "courtship rituals." If you're willing to do that, the article raises several promising possibilities:

1. The article on courtship tells you what the one on bowerbird doesn't, namely, that in the animal world members of one sex use bright colors and objects (among other things) to stimulate members of the other sex to sexual activity. Given that information, you should begin wondering whether that isn't the reason for the bowerbird's marvelously humanlike activities. If the answer to the question is "yes" (and it probably is), you have a thesis: "The bowerbird's incredible nest building activities are part of the courtship ritual."

2. You'll also notice that the article speaks of "marriage systems" and monogamous and polygamous birds. You might wonder whether bowerbirds are monogamous or polygamous. Your second question (inspired by the last sentence of the article) might be whether a bird's preference for monogamy or polygamy has any bearing on the nature or elaborateness of the courtship rituals. Is there a correlation? Elaborate rituals go with polygamous birds, plain rituals with monogamous? Or vice versa? And where does the bowerbird fit in? A tentative thesis, therefore, might be the following: "The elaborateness of the bowerbird's nest is an example of the rule among birds that the more elaborate the courtship ritual the shorter/longer the relationship between the mating birds."

COMICS

Comics, kom′iks, are cartoons arranged either in a single panel or in several boxes (in which case they are called "comic strips"), which are a popular feature of most American newspapers. Generally, comic strips have a continuing cast of characters. Depending on the nature of the strip, these characters may appear either in short, humorous incidents or in longer narratives employing suspense, drama, and adventure. The term "comics" is also applied to *comic books,* a carry-over from the cartoon strips from which they developed. A distinctive feature of most comic strips and comic books is the enclosure of the dialogue in "balloons" that seem to emerge from the speakers' mouths.

Daily and Sunday comic strips are read by millions of Americans
1 from all segments of society. The comics, with their use of familiar
folk themes and motifs, may be likened to 20th century versions of fairy
tales, myths, and fables. They draw upon the folklore of American life
2 and create their own gallery of folk characters. The comics are an
American institution, and from their beginning they have influenced the
American language. Cartoonist Thomas A. Dorgan, for example, created many expressions that became part of American slang. Dorgan's strips *Indoor Sports* and *Judge Rummy* introduced such phrases as "twenty-three skiddoo," "cat's pajamas," "drugstore cowboy," and "yes, we have no bananas."

In his book *The American People: A Study in National Character,* the British anthropologist Geoffrey Gorer observed: "With the notable exception of the New York *Times,* almost every American newspaper carries comic strips. They are one of the few important bonds (the films being another and the presidential elections a third) uniting all Americans in a common experience."

From their beginning in the 1890's, the comics appealed both to
young readers and to adults. Research conducted by Charles Swanson
indicated that in the period from 1939 to 1950 the comic strip page was
3 by far the most widely read section of the newspaper. Analyzing the
appeal of approximately 40,000 news and feature items that appeared in 130 American newspapers, Swanson found that the comics ranked highest, with an average male readership of 56.3% and an average female readership of 56.6%. The next highest category was war (World War II, of course, occurred dring the period of these surveys), with an average readership of 34.6%. Swanson did not conclude that the comics were more important to the average American newspaper reader than news about the greatest war in history. But his study did indicate that comic strips had a very great appeal to the American people.

A strong case could be made for the comics as the most widely read mass medium in the United States. For example, a comic strip such as *Blondie,* a leader in popularity for nearly four decades, quite possibly may have been read more than 300 billion times. This enormous figure is based on the assumption that 40 or 50 million *Blondie* devotees habitually read this strip each day. By reestablishing itself daily with its reader, the comic strip reinforces its hold on him.

American comic strips have been widely circulated throughout the world. In turn, the success in the United States of such strips as Britain's *Andy Capp* signifies that the medium serves as agent for the exchange of mass culture. American comics have achieved wide popularity in Latin America, where in Buenos Aires the prestigious *La Prensa* has carried several American strips. They have been accepted in Europe, even in such Communist countries as Yugoslavia, Poland, Czechoslovakia, and Hungary. Australia and South Africa have also proved to be good markets for American comics.

Origins and History

4 Newspaper comic artists are the spiritual descendants of the Egyptian artists of 3000 B.C., who drew amusing cartoons of animals on papyrus, and of the Romans of Caesar's time, who hawked satiric cartoons on *tabulae*. In England, broadsheets and pamphlets of Punch and Judy characters were sold at fairs in the 17th century, and thus might be called the first comic books. Perhaps the most clearly traceable influence on modern comic strips is Wilhelm Busch's *Max und Moritz* (1870), a classic story of two mischievous boys. It was translated by an American clergyman, Charles T. Brooks of Salem, Mass., and published in comic book form in the United States. Busch's creation undoubtedly served as the inspiration for *The Katzenjammer Kids* a few years later.

from *The Encyclopedia Americana,* 1986

The excerpt above from *The Encyclopedia Americana* is the first page of a six-page overview of comics; it offers four possibilities that conveniently cover the various kinds of statements that you will be confronting in your preliminary research and the mental notes you should be making as you study the overviews.

1. *The dual-subject thesis.* The first statement (already phrased as a thesis) involves a subject that requires research in two separate areas: American comics (or comic) and fairy tales, myths, and fables. If you were dealing with the comic strip *Orphan Annie,* for example, your aim would be to discover what it has in common with fairy tales, myths, and so on.

This kind of topic, in which you have to draw on information from *two* separate fields of study, is particularly good in keeping you from the pitfall of overdependence on your sources. You will be forced to make many of the connections yourself between what you read about American comics (*Orphan Annie,* for example) and about fairy tales in general. You'll be doing a great deal of thinking for this topic, and that, of course, is the ideal research situation.

2. *The already researched thesis.* The second sentence (also phrased as a thesis) has a snare. It's the sort of statement that sounds like the thesis of some existing book or article. Your research paper will be forced merely to restate or summarize it. Therefore, you would have to check out just how much has been written on it. Is it just one book or article? Discard the thesis. A number of books and/or articles? Take the thesis but narrow it even further so that you aren't merely summarizing the books (not really any better than summarizing just one) but zeroing in and elaborating on *one* aspect of the thesis. Thus in the end after having explored the field, you'd settle on something like the following thesis sentence: "From their beginning comics have influenced the sexual vocabulary of Americans."

3. *The question-raising thesis.* The third statement gives statistical facts. So, of course, it can't be a thesis. However, there is an idea embedded in the facts that could be formulated into a thesis: "Comics *appeal* to newspaper readers." While the statement above *is* a thesis, it obviously also implies a question: why? *Why* do comics appeal to readers? You don't know. So you use the above as a tentative thesis with the understanding that when you find out in the course of your research, you will reformulate your thesis indicating the reasons for their appeal. Needless to say, this is an excellent way of approaching your research—with questions that need to be answered. Half way through your research you would probably be able to formulate something like the following statement: "American newspaper comics appeal to their readers because of their humorous exaggeration of American life and manners."

4. *The correct-a-misconception thesis.* The fourth statement suggests the unusual angle that is always tantalizing to work with because it corrects a misapprehension. It's the kind of thesis that proves the opposite of what most people think. This sort of thesis will always have as part of its angle what the average person thinks about the subject. In fact, the misconception provides the paper with the angle from which it is launched; in other words, your paper begins by discussing the misconceptions and then moves on to correct them. Hence the following thesis: "Cartoons are not a modern invention but were found in Egypt as far back as 3000 B.C. and in the Rome of Caesar's time."

The Biographical Topic

If you've chosen to write on a person's life, narrowing your topic is particularly vital. You can't deal with straight biography in your paper because it would mean turning your essay into straight summary. One way to avoid formulating a thesis that leads to straight summary while engaging in preliminary research is to scan the encyclopedia and biographical dictionary entries for some point or fact for which the person is not principally famous. For example, a paper on Michelangelo as sculptor or painter would cover too large a span of his life. But one on Michelangelo as military engineer who undertook the defense of Florence would be both manageable in size and avoid summarizing the larger part of his life. Similarly, the subject of Churchill's political career is too large in scope, but *Chambers's Biographical Dictionary* points out that he was also a "zestful social reformer." There's a connection that the average person does not make with Churchill. It thus provides you with a narrow angle that doesn't require summarizing either his life or his long political career.

If you can't find a sideline that the person was engaged in, then look for a narrower aspect of his or her principal career: Rembrandt's studies of old age, for instance, instead of just Rembrandt's paintings; or the bloodshed that Gandhi's critics claim his "nonviolent" campaigns instigated rather than the civil disobedience campaign itself.

Like nonbiographical topics, the lives of famous people may also suggest the kind of thesis that involves the correction of some misapprehension or simply a reinterpretation of a person's life. Therefore, look for angles in which modern scholarship has shed new light on some old facts.

JUDAS ISCARIOT

Judas Iscariot, jo͞o′dəs is-kar′ē-ət ("man of Kerioth," or "the false"), the son of Simon and an intimate disciple of Jesus, whom he betrayed. Tradition, not unnaturally, has dealt harshly with him; hence, details are obscure and far from trustworthy. He was "treasurer" for Jesus' followers, and John says he stole money from the common purse (John 12:6). He contracted with the Jewish priests to betray Jesus for 30 pieces of silver (Matthew 26:14–16; Mark 14:10–11; Luke 22:3–6). At the Last Supper when Jesus pointed to him as a traitor Judas left, and shortly thereafter identified his master with a kiss in the Garden of Gethsemane. Matthew says that he returned the money and hanged himself (Matthew 27:3–10). According to Acts, he used it to buy a field, fell headlong, and burst asunder (Acts 1:16ff).

Greed perhaps influenced Judas. But disappointment at Jesus' refusal to assume the role of a military leader, as some expected the Messiah to do, may have dulled his initial enthusiasm and destroyed his allegiance. He may simply have intended to force Jesus' hand, believing that Jesus, once arrested, would surely assert his heavenly power and lead the Jews to victory over their enemies.

O. Sydney Barr, *The General Theological Seminary*
from *The Encyclopedia Americana*, 1986

According to the biographical sketch of Judas Iscariot, Judas may have been misrepresented. Since Biblical times he has been the archetype of betrayal, the man who sells out his friend for money. While the sketch doesn't suggest that Judas did not betray Jesus, it does suggest that the betrayal may not have been an act of greed but possibly political manipulation. Can such a speculation about Judas' motives be verified through an examination of the political climate of Jesus' day? Tentative thesis: "Judas' betrayal of Jesus was not an act of greed but an act of politics."

EXERCISE 1

Look at the following passages that have been taken from various general reference works. What restricted topics and thesis statements can you derive from them?

EVERGLADES

Everglades, The, in southern Florida, a low region of periodically flooded sawgrass prairies and swamps in a shallow basin that slopes gently in a broad arc from Lake Okeechobee to the Gulf of Mexico. The basin ranges from 35 to 50 miles (56–80 km) in width and covers some 4,000 square miles (10,300 sq km). The slowly moving water ranges from a few inches to several feet in depth. Much of the region is included in the Everglades National Park. The name is thought to be a corruption of "river glades," attributed to a British surveyor who visited the region in the early 18th century.

Situated at the edge of the tropics, the Everglades are a wilderness that is unique in the United States. Its diverse habitats have supported a teeming array of wildlife. Some plants and animals exist nowhere else in the country.

Man is seldom willing to coexist with a natural landscape, particularly if he has the power to modify it. A network of canals, locks, pumping stations, and dams has been built to drain extensive areas of the Everglades for agriculture and real estate development. The effect upon the region's ecology has been serious. . . .

Ecology

The Everglades are a dynamic ecosystem in which all parts—plants, animal, and physical landscape—are connected in an interdependent network of energy flows and mineral cycles. Each part, whether it is an entire sawgrass prairie or a single species of reptile, has a place in the system.

The sawgrass and the mangroves, which grow nearer the coast, are not consumed by grazing animals. Nevertheless they are extremely important because fungi and bacteria attach themselves to the fallen leaves and provide food for larger animals. Algae growing on submerged sawgrass stems are eaten by herbivores, such as snails, which are the basic diet of limpkins and kites. Similarly, minnows support larger fish and wading birds. Eagles, ospreys, alligators, and man are among the top carnivores. Mangrove forests drop about 12 tons of organic detritus per acre each year, providing the basis for many food chains. These chains include some 80 species of marine fishes.

ROLE OF THE ALLIGATOR. The role of the alligator illustrates the interdependence of organisms in the Everglades ecosystem. The alligator is a top carnivore at which various food chains converge. It eats any animal smaller than itself, including other alligators, thus providing a valuable population control and selection service. It creates and sustains ponds in its territory. Its flailing about in pursuit of food continually deepens and enlarges the pond, or "gator hole," as it is called locally. In nesting, the female heaps up mud and vegetation, further enlarging the hole. In times of drought, these holes provide a refuge where water-dependent animals can survive until the rains come and they can move out and repopulate their original habitats. The few inches of material piled up by the alligator around its hole can provide the necessary substratum for a new tree island in the sawgrass prairie. In turn, the trees provide new feeding, roosting, and nesting sites for birds. Success in nesting can be dependent upon the presence of alligators to reduce predation on eggs and fledglings by raccoons and snakes. Finally, the food the alligator eats, and eventually its own body, are mineralized by bacteria and returned to the system for uptake by plants.

WATER AND FIRE. The seasonal timing, amount, and duration of water upon the landscape contribute to shaping the unique ecosystem. The system is attuned to cycles of summer flooding and winter drought, dry years and hurricanes. The Kissimmee River basin, which feeds into Lake Okeechobee to the north and is an area nearly as large as the Everglades, once supplied a significant quantity of water. Now the southern edge of the lake has been diked, and this water is wasted to the sea in times of potential flood rather than allowed to flow south through the sawgrass. About one third of the Everglades' water comes from the Big Cypress Swamp to the west.

Fire is second only to water in importance to the Everglades' ecosystem. Long before man came on the scene, lightning-caused fire played a significant role in shaping the landscape. Hammocks are continually trimmed back around the edges by fires that whip through the dry sawgrass. Without fire the open pinelands with their understory of seed-bearing and succulent plants would be replaced by dense stands of hardwoods, which contain little food for deer, many species of birds, or ranchers' cattle. Fires are more frequent and intense today because of drainage.

from *The Encyclopedia Americana*, 1986

GRAFFITI

Graffiti, gra-fē′tē, an Italian word meaning "scratchings" or "scribblings," was originally applied by archaeologists to a class of casual writings found in Pompeii, in Roman catacombs, and elsewhere. They were scratched onto walls or written on them with chalk or charcoal. An early example in Pompeii consisted of the words "Sodoma, Gomora." Other graffiti were messages by lovers, poetry, obscene terms, and political slogans.

The word "graffiti" is now often a general term for any obscenities, and at other times refers to inscriptions or designs scratched on walls. Both uses are a departure from the technical meaning, which was restricted to wall scratchings, but of an unauthorized and casual nature. Graffiti are found in public toilets, on sides of buildings, and on rocks in parks and in the countryside. Sometimes they consist of a single word, often obscene; sometimes a name and date; often a brief poem, a sexual solicitation, or a political statement. During periods of revolutionary action, graffiti may be used to express party loyalties or opposition to the ruling powers. The political use of graffiti is seen in racist slogans in the United States and in anti-American slogans in many parts of the world, of which the best known is probably "Yankee Go Home."

Edward Sagarin, *The City College, New York*
from *The Encyclopedia Americana,* 1986

HANSEL AND GRETEL

Hansel and Gretel, han′səl, gret′əl, is a German folktale appearing in the collection by the brothers Grimm (q.v.). A brother and sister are deserted in the woods by their impoverished father and wicked stepmother. They come upon a gingerbread house, guarded by a wicked witch. She locks Hansel up, preparing to roast and eat him, but Gretel tricks the witch and burns her in her own oven.

The story is found in the children's literature of India, Japan, and the West Indies, as well as northern Europe. The motifs of the abandoned children, the wicked stepmother, and the stupid ogre deceived by the innocent children are familiar folkloric elements.

from *The Encyclopedia Americana,* 1986

MARRIAGE

Forms of Marriage

An enormous variety of relationships between men and women, singly and in groups, meet the definition of marriage. Often the forms of marriage sanctioned by a society are related to the needs of that society. Marriage between two individuals, one male and one female, is known as *monogamy.* Marriage of three or more individuals is known as *polygamy.*

Polygyny is a form of polygamy in which one male is married to more than one female. *Polyandry* is a form of polygamy in which one female is married to more than one male. Still another form of polygamy is *group marriage,* in which two or more males are married to two or more females. In some societies a polyandrous marriage of two men with one woman may become a group marriage through the addition of a second woman. Not uncommonly in these marriages, the co-husbands are brothers and the added woman is the first wife's sister. . . .

PROBLEMS OF MARRIAGE. Both polygynous and monogamous unions have been criticized by those concerned with equal rights for women. Polygynous marriage has been condemned on the ground that it debases women. Monogamous marriage also has been condemned on the ground that it keeps the wife dependent on, and therefore unequal in status with, the husband.

Marriage is intimately connected to other aspects of society. The consequences for the men and women involved depend on a host of economic, ideological, and demographic factors. In no setting can marriage solve the larger social problems of economic exploitation and the institutional factors of sexism.

Each marital form presents a different structural problem to the marital partners. In monogamous unions, particularly in Western society, the dominant relationship is the married couple. The marriage is expected to fulfill virtually all the social and psychic needs of the partners.

By contrast, in a polygynous society marriage is not viewed as an independent tie between two individuals. Polygynous marriages are seen in relation to group interests that take precedence over individual interest. Polygyny is enmeshed in a larger kinship unit in which the marital tie is not expected to be the dominant one. Husband and wife have little opportunity for intimacy. They do not expect to receive love, companionship, sexual satisfaction, economic sustenance, or domestic support from one individual, as in a monogamous marriage.

from *The Encyclopedia Americana,* 1986

CLOTHING

Clothing and Status

An important function of clothing is that of defining a person's status and position in his society. For example, in some societies small children wear no clothing at all, and the adoption of clothing by a child marks a change in age status. In Turkistan small boys wear clothing like that of their fathers except that they do not wind a turban over their skullcap until they become men. In East Africa a boy's developing status is indicated through a number of stages: at one age a front tooth is knocked out, later he undergoes scarification, and when he becomes eligible to look for a bride, the regalia he wears at once identifies this status. Among the Ainu of Japan the tattooing of a woman's moustache was done just before her marriage. Tattooing and scarification, which are usually completed by the time of marriage, may have other status significance. Among Australian aborigines the scars on a man's back indicated the totem group to which he belonged, while in Borneo the symbols tattooed on a Dayak's legs were supposed to identify him to his ancestors in the afterworld when he died.

Hairdress serves as a status symbol almost everywhere. Men and women dress their hair differently, and girls often change their hairdress after marriage. In Turkistan, for example, a girl wears her hair in 40 tiny braids until marriage, changing to 2 large braids after the birth of the first child. In a number of societies a widow shaves her head, rubs ashes in her hair, or leaves it unkempt to denote her bereaved status. Among the Iroquois Indians, the warrior shaved his head except for a scalp lock.

Among the Witoto a necklace of human teeth denoted the successful warrior, and chiefs wore a necklace of jaguar teeth. In the Philippines, Mandaya warriors were distinguished by their red clothing, as were women shamanistic mediums.

Local group affiliations are often indicated by variations in costume. Among the Plains Indians each tribe had its own conventions in making the traditional skin clothing. In the Burmese highlands each locality had its own colors and patterns of stripes or plaids, and a woman's locality could also be identified by her headdress. Originally, the Scottish tartan indicated the locality in which the wearer lived. Later the clan tartan denoted membership in a larger kin group and could be worn by clan members who had left the highlands.

As societies become more complex, class differences develop and are reflected in the people's clothing. Among the authoritarian Incas of Peru, only officials, nobles, and priests were allowed to wear fine fabrics of alpaca and vicuña. Also forbidden to commoners were gems, feathers, and ornaments of gold and silver. In 19th century Turkistan, a man's status was measured by the number of robes he wore in public and by the elaborateness of his silver girdle.

from *The Encyclopedia Americana*, 1986

Formulating the Preliminary Thesis

As you are aware by now, the thesis statement must be phrased as a sentence: "In East Germany athletes for world class competition are trained like professionals not amateurs," *not* "the way athletes are trained in East Germany." To give another example, the following is a properly phrased thesis: "Gunpowder was not used in warfare in China as it was in Europe because the Chinese had a different attitude to death, battle, and personal honor than did the Europeans." This isn't a thesis: "the Chinese use of gunpowder versus Europe's." Another sample thesis: "Expensive cosmetics are essentially the same as cheap cosmetics." Not a thesis: "how the cosmetic industry rips you off."

To be valid for a research paper a thesis must satisfy all the following requirements:

1. It must be narrow.
2. It must require library research.
3. It must avoid making a statement that will lead to straight summary.
4. It must be a general statement of opinion rather than a self-explanatory statement of fact.
5. It must be phrased as a sentence.

EXERCISE 2

Examine the following sentences submitted as thesis statements by students. Indicate which are valid for a research paper and which are not. Use the guidelines given above.

1. Dyslexia is a handicap shared by millions.
2. A light-weight bullet has as much or more knockdown force than a heavier one.
3. The causes of child abuse and what's being done.
4. My own personal experiences while in Greece during the war with Turkey.
5. The Great Wall of China was originally built as a barrier against invasion but had far-reaching consequences in Chinese history.
6. If more people experienced empathy, it would be a better world.
7. The nineteenth-century Russian writer Fyodor Dostoyevsky suffered from epilepsy.
8. The impersonality of urban living is an important cause of urban suicides.
9. How kudzu weed has taken over the state of Florida.
10. Railroads have gone bankrupt in the United States because of government mismanagement.

Suggested Research Paper Topics

Arts/Crafts/Hobbies

stained glass
doll houses
Oriental rugs
scrimshaw
Kachaturian
kaleidoscopes

topiary gardens
Picasso
Japanese flower arranging
commemorative stamps
tattoo
caricature
Andrew Wyeth

Commerce/Industry

strip mining
seal hunts
pearl divers
tree farming
home computers
cottage industries
oil prices
meat packing
frozen foods

Communications

spy satellites
political cartoons
body language
bumper stickers
bilingual education
world fairs
cable television

Entertainment

ragtime
foreign films
commedia dell'arte
pleasure piers
theme parks
Calypso
Mardi Gras
Casbah
circus
Ziegfeld
Isadora Duncan

Food

fish farms
baby food
caviar
migrant farm workers
windmills
hydroponics
fad diets
designer label chocolates
Vichy water
Cognac

History

Roman aqueducts
Indian reservations
cliff dwellings
Etruscans
Attila the Hun
Minoan civilization
Machu Picchu
Khmer Rouge
samurai
Hawaiian royalty
medieval fairs

Law/Order

Interpol
capital punishment
terrorism
juvenile delinquency
police brutality
missing children
Mothers Against Drunk Drivers (M.A.D.D.)
scoff laws
astro law

Modern Life

toxic waste disposal
singles bars
draft registration
mail-order Asian brides
international weapons trading
over-the-counter terrorism

Nature

hurricanes
caves
barrier reefs
comets
rain forests
Scottish moors
Great American Prairie
coyotes
Chesapeake Bay
animal hibernation

Religion

TV evangelists
cults
Salem witches
dissident theologians
creationism
catacombs
charismatics
Dead Sea Scrolls
Koran
voodoo

Science/Medicine

generic drugs
animal experiments
Agent Orange
Einstein
Interferon
laser surgery
acupuncture
the golden section

Sports

ballooning
sports medicine
kites
Mt. Everest
water polo
ice fishing
falconry
horse shows

Transportation

electric cars
camels
luxury ocean liners
Lindbergh
subways

Travel

Appalachia
Amazon jungle
Southern plantations
Taj Mahal
Mississippi River
Lapps
Crete
Venice
oasis

ASSIGNMENT

Select a general topic for your research paper, then narrow it, and formulate a thesis with the help of some preliminary research in various encyclopedias and other reference books. A simple way to assure a properly phrased thesis statement is to use the following formula when submitting your tentative thesis for your instructor's approval:

Research Paper Proposal

I have chosen to write on the subject of ______________

____.

After some preliminary research, I have narrowed it

down to ____

____

and decided that it would be interesting and worthwhile

to corroborate or substantiate the fact that __________

____ **This is your thesis statement.**

____

____.

Here is a sample proposal:

I have chosen to write on the subject of Siberian huskies.

After some preliminary research, I have narrowed it down to their use on polar expeditions

and decided that it would be interesting and worthwhile to corroborate or substantiate the fact that the lack of sled dogs was responsible for Scott's failure to beat Amundsen in their race to the South Pole in 1911.

4
Using the Library

Preparing a Working Bibliography

Now that you have a topic, have restricted it, and have formulated a thesis, it's time to move to stage two. Your next goal is finding the material (data, ideas, and expert opinions) that will corroborate your thesis. Such material can be found in two kinds of sources—primary and secondary. **Primary sources** are original material that include literary works (novels, short stories, plays, poems, autobiographies), historical documents (speeches, diaries, letters), as well as interviews, surveys, observations, and experiments. **Secondary sources** are works that analyze and report information from primary as well as other secondary sources. In other words, secondary sources are books, magazines, journals, and newspapers that derive their material from observations, interviews, surveys, and/or experiments; studies of literary works and/or historical documents; and other books, magazines, journals, and/or newspapers.

When a research paper is brief, most of its information will be drawn from secondary sources, and for the purpose of *this* particular research paper, secondary sources will be adequate. However, generally speaking, you are encouraged to use primary sources whenever possible in doing research. In fact, sometimes, as in the case of a literary analysis, primary sources (novels, short stories, poems, plays) are indispensable. However, in this research paper you may rely on secondary sources exclusively. What is more, all your secondary sources as well as the resources for finding them are in the *library,* which should be the focal point of your search—*not,* for example, the State House, the Chamber of Commerce, Alcoholics Anonymous, or your roommate, "whose father has cancer, and so he has a lot of books on the subject."

Library Resources

The library contains three kinds of reading materials: general books, periodicals, and reference books. **General books** are those found in the stacks of the library that circulate. In the discussion of their subject, they aim for depth, of course, but also breadth, covering many aspects of a single subject.

Periodicals are magazines, journals, and newspapers that are published periodically (daily, weekly, bimonthly, monthly, and quarterly) and are found in a periodicals room or section of the reference area. **Magazines** are popular in nature and address a general audience (for example, *Science Digest, Time, Seventeen*). **Journals** are scholarly publications intended for a professional or learned audience (for example, *Yale Review, American Journal of Sociology, Scientific American*). **Newspapers** are just that. But what you should recognize about them is that some newspapers are more authoritative than others; five of the nation's most respected and influential newspapers from different regions are the *New York Times, The Washington Post, The Chicago Tribune, The Los Angeles Times,* and the *New Orleans Times-Picayune.* Periodicals are more up-to-date than books and have a narrower focus. For these reasons, you should rely on them as much, if not more sometimes, as on books. The most current issues of periodicals do not circulate; in fact, sometimes libraries do not allow any periodicals to circulate.

Reference books are the guides, encyclopedias, biographical and word dictionaries, almanacs, yearbooks, atlases, gazetteers, bibliographies, and indexes found in the reference area; they are noncirculating. Unlike circulating books and periodical articles, which are read for their own sake, reference books are not "read"; they are consulted. Their special characteristic is breadth and brevity—the all-in-a-nutshell approach. They are arranged always with the purpose of facilitating the retrieval of information. You have already used some of the reference books to retrieve a quick overview of a subject for the purpose of formulating a thesis. You will now turn your attention to the reference books that you have not yet consulted to retrieve information of a different kind: namely, information indispensable to finding the books and periodicals you need to support your thesis and write your paper.

As you can see, the resources of the library are considerable. However, they are of no use to a reader who doesn't know how to find the reading material he or she needs. The trick is to know how to tap into the library's resources; specifically, how to retrieve the data you need without personally examining every book, magazine, journal, and newspaper for information relevant to your subject.

Locating Books and Articles on Your Subject

The library makes available to you three kinds of resources that are indispensable in tracking down books and articles on your subject. How thoroughly and how many of these resources you examine will depend on the length, nature, and requirements of the research assignment as well as on the availability of the secondary sources. (You're expected to keep tracking until you find what you're looking for.) The purpose of the information on library reference materials in this chapter and in the Appendix is to provide you with a ready reference guide that you can use now in a limited fashion and, more importantly, can refer to later when doing more comprehensive research in other courses.

Use the following sources in locating information on your subject:

1. Subject card catalog (list of books).
2. Bibliographies (lists of books and sometimes periodical articles).
3. Indexes (lists of periodical articles—primarily).

The Subject Card Catalog

A natural place to start, since you're already familiar with it, is the card catalog; it lists general books alphabetically by names of authors, titles of books, and subjects. Since you don't have the titles or authors of the books yet, the place to look is in the **subject** card catalog (a systematic list of the library's books arranged alphabetically by subject). As a resource for locating data on your subject, it yields three types of information. If you look up your subject, you will find some or all of the following:

1. Books that deal with your subject.
2. Books dealing with your subject that also contain a bibliography on your subject.
3. A bibliography devoted entirely to your subject and published separately as a book.

Suppose you look up the following topics in the subject card catalog: bathing, diving, plazas, and divorce. (See Figures 4.1 and 4.2.) Here's what the results of your search *might* be:

- On the subject of *bathing:* no cards at all.
- On the subject of *diving:* four or five cards; no books containing a bibliography; no separate bibliography.
- On the subject of *plazas:* several cards; no separate bibliography, but one of the cards shows that the book contains a nineteen-page bibliography.
- On the subject of *divorce:* many cards; one of them shows a separate bibliography.

Thus a search through the subject card catalog can yield one or more relevant titles of books and/or leads to other lists (bibliographies) of relevant readings.

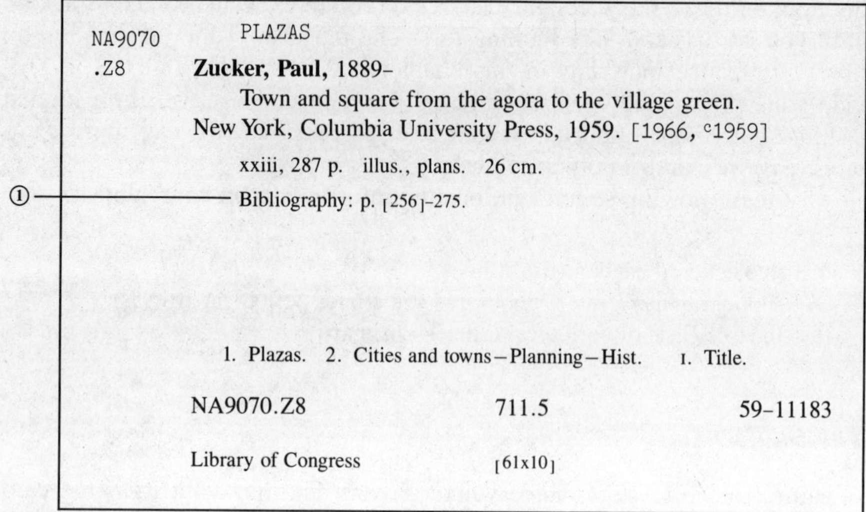

NA9070 PLAZAS
.Z8 **Zucker, Paul,** 1889-
Town and square from the agora to the village green.
New York, Columbia University Press, 1959. [1966, ©1959]
xxiii, 287 p. illus., plans. 26 cm.
① Bibliography: p. [256]-275.

1. Plazas. 2. Cities and towns–Planning–Hist. I. Title.

NA9070.Z8 711.5 59-11183

Library of Congress [61x10]

Figure 4.1: Subject Card 1. Bibliography to be found in the book on pp. 256–275.

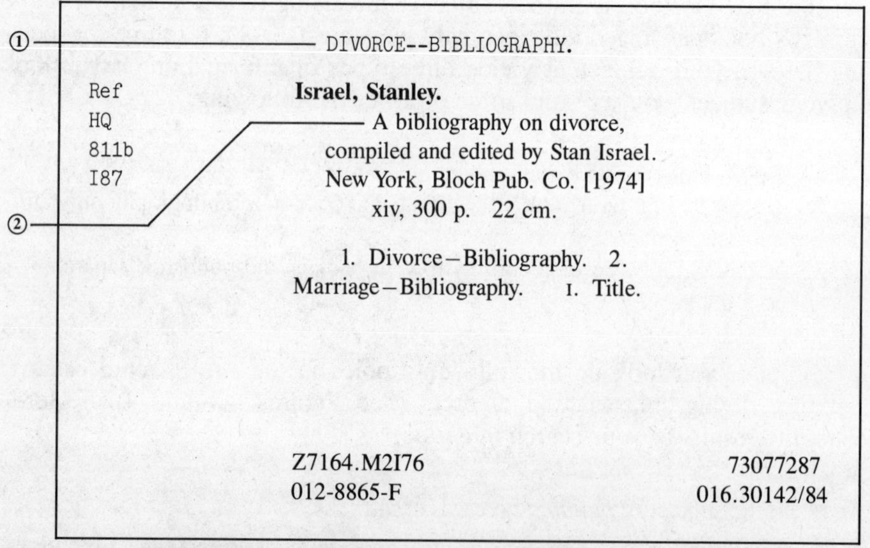

① DIVORCE--BIBLIOGRAPHY.

Ref **Israel, Stanley.**
HQ A bibliography on divorce,
811b compiled and edited by Stan Israel.
I87 New York, Bloch Pub. Co. [1974]
② xiv, 300 p. 22 cm.

1. Divorce–Bibliography. 2.
Marriage–Bibliography. I. Title.

Z7164.M2I76 73077287
012-8865-F 016.30142/84

Figure 4.2: Subject Card 1. Subject heading showing the book is published as a bibliography. 2. Title of book indicating a bibliography.

Bibliographies

The second area to consult in choosing books on a particular topic is the following set of reference works, most of which are called **bibliographies** (lists of readings arranged alphabetically usually by subject). The following is a selection of the most general bibliographies, not confined to any one field.

For a somewhat more selective list of reference works, arranged by subject field, see the Appendix.

Bibliographic Index: A Cumulative Bibliography of Bibliographies, 1937– . This "superbibliography" is unique: It does not list titles of books and articles on a given subject. Instead it lists bibliographies that are published separately as books as well as books and articles that contain bibliographies in them. It is so comprehensive that it includes every topic on which a bibliographical list has ever appeared.

Encyclopedias and Biographical Dictionaries. The longer articles found in these two reference works, with which you're already familiar, often carry a bibliography at the end of the entry or, as in the case of *Collier's Encyclopedia,* for example, in a separate volume at the end of the series.

Subject Guide to Books in Print, 1957– . Provides an annual list of books published in the United States on all the subject headings set up by the Library of Congress.

British Books in Print, 1967– . Provides an annual list of books published in Great Britain.

Public Library Catalog, 1973. Lists, according to subject, basic books in all fields suitable to a public library.

The United States Catalog, 1928; and the *Cumulative Book Index,* 1928– . Together list all books in print since 1928.

U.S. Superintendent of Documents, 1895– . Lists government publications.

Poore, Benjamin P. *A Descriptive Catalogue of the Government Publications of the U.S.,* 1774–1881. Lists government publications during the first century of the republic.

Ames, John G. *Comprehensive Index to the Publications of the U.S. Government,* 1881–1893. Bridges the gap between the above two publications.

Indexes

The last of the traditional resources are the **subject indexes** (lists of articles in periodicals and essays in books, arranged by subject). The following is a partial selection of fairly general indexes not confined to a particular subject field. For a more selective list, consult the Appendix.

VERY GENERAL INDEXES

Readers' Guide to Periodical Literature, 1900– . Lists articles in magazines for the general public. Some of these, *Ladies' Home Journal,* for instance, are not suitable for a college-level research paper and will have to be overlooked.

Magazine Index, 1976– . A microfilm index to more than double the number of general magazines and business periodicals found in *Readers' Guide.*

Ulrich's International Periodicals Directory, 1975/76. Does not index articles but periodicals (approximately 57,000) by subject. However, it also gives the names of the periodical indexes in which each periodical listed can be found; therefore, you can find the periodicals relevant to your subject and then consult the indexes named for the articles.

Essay and General Literature Index, 1900–1933; Supplements, 1934– . Lists essays and articles on given subjects that are found within collections of essays and miscellaneous books with possibly misleading titles; that is, the book titles may not hint at your subject so that you would not normally check them out.

Biography Index: A Cumulative Index to Biographical Material in Books and Magazines, 1947– .

GENERAL INDEXES

Poole's Index to Periodical Literature, 1802–1881. Lists by subject, articles in nineteenth-century American and British periodicals.

Social Sciences and Humanities Index, 1965–1974. *Humanities Index,* 1974– . Lists articles in the following fields: archaeology, classics, folklore, history, language, literature, performing arts, philosophy, religion, and theology. *Social Sciences Index,* 1974– . Lists articles in the following fields: anthropology, criminology, economics, environmental science, geography, law, medicine, political science, psychology, public administration, and sociology.

The New York Times Index, 1913– . *The New York Times* newspaper provides a comprehensive coverage of national and international news and commentary. This index is particularly helpful because it includes a brief summary of each article it lists, *and* by providing the date of a newsworthy event, it enables you to look up concurrent issues of other newspapers running a story of the same news event.

Newspaper Index, 1972– . Indexes the remaining four major American newspapers (i.e., *The Washington Post, The Chicago Tribune, The Los Angeles Times,* the *New Orleans Times-Picayune*). Indexes to the *Detroit News,* the *Houston Post,* the *Milwaukee Journal,* and the *San Francisco Chronicle* added in 1976. The *London Times,* the *National Observer,* the *Christian Science Monitor,* and the *Wall Street Journal* have their own indexes.

SPECIAL INDEXES

Applied Science and Technology Index, 1958– . From 1913 to 1957 called *Industrial Arts Index.*

Art Index, 1929– .

Biological Abstracts, 1926.

Biological and Agricultural Index, 1964– . From 1916 to 1963 called *Agricultural Index.*

Business Periodicals Index, 1958– .

The Education Index, 1929– .

Index Medicus, 1899–1926 and 1960– . From 1927 to 1959 called *Quarterly Cumulative Index Medicus.*

MLA International Bibliography of Books and Articles on the Modern Languages and Literatures, 1921– .

Science Citation Index, 1961– .

Social Sciences Citation Index, 1970– .

Computer Searching

The computer searching service is an electronic resource that college and university libraries across the country are making increasingly available to the academic community and public at large. It is a computerized way to find bibliographical information on a specific topic. The service provides access to hundreds of databases. In this context, a database is a reference work such as a bibliography or index. In fact, some of the databases the computer searches are the very same ones that are listed in this chapter and in the Appendix, for example, the *MLA Bibliography,* the *PAIS International, Sociological Abstracts,* and *Books in Print,* to cite just a few. The search result is a customized bibliography, which, for the purpose of long-range research projects, can be updated periodically.

Although the databases currently online (connected with a main computer) do not cover all disciplines, they do cover a wide variety of them. Here's a partial list of some of the major subject fields: biological sciences, business and management, chemistry, education, geography and geology, humanities, law and government, medicine, technology, and the social sciences.

The biggest advantages of computer searching are comprehensiveness and speed. One search can cover many years on very complex and multifaceted topics, and it has access to extensive files of information. It is also fast. The actual search online is usually less than fifteen minutes, though designing a search strategy takes longer. It involves filling out a search request form, conferring with the reference librarian who will be conducting the search, and most importantly, selecting the key words to be searched. You should plan on an hour of search time. The resulting bibliography may be printed online (that is, the terminal produces a printout at the time of the search) or offline (the citations are printed during the off hours of the main computer and mailed to you). Thus offline printing takes a few days longer.

One of the few disadvantages of computer searching is a consequence of its electronic nature: it does not allow browsing, which is usually a desirable stage in the research process because it suggests ideas. When you scan titles and related subject headings for pertinent information during a manual search, you often make profitable discoveries. (Look at the practical example provided on researching "wine" in Chapters 4 through 6.) With a computer, however, browsing is eliminated because the computer does the scanning for you. Therefore, computer searching will probably never replace manual searching entirely, especially in its preliminary stages. The reason is that some manual searching is useful in providing a researcher with a sense of the field and even the key words that are going to be indispensable to electronic searching.

The other disadvantage is cost. Computer searching is not free. The library charges patrons all the identifiable costs of a search: a fee for each minute of time connected to the computer; a charge, in the case of offline printing, for each bibliographic citation; and other fees, which may include communication calls and mailing charges. What's more, since the library is paying for computer time, it passes the fee on to you whether relevant citations are found or not. Actual rates, however, vary considerably not only from search to search but also from database to database.

To initiate a search, contact your reference librarian, who will explain the procedure in detail, apprise you of the approximate charges, arrange a convenient time to discuss the topic you want searched, and provide you with a request form. (See sample search request form.)

SAMPLE SEARCH REQUEST FORM

Patron name ______________________________ Date ______________

Department ____________________ Tel. __________ Status:

Campus address ______________________________ ___ Faculty

___ Grad student

(or address if non-college patrons) ______________ ___ Undergrad student

____ ___ Administration

___ Staff

City, state, zip ______________________________ ___ Non-college

---

Short title of search topic ____

1. SEARCH TOPIC: Describe the subject/topic you want searched. Here is an example: Citations that deal with the effects of any mutation on the eye color of the fruit fly (Drosophila melanogaster).

   ____

   ____

   ____

   ____

   ____

2. KEYWORDS: list key terms, phrases, or concepts that describe your topic or research. Give synonyms and spelling variations. Specify terms you do NOT want used in retrieving items.

   ____

   ____

   ____

   ____

   ____

3. Please list two or three of the most important authors (and/or organizations) publishing on your topic; complete names, if known, are helpful. Please indicate

if you wish to exclude documents by any of these (or other) authors or organizations because of prior familiarity with their publications.

____

____

____

4. Please list two or three of the most important journals covering your problem. Please indicate if you wish to retrieve references to documents from these journals only. Please indicate if you do NOT wish to retrieve references to documents from any particular journal (perhaps because you subscribe to journal).

____

____

____

____

5. LANGUAGES: English only ________
any language ________
specific languages ______________________

6. RANGE OF YEARS WANTED: All years available ________
No items before 19________

7. ABSTRACTS NEEDED: (if present in file searched) yes ________
no ________

8. SCOPE OF SEARCH: Check the kind of search you want.

________ Comprehensive: in which an attempt will be made to retrieve the maximum number of items with the possibility that there may be a relatively high percentage of nonuseful items.

________ Limited: in which an attempt will be made to retrieve a minimum acceptable number of items with the possibility a number of items that would be in a comprehensive search will not be retrieved.

9. FEE LIMIT: Give the approximate amount acceptable as a maximum fee. This will guide the searcher in the selection of databases and in determining the scope of the search. $____________________

PLEASE NOTE: THE FEE PAYS FOR A SEARCH. IT IS POSSIBLE THAT NO RELEVANT CITATIONS WILL BE FOUND.

10. DEADLINE: state the latest date beyond which the search will not be useful to you. NOT USEFUL AFTER____________________

11. AUTHORIZATION: I authorize the library to perform the search described above and agree to the charges incurred in doing the search. Payment will be made by: Check________ Cash________

Signature ____________________________________ Date __________________

—Courtesy of the Clement C. Maxwell Library
at Bridgewater State College

Evaluating Your Sources

You can assume that not all the sources you find on a given subject are going to be equally *useful* or equally *reliable.* Therefore, you will *not* be using every source you locate in the card catalog, bibliographies, and indexes. Instead, you will want to screen the sources and choose only those that are not only reliable but also useful to you.

What Makes a Source Useful?

1. *Is it duplicating any other source you're using?* Books, which survey a subject, will duplicate each other more frequently than articles with a specific focus. Therefore, when a number of titles seem to cover the same ground, pick just one of them. For example, Walter Sullivan's *Black Holes: The Edge of Space, the End of Time* and John Taylor's *Black Holes: The End of the Universe?* both seem to provide overlapping coverage of the black hole phenomenon. Therefore, one of them would do—usually the more authoritative one. (For what makes a source authoritative and, therefore, reliable, see the discussion below.)

2. *Is it too specialized for you* or *your audience?* Books and articles that go over your head because of the technical language are not going to be much help. In fact, if you can't understand what an author means, you will be tempted to pass that information on to another reader by quoting wholesale.

An obvious solution is to change the topic or the thesis. But usually less drastic solutions are possible. That is to find less technical sources. For example, *Science 84* and *Scientific American (SA)* are both quality periodicals with a focus on science. But a brief look at their tables of contents should quickly alert you to the difference in their level of sophistication:

- *Science 84* "Taming a Star"
  "The Heartbreak Gene"
  "Fire in Iceland"
- *Scientific American* "The Packing of Spheres"
  "The Control of Ribosome Synthesis"
  "Quantum Gravity"

The titles in *SA* are a good clue to their inaccessibility to the average reader and probably to a number of you. So you should overlook articles in *Scientific American* in favor of ones in *Science 84, Smithsonian, Audubon, New Scientist,* and others. Needless to say, if your level of sophistication in your chosen topic is higher than that of the general reader, use the technical journals and books, but remember to keep the reader in mind when you write. (See "Consideration of Audience" in Chapter 1.)

What Makes a Source Reliable?

1. *What kind of an audience is the book, journal, magazine, or newspaper targeting?* All publications have a specific readership in mind and can be ranked accordingly—from those addressed to a mass audience at the bottom of the scale to others addressed to a highly learned and specialized audience at the top. The magazines and newspapers, for example, found at the supermarket checkout counter would be in the lowest category (for the most part), while the ones in a college/university or large city library would be at the top. Thus reliability would be determined accordingly: the more knowledgeable the intended reader, the higher the degree of reliability expected. What that means in practical terms is that a women's magazine, for example, devoted to the mass interests of music, film, sex, food, fashion, and cosmetics is not the place to go for information on, say, nutrition—even if there were an M.D. or some other label like "top nutritionist" attached to the author's name. That is not to say such a magazine necessarily promotes false or distorted information, merely that an uncritical readership makes such promotion possible.

If you have any doubts regarding the intended audience of a periodical, observe the amount of advertising and length of the articles. If the articles are brief and you have difficulty identifying them among the ads, you're looking at a periodical addressed to a consumer who is regarded as gullible and limited in attention span.

At the other end of the spectrum are periodicals that cater to specialists, like the *Journal of Nursing* for nurses, *Botanical Review* for botanists, *Renaissance News* for historians; consequently, "quality control" is going to be high and information consistently reliable since the reader is often as knowledgeable as the writer.

In between *People* magazine and *Renaissance News,* however, there is also a whole range of periodicals addressed to readers who are not experts in the field but sufficiently intelligent and educated to have a serious interest in the subject. A magazine like *House & Garden,* for example, falls into this category; building and landscape architecture are the only subjects featured in the magazine. By contrast, *House Beautiful,* with its recipes, decorating tips, and plentiful ads, addresses an audience whose interest is practical (homemaking and gardening) rather than intellectual (architecture).

2. *Who is the author?* While you may not think you have the expertise to evaluate the writer, you, in fact, can make some valid observations regarding his or her knowledgeability, objectivity, and thoroughness, qualities that confer reliability on an author.

First, consider how often you've encountered the author's name in the card catalog, bibliographies, indexes, and readings so far. Frequent writing on a subject points to knowledgeability. Look for credentials somewhere on the book jacket, in the front matter of a book, or at the beginning or end of an article. In the absence of credentials, look for excerpts of reviews.

Finally, be wary of celebrities writing in a field other than the one they're famous in, like a comedian on politics, a politician on religion, and so on.

Second, ask yourself whether the author (or publication) is known for any biases by reason of his or her personal experiences, vested interests, and political or religious ideologies. Although a biased individual or publication can still be authoritative, information and conclusions coming from such a source should be evaluated in light of a possible bias. In such cases, pay particular attention to the author's reference to outside sources. If you're reading what appears to be an objective study of sexuality by the British feminist Germaine Greer, for example, notice the sources she's using to develop and substantiate her thesis. If you find references to sources like Freud, anthropologists doing field study in Indonesia, researchers at the Emory School of Medical Psychiatry, and recent studies of American prison populations, you at least have the assurance of scholarly support for the thesis and, therefore, sources that you can check out yourself, if necessary. Beware of articles that ask or suggest you "take it from someone who knows"; personal experience is not always an advantage if it's the only thing the author is relying on. "One Woman's Story on Amniocentesis" is not going to be an objective study of the subject.

Third, see whether the author has been as thorough as the subject requires. Often a simple look at length will tell. Although the length of a short newspaper column on the results of a wine competition in San Francisco is probably adequate to the subject, a half-page article entitled "Should You Be Friends with Your Boss?" is not long enough to provide a thorough, well-researched analysis of employer–employee relations.

3. *What purpose is the book or article serving?* Sometimes the biases discussed above are not obvious. If they aren't as obvious as in the case of, say, Shell Oil publishing a study on the rise in oil prices, examine purpose. Authors do not always write to inform; sometimes they write to persuade—and sell you on a product or idea. Obviously such a purpose does not automatically invalidate their findings or conclusions, which require more critical scrutiny than purely informative purposes; since a lot is to be gained by getting the reader to agree, the writer may be tempted to manipulate the evidence. Look for the sales pitch in the title—"Save Energy: Build a Passive-Solar Sun Room"—as a clue to the publication's marketing intentions. Investigate any financial interest that the author and/or publication may have in the subject, for example, a magazine writing about vitamins *and* selling them.

4. *What is the date of the publication?* Using recent material is a good rule of thumb in many instances. In the case of scientific, medical, and technological fields, in which "breakthroughs" occur almost daily, information that's only a year old can actually be dated. Even in other fields, in which schools of thinking and research methods change or new evidence is unearthed invalidating previous assumptions, current research is more reliable than past research. Thus you'd look for current data on topics like prenatal testing, video-display terminals, and rock hopper penguins. However, there can be exceptions to the use-the-most-recent-source guideline. A study done in 1914 on the fighting prowess of the Roman Legion can still be the best study around—unless your research leads you to suspect otherwise.

5. *What are the author's sources?* Scholarly, and hence most reliable, sources will provide documentation, which can be checked. Therefore, look at the end of the book or article for a bibliography or notes to chapters. In magazines and newspapers that do not supply documentation, look for references to sources in the text. In books check out the introduction, afterword, and acknowledgments for the light they can shed on the author's sources. Take William W. Warner's *Distant Water: The Fate of the North Atlantic Fisherman,* which offers no credentials or documentation. However, in the foreword at the beginning and acknowledgments at the end, Warner tells the reader where and how he gathered his information on North Atlantic fishery. He informs the reader that he went out on commercial fishing vessels; he gives the exact sources of his fish-catch statistics; he acknowledges his debt to university departments, biologists at Canada's Department of Fisheries, and individuals supplying him with invaluable fishing journals.

Preparing a Working Bibliography

In the process of searching through the library's resources, you will also be compiling your own bibliography, that is, your own list of relevant titles derived from your investigation of the subject card catalog, bibliographies, indexes, or possibly a computer search. At this point, it's best to make two lists: one for books and one for articles. Even though the final bibliography to be attached to your finished research paper integrates all books and articles into a single list, you'll find it more convenient at this stage to use two lists because books and articles are found in two different sections of the library. Since you'll be working on your book list in one place and your periodicals list in another, two separate lists are handier than one.

List of Books

Take your list of books to the author card catalog, look up each book according to the author's last name (Figures 4.3 and 4.4), and if you find an entry card for it, jot down the following information: (1) bibliographical data that include the author's name, title of the book, city of publication, publisher, and date; (2) the call number taken from the top left-hand corner of the entry card.

The presence of the entry card means, of course, that the book is in the library. If you do not find an entry card, you should do one of two things: if you think that you can get along without the book, cross it off your list and

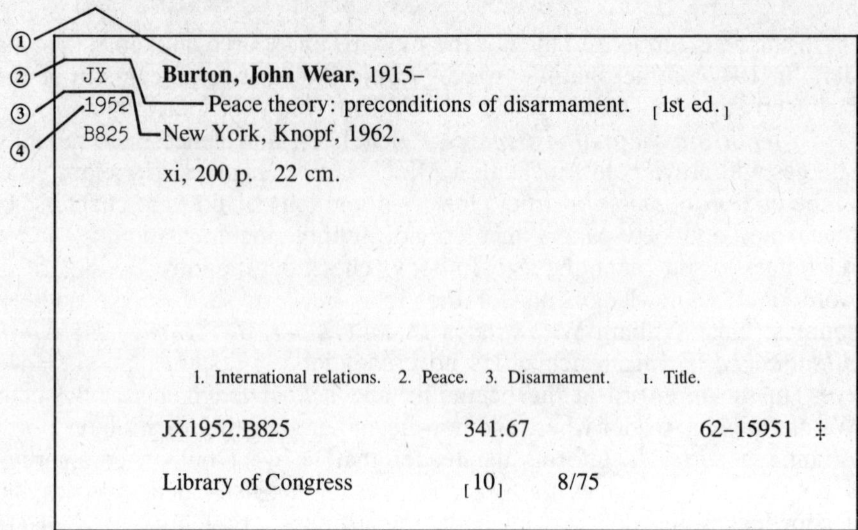

JX Burton, John Wear, 1915–
1952 Peace theory: preconditions of disarmament. [1st ed.]
B825 New York, Knopf, 1962.
xi, 200 p. 22 cm.

1. International relations. 2. Peace. 3. Disarmament. I. Title.

JX1952.B825 341.67 62-15951 ‡

Library of Congress [10] 8/75

Figure 4.3: Author Card 1. Author. 2. Title. 3. City, publisher, date of publication. 4. Call number by which book can be located in the library.

forget about it; if the title seems really pertinent to your subject, check with the librarian about having the book traced to another library in the area and borrowed through the interlibrary loan system, a service college libraries usually provide. You should plan well in advance to use interlibrary loan; the process can take as long as three weeks.

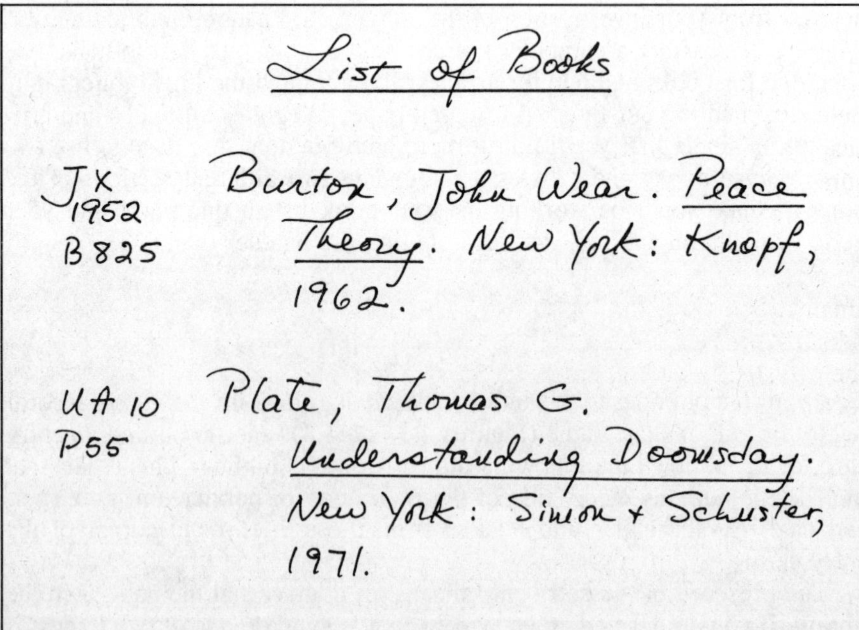

List of Books

JX 1952 B825 Burton, John Wear. Peace Theory. New York: Knopf, 1962.

UA 10 P55 Plate, Thomas G. Understanding Doomsday. New York: Simon + Schuster, 1971.

Figure 4.4: Sample from Student's List of Books

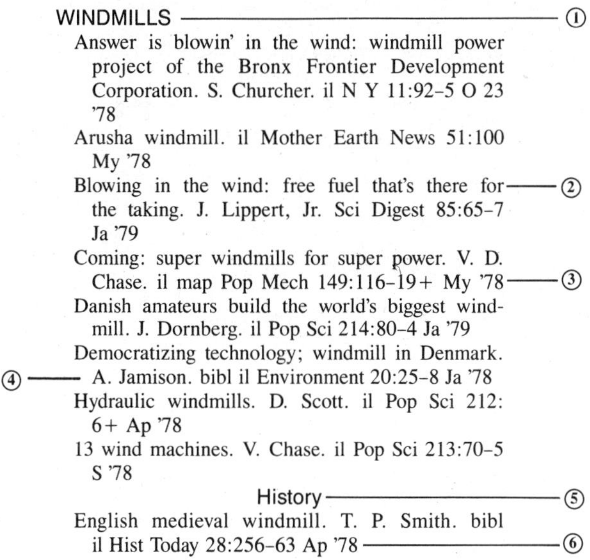

WINDMILLS ①
Answer is blowin' in the wind: windmill power project of the Bronx Frontier Development Corporation. S. Churcher. il N Y 11:92–5 O 23 '78
Arusha windmill. il Mother Earth News 51:100 My '78
Blowing in the wind: free fuel that's there for the taking. J. Lippert, Jr. Sci Digest 85:65–7 Ja '79 ②
Coming: super windmills for super power. V. D. Chase. il map Pop Mech 149:116–19+ My '78 ③
Danish amateurs build the world's biggest windmill. J. Dornberg. il Pop Sci 214:80–4 Ja '79
Democratizing technology; windmill in Denmark. ④ A. Jamison. bibl il Environment 20:25–8 Ja '78
Hydraulic windmills. D. Scott. il Pop Sci 212:6+ Ap '78
13 wind machines. V. Chase. il Pop Sci 213:70–5 S '78
History ⑤
English medieval windmill. T. P. Smith. bibl il Hist Today 28:256–63 Ap '78 ⑥

Figure 4.5: From *Readers' Guide to Periodical Literature* 1. Subject. 2. Title of article. 3. Illustrated with map. 4. Author. 5. Subheading. 6. Title of periodical and publication data: volume, pages, month, year.

List of Periodicals

When making your list of periodicals, be sure to copy down author, title of article, title of periodical, volume number (if any), date, and page numbers from the indexes (Figure 4.5).

Copy the bibliographical data from the indexes onto your list. Use only one side of the page in preparing the two lists. You'll find it much easier to scan them later and take in at a glance the information they provide. Make sure this information is complete and accurate since these are the lists you'll be using when you prepare your final bibliography for the finished essay. (See Chapter 14 for the correct bibliographical format.)

Now take the periodicals list to what some libraries call a **cardex** (a small, rotating catalog of cards, like a spindle, devoted exclusively to periodicals). It's the equivalent to the card catalog and does for periodicals what the card catalog does for books: provides the information whereby you can locate the articles you need in the library. Look up the title of the *periodical* (not the article) in the cardex. If you find a card on it, that means that the library carries the periodical and you should check for the following information: the date the library first began subscribing to it, the dates of the missing issues (if any), and the date the library stopped subscribing to it (if it did stop). If, according to this information, the library has the issue you need, make a notation (some sort of abbreviation) in the left-hand margin of your list alongside the periodical in question to tell yourself that your article is available in the library (Figure 4.6).

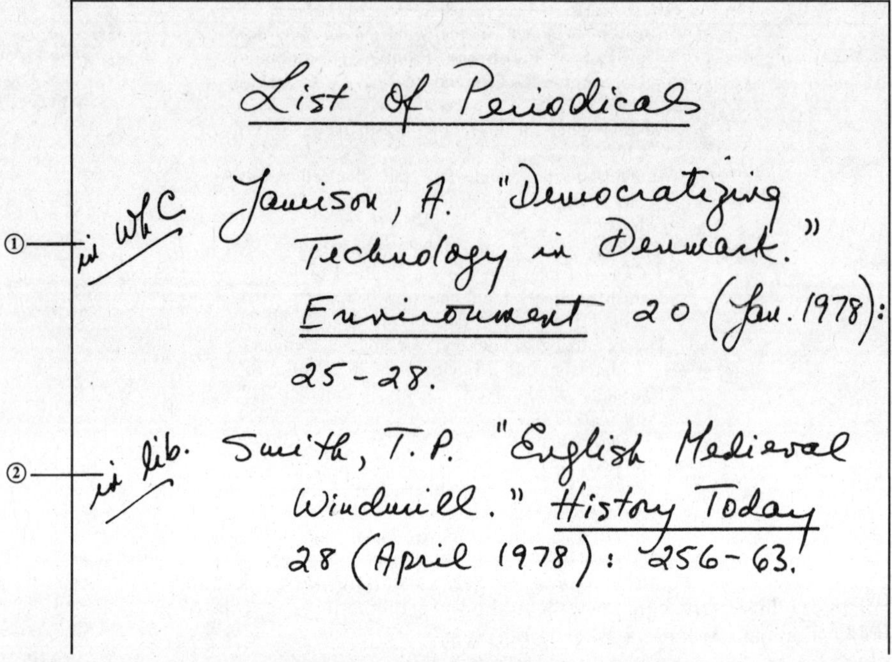

List Of Periodicals
① in W&C Jamison, A. "Democratizing Technology in Denmark." Environment 20 (Jan. 1978): 25-28.
② in lib. Smith, T.P. "English Medieval Windmill." History Today 28 (April 1978): 256-63.

Figure 4.6: Sample from Student's List of Periodicals 1. Student's notation of holding in area library. 2. Student's notation of college library holding.

If you do *not* find an entry card for the periodical, do one of two things: cross it off your list if the title only seems vaguely relevant or check with the librarian again. Ask the librarian for a catalog that lists the holdings of periodicals in area libraries. Should you find the periodical (and issue you need) listed in this catalog, make a notation alongside your entry as to where it can be found and then order a photocopy of the article through your library.

If you do not find the periodical listed in this catalog, you may want to check out a much more comprehensive listing of magazines and newspapers: *The Union List of Serials in Libraries of the U.S. and Canada, 1965.* An important reference tool, it lists some 156,000 periodicals and points out the nearest library carrying a given periodical. If the library is inaccessible, you can usually obtain a photocopy of the article. But remember to allow for the several weeks it might take to receive it.

Researching the Subject of Wine

Just as an example, let's say that, like the student whose essay has been used as a sample research paper in Chapter 15, you selected wine as a subject. As instructed, you headed for the shelves of encyclopedias to acquire an

> *The United States.*—Most wine of North America comes from the United States. Prohibition from 1919 to 1933 destroyed an industry that was becoming respected even in Europe. Carefully chosen vines and locations were grubbed up or returned to wilderness. Establishing vineyards is a lengthy process; hence the first products after prohibition were usually coarse and heady and marketed under such names as Chablis or Sauternes to which they had no technical right. After World War II production began to recover. Great improvements in quality were made and selling of wines with labels showing place of origin and grapes used increased. Most states produce wines, but California is far ahead of the others. The best wines are chiefly from the San Francisco area, in the districts of Napa Valley, Sonoma, Livermore, and Santa Clara Valley; some of these compare with Europe's, but there are as yet no great wines. The best established districts in the east are the Erie Islands area near Sandusky, Ohio, and upper New York state where interesting projects with native vines not of the *V. vinifera* were being carried on.

Figure 4.7: From *Encyclopaedia Britannica*

overview of the topic that would enable you to restrict it and arrive at a thesis. Most of what you found in *Britannica* was technical: on tasting, classification, chemistry, wine making, and so on. You did find a section on the history of wine that offered some possibilities, but what intrigued you most was one particular statement that was made about U.S. wines (Figure 4.7).

You read *Britannica*'s opinion that America had no great wines and naturally wondered why. You also wondered whether that wasn't just European snobbishness and whether the situation hadn't changed since 1972 (the date of the encyclopedia). In short, your interest had been aroused, and, what's more, you had a tentative thesis: "While some American wines can compare with Europe's, there are as yet no great American wines." You knew your thesis was tentative; research might prove (you secretly hoped) just the opposite. (It might also prove that your topic needed further narrowing—maybe to one particular wine.) But for the time being you were set; you were now ready to search the subject card catalog, bibliographies, and indexes for titles of books and articles that dealt with wine.

The Subject Card Catalog

You found only one card in the catalog (Figure 4.8). At first, you were disappointed but then noticed the bibliography.

So while the catalog didn't yield many titles, it did give you a book with a three-page bibliography. What is more, in its obviously general approach, *The World of Wines* sounded like just the kind of book you needed to give you background in the subject.

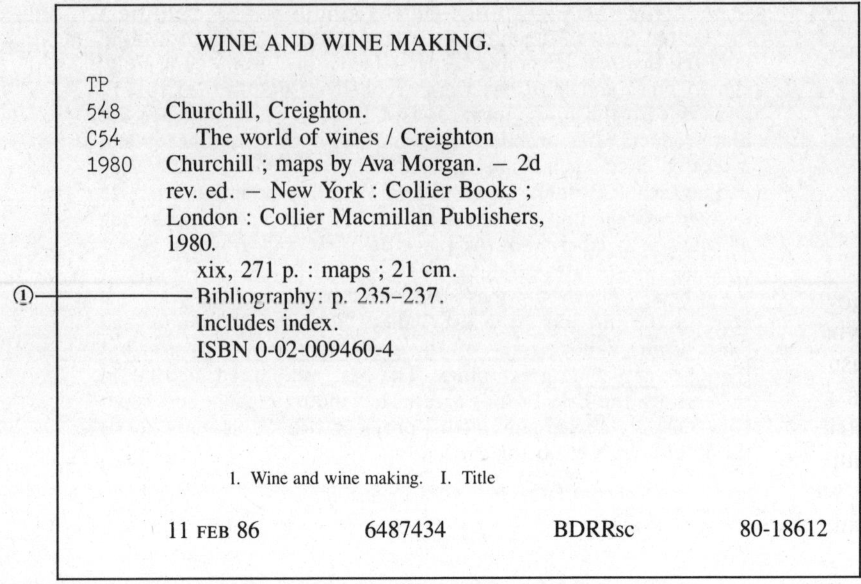

WINE AND WINE MAKING.

TP
548 Churchill, Creighton.
C54 The world of wines / Creighton
1980 Churchill ; maps by Ava Morgan. – 2d rev. ed. – New York : Collier Books ; London : Collier Macmillan Publishers, 1980.

xix, 271 p. : maps ; 21 cm.
(1) Bibliography: p. 235–237.
Includes index.
ISBN 0-02-009460-4

1. Wine and wine making. I. Title

11 FEB 86 6487434 BDRRsc 80-18612

Figure 4.8: Subject Card 1. Bibliography on pp. 235–237.

The Encyclopedias

You now return to *Britannica* in which you remember seeing a list of books at the end of the article on wine (Figure 4.9).

What you find are some technical books on wine making and some general overviews like the Churchill book above; what makes the latter less useful to you than Churchill's book, however, is the fact that they are less recent. However, you do notice a primer on wines and books on the wines of specific countries. These might be useful if you decided to narrow "European wines" to just "French wines." So you jot them down into your list.

Next you decide to check out *Collier's Encyclopedia* because the edition is somewhat more recent in your college library (1977). Because *Collier's*

BIBLIOGRAPHY.—R. Postgate, *Plain Man's Guide to Wine* (1957); H. Grossman, *Grossman's Guide to Wines and Spirits,* 4th rev. ed. (1964); A. Lichine and W. Massee, *Wines of France* (1955); F. Schoonmaker, *The Wines of Germany* (1956), *Dictionary of Wines,* ed. by Tom Marvel (1951); C. Bode, *Wines of Italy* (1956); G. Rainbird, *The Wine Handbook* (1963); A. Simon, *A Wine Primer,* rev. ed. (1950), *A Dictionary of Wine, Spirits and Liqueurs,* rev. ed. (1958); T. Layton, *Winecraft,* 2nd ed. (1956); L. Larmat, *Atlas de France Vinicole* (1949); L. Adams, *The Commonsense Book of Wine* (1958).

Making of Wine: W. V. Cruess, *The Principles and Practice of Wine Making,* 2nd ed. (1946); J. Ribéreau-Gayon and E. Peynaud, *Traité d'Oenologie* (1960); L. W. Marrison, *Wines and Spirits,* reprinted (1962); M. A. Amerine and W. V. Cruess, *The Technology of Wine Making* (1960).

Figure 4.9: From *Encyclopaedia Britannica*

has integrated all its bibliographies into a single list in volume 24, that's where you look: first, at a list of subjects in its index to locate "wine"; then down the column under "wine" to locate the bibliography. Remember that each reference work explains its system of abbreviations and symbols in its preliminary pages. You should refer to them if you can't decipher any part of the entries.

What you find in the bibliography under "Wines and Liquors" are the following four titles: *The Great Wines of Europe, Grapes and Wines from Home Vineyards, Wines of France,* and *The Wonder World of Wines.* By now, you're not surprised to find that books on wine are going to be general; what's more, none of them seems to deal exactly with your thesis. (That's usually true of all books; their subject matter is broad, while that of articles is relatively narrow.) Yet the first title, *The Great Wines of Europe,* does strike you as potentially useful for an overview of the subject and for those authoritative opinions you know you are going to need on what makes a wine "great," so you jot it down (along with the rest of the bibliographical information).

The Bibliographies

You start with the *Bibliographic Index* since it is listed first in the list of bibliographies on page 57. The most recent (as yet unbound) volumes yield no titles of bibliographies, just the information given in Figure 4.10. But your search has not been a total loss here. You've discovered that the learned name for wine and wine making is "viticulture" (you can now look that word up to see what it yields). You've also learned that there's an actual journal on wine: *American Journal of Enology and Viticulture.* Finally, you've also discovered that each issue of the journal provides a bibliography since it includes "Abstracts" (summaries) of books and articles. It seems like a useful source so you include the title of the journal in your periodicals list. You then check out the last five years of volumes but do not find anything you can use.

You move on to *The Subject Guide to Books in Print* (Figure 4.11). From a three-page list on wine, you find the same topics treated repeatedly: how to make wine, how to choose wine, a history of wine, a guide to wine, and so on. You choose only one to jot in your list because it seems particularly appropriate to a study of "great" wines.

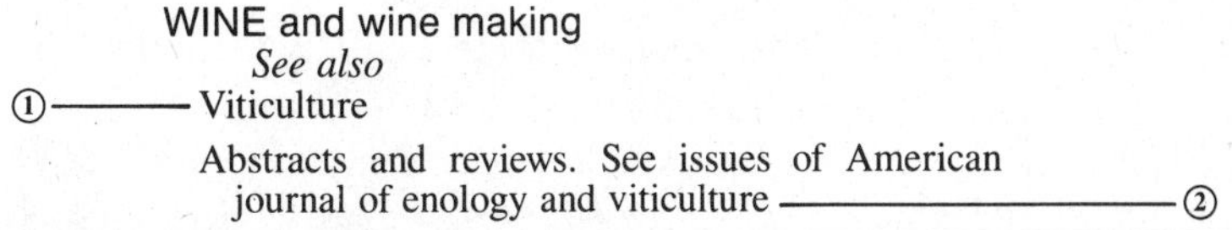
WINE and wine making
See also
① Viticulture
Abstracts and reviews. See issues of American journal of enology and viticulture ②

Figure 4.10: From *Bibliographic Index* 1. Cross-reference. 2. Title of journal.

Price, Pamela V. Enjoying Wine: A Taster's Companion. (Illus.) 256p. 1983. 18.95 (ISBN 0-434-82545-X, Pub. by W.Heinemann England); pap. 12.95 (ISBN 0-434-82546-8). David & Charles.

Programme Ideas for Amateur Winemakers. 1973. pap. 1.95 (ISBN 0-8277-1303-7). British Bk Ctr.

Quimme, Peter. The Signet Book of American Wine. 3rd rev. ed. 1980. pap. 2.50 (ISBN 0-451-09178-7, E9178, Sig). NAL.

Ramey, Bern C. The Great Wine Grapes & the Wines They Make. (Illus.). 49.95 (ISBN 0-8436-2257-1). Great Wine Grapes.

Ramos, Adam & Ramos, Joseph. Mixed Wine Drinks: Seven Hundred Recipes for Punches, Hot Drinks, Coolers & Cocktails. 2nd ed. LC 74-25080. (Illus.) 1982. pap. 9.95 (ISBN 0-914598-60-0). Padre Prods.

Read, Jan. The Wines of Portugal. (Books on Wine). 192p. 1983. 11.95 (ISBN 0-571-11951-4); pap. 5.95 (ISBN 0-571-11952-2). Faber & Faber.

–The Wines of Spain. (Books on Wine). (Illus.) 272p. 1983. 11.95 (ISBN 0-571-11937-9); pap. 6.95 (ISBN 0-571-11938-7). Faber & Faber.

Reingold, Carmel B. California Cuisine. 192p. 1983. pap. 5.95 (ISBN 0-380-82156-7, 82156-7). Avon.

Roate, Mettja C. How to Make Wine in Your Own Kitchen. 12th ed. (Orig.). 1979. pap. 1.75 (ISBN 0-532-17241-8). Woodhill.

Robards, Terry. California Wine Label Album. LC 81-40502. 176p. 1981. looseleaf 16.95 (ISBN 0-89480-183-X). Workman Pub.

Figure 4.11: From *The Subject Guide to Books in Print*

Even though you haven't done much research yet, you're already feeling just a shade less ignorant than you did before. You still don't know what makes a wine great or why American wines are or aren't, but judging from the titles you've encountered, you know now that there are such things as "great wine grapes" and that there are obviously ways of tasting, judging, and evaluating wines. As a result, you can now be on the lookout for articles dealing with the quality of grapes and wine tastings.

The Indexes

Given your topic and a look through the list of general and special indexes listed earlier (pages 57–58), you decide to check out the *Readers' Guide to Periodical Literature* and *The New York Times Index*.

You begin with the most recent volume (usually unbound) of *Readers' Guide* and work your way back (Figures 4.12–4.14).

At this point, you feel a little disheartened because you think you haven't found enough material on your *precise* thesis; it seems that none of the titles suggests a comparison of American and European wines; and only a few

WINE Industry

Alors! American wines come of age. L. Langway and others. il Newsweek 96:56–7+ S 1 '80

Brothers Christian [California winery] N. Hazelton. Nat R 32:546 My 2 '80

California: a wine is born [Jordan Vineyards and Winery's Alexander Valley cabernet sauvignon] R. L. Balzer. il Trav/Holiday 153:6+ Je '80

California find [Chateau St. Jean Winery] T. Robards. il N Y Times Mag p54 Je 22 '80

California high. N. Hazelton. Nat R 32:305–6 Mr 7 '80

Central coasting: California's new wineries. A. Bespaloff. map N Y 13:50 S 1 '80

Living the wine lover's fantasy [executives-turned-vintners] C. G. Burck. il Fortune 102:100–5 N 3 '80

Figure 4.12: From *Readers' Guide* March 1980–February 1981

No wines in Africa? Tut, tut. S. Aaron and C. Fadiman. il Sat R 6:38 N 10 '79

Picnic wines. F. J. Prial. il N Y Times Mag p58 My 27 '79

Quality from California. F. J. Prial. il N Y Times Mag p93 S Je 10 '79

Season for hunting bargains. F. J. Prial. il N Y Times Mag p95 S 16 '79

Top California wines for under $10. A. Fraser Mademoiselle 85:108+ Ap '79

White wines of summer. B. J. Cutler. il House & Gard 151:176+ Je '79

Who says American white wines are sour grapes? J. White il Essence 10:112+ My '79

Wine:

Burgundy blues. A. Bespaloff. il N Y 12:84–7 O 15 '79

Figure 4.13: From *Readers' Guide* March 1979–February 1980

WINE

Beaujolais: the younger the better. F. J. Prial. il N Y Times Mag p76 N 12 '78

Bottles to begin with; collecting red wines. F. J. Prial. il N Y Times Mag p52+ F 19 '78

California's extraordinary ordinary wines. R. Finigan. il Money 7:56–8+ N '78

Christmas vineyards. N. Hazelton. Nat R 31:41–2 Ja 5 '79

Cultivating weinsmanship; German wines. F. J. Prial. il N Y Times Mag p 178+ D 10 '78

Days of wine and roses. F. J. Prial. N Y Times Mag p 112 Je 11 '78

Expert answers to your questions about wine; interview; with recipes. H. Lembeck. Redbook 150:132+ Ap '78

French experts' favorite wines. Atlas 25:54–5 Ja '78

French tradition becomes American ... accenting wines from the golden West with recipe. R. L. Balzer. Trav/Holiday 149:69–71 Je '78

Good wines at bargain prices. A. Fraser. Mademoiselle 85:140 Ja '79

Grape white way. F. J. Prial. il N Y Times Mag p68+ Mr 19 '78

Figure 4.14: From *Readers' Guide* March 1978–February 1979

titles hint at the quality of American wines. And you only have one more index to go. But, in fact, you shouldn't feel disheartened at all. In terms of the number of titles you have found, you have quite enough for a four- to six-page paper and possibly longer. The fact that none of the titles suggests your actual thesis shouldn't discourage you; on the contrary, you should be relieved to find that you will be in no danger of doing straight summary of a source that has the same thesis as yours. You should even feel challenged by the fact that the authors you've discovered aren't going to prove your thesis for you; they will just provide you with the data to prove it on your own.

Time to move on to *The New York Times Index* (Figures 4.15–4.18).

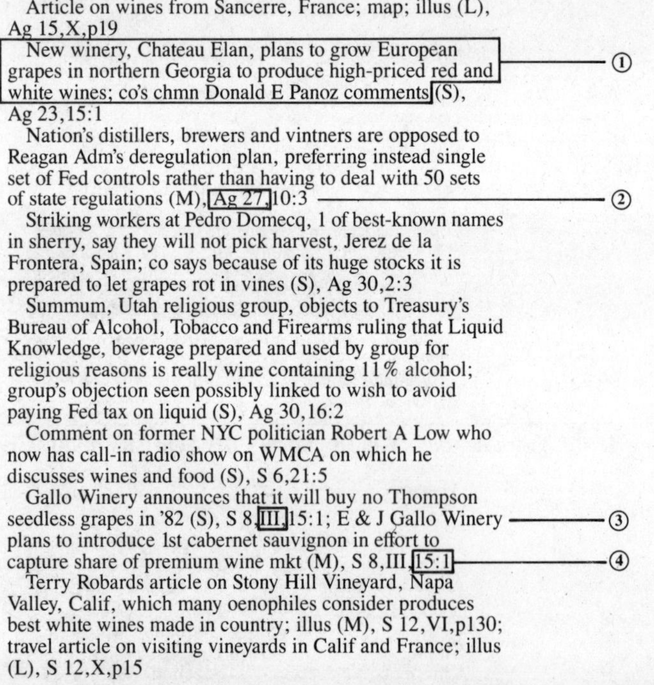

Article on wines from Sancerre, France; map; illus (L), Ag 15,X,p19

New winery, Chateau Elan, plans to grow European grapes in northern Georgia to produce high-priced red and white wines; co's chmn Donald E Panoz comments (S), Ag 23,15:1 ①

Nation's distillers, brewers and vintners are opposed to Reagan Adm's deregulation plan, preferring instead single set of Fed controls rather than having to deal with 50 sets of state regulations (M), Ag 27,10:3 ②

Striking workers at Pedro Domecq, 1 of best-known names in sherry, say they will not pick harvest, Jerez de la Frontera, Spain; co says because of its huge stocks it is prepared to let grapes rot in vines (S), Ag 30,2:3

Summum, Utah religious group, objects to Treasury's Bureau of Alcohol, Tobacco and Firearms ruling that Liquid Knowledge, beverage prepared and used by group for religious reasons is really wine containing 11% alcohol; group's objection seen possibly linked to wish to avoid paying Fed tax on liquid (S), Ag 30,16:2

Comment on former NYC politician Robert A Low who now has call-in radio show on WMCA on which he discusses wines and food (S), S 6,21:5

Gallo Winery announces that it will buy no Thompson seedless grapes in '82 (S), S 8,III,15:1; E & J Gallo Winery ③ plans to introduce 1st cabernet sauvignon in effort to capture share of premium wine mkt (M), S 8,III,15:1 ④

Terry Robards article on Stony Hill Vineyard, Napa Valley, Calif, which many oenophiles consider produces best white wines made in country; illus (M), S 12,VI,p130; travel article on visiting vineyards in Calif and France; illus (L), S 12,X,p15

Figure 4.15: From *The New York Times Index* 1982 1. Description of article. 2. Month and day. 3. Section number of newspaper. 4. Page and column.

Article on revival of Chateau Ausone, '1 of great' St Emilion (France) vineyards; illus (L), Ja 18,VI,p38; Terry Robards article on blind taste test in which Calif wines defeated French wines; test, hosted by Society for American Wines, took place in Ottawa (M), Ja 21,III,12:1; Terry Robards article on visit to Chablis (France), town with most famous, most copied name in entire world of wine; illus (L), Ja 25,VI,p50

Article on wineries in GB; notes some 200 wineries are operating in country, most of them very new; illus (M), Ja 28,III,14-6

continued

Gov Carey backs sale of liquor, wine and beer in NYS supermarkets, news conference; reiterates his intention to abolish State Liquor Authority, despite objections from Anthony Papa, head of Association of State Liquor Authority Enforcement Agents (S), Ja 30,1:2

Article on wine-tasting courses in Manhattan; classes listed; illustration (L), F 4,III,14:1

Article on finding low-priced wines (M), Ap 8,III,1:1

Terry Robards article on NYS's '80 vintage; finds they are 'best wines made in state since World War II and may be best of century'; illustration (M), Ap 8,III,16:3

1,000 bottles of wine are stolen from Amouroux wine-growing estate (Chateauneuf-du-Pape, France); loss estimated at $10,000 (S), Ap 12,14:1

Terry Robards article on South African wines on sale in US (M), Ap 15,III,16:5

Article on wine tasting competition between French and Calif wines organized by Paul Draper, winemaker at Ridge Vineyards (Calif); results noted (L), My 20,III,20:5

Article on wines from Mosel Valley, Germany; illustration (L), My 24,VI,p62

E & J Gallo Winery plans commercial production of fine premium wine (L), My 27,III,16:3

Article on Euroblend wines; EEC rules allow these blends to be labeled tafelwin–German for table wine (M), My 27,III,18:4

Travel article on visiting Napa Valley–Calif's wine country; map; illustration (L), My 31,X,p11

Article on ritual of wine service in restaurants; drawing (M), Je 3,III,14:4

Article on 13th annual Heublein auction of rare wines recently held in New Orleans; notes prices appeared somewhat lower than in previous years (M), Je 3,III,15:3

Article on Alsatian wines and Alsatian wine society Confrerie Saint-Etienne; illustration (L), Je 7,VI,p86

Taylor California Cellars to market Light Chablis, wine with 25% fewer calories than company's regular Chablis; illustration (M), Je 9,IV,22:3

Article on new guides to wineries in NYS; guides are published by NYS Agriculture Dept and by American Vintners Assn (M), Je 10,III,16:5

Policy of some restaurants when 'unsound' wine is served accidentally noted, Je 10,III,17:1

Impact survey shows wine has outsold liquor for 1st time in US in '80; wine shipments in '80 were 475.8 million gallons, up 7.1%, while shipments of distilled spirits were 455 million gallons, down 3.7% (S), Je 14,70:1

Article on experiment by Dr Philip J Wyatt (Science Spectrum Inc) in which he pitted laser instrument against panel of people in assessing flavor of 7 different wines; Wyatt found that panel and machine agreed almost perfectly; results are published in journal Science (S), Je 16,III,2:5

Article on drop in price of wines imported from Europe because of soaring US dollar on world currency markets; drawing (L), Je 17,III,1:1

Article on Beaujolais wines; drawing (L), Je 21,VI,p58

Wine merchant Charles F Mara bids $24,000 for 12-bottle case of Calif red wine at Christie's auction, highest price ever recorded for American wine; illustration (L), Je 24,15:1

Article on estate-bottled French burgundies, which are held to be superior to other burgundies; drawings (M), Ag 2,VI,p64; article on cabernet sauvignons from California (M), Ag 5,III,14:1; article on California zinfandels (M), Ag 12,III,16:1

continued

Article on California's Beaulieu Vineyard, which produces 1 of finest red wines in US; photo (M), Ag 16,VI,p54; interview with Ben Feder on how his Clinton Vineyards winery is struggling back from bad winter; illus (M), Ag 19,III,13:1

New Massachusetts law allows customers to sample wine in retail liquor stores (S), Ag24,12:6

Many small shops have been hard hit by abolition of retail price controls on wine in several states (M), Ag 26,III,15:1

Topics editorial on marketing of wine in cans in California, Ag 28,22:1

Article on NJ wineries; illus; map (M), Ag 30,XI,2:1

Article on Calif vintner William Hill; illus (M), S 9,III,18:3

Frank J Prial article holds Calif wines are overrated (M), S 16,III,1:1

Weibel Vineyards, Calif, will begin marketing 6.3-oz bottles of champagne in 6-packs; drawing (M), S 20,III,19:3

Article on Conn's wine indus (M), S 20,X,p.3

Article on award-winning wines produced at Durney Vineyard, Monterey County, Calif; illus (L), S 27,VI,p86; Thomas M La Chine lr on Aug 16 article on Calif wines, S 27,VI,p110

Article on North Salem, NY, vintner George Naumberg; illus (M), S 27,XXII,8:5

Terry Robards article on bright outlook for '81 wine harvest in NYS despite last winter's freeze (M), D 2,III,20:5; Terry Robards article on wines that are popular during winter; drawing (M), D 16,III,19:1

NYS Equalization and Assessment Bd proposal that orchards and vineyards be valued at separate and higher rate than land used for other purposes stirs dispute among fruit and grape growers in state (M), D 20,59:1

Figure 4.16: From *The New York Times Index* 1981

Case & McGrath launches ad campaign for Keller-Geister, W Ger white wine mktd by Natl Distillers; illus (M), Mr 8,IV,15:1

NYS Assemblyman Rolland E Kidder and Sen Jess J Present introduce bill that would allow sale of table wines in grocery stores (M), Mr 20,II,8:3

Article on Dr Konstantin Frank, pres of Vinifera Cellars, Hammondsport, NY, who embarked on career as wine-grower after retiring at age 65; Frank, who will be 80 on July 4, was honored at birthday party given by NYS Commerce Dept for his contributions to wine indus; Frank illus (L), Mr 21,III,1:1

Article on Chateau Lafite-Rothschild wines (L), Mr 30,22:1

Prices of imported and Amer wines will rise sharply over next few mos; series of relatively small grape harvests in Eur, combined with steadily rising consumer demand, has exerted strong upward pressure on wine prices (S), Mr 31,36:2

Frank J Prial article, part of series entitled The Mood Makers, discusses varied moods evoked by different wines; illus (L), Ap 1,VI,p88

Frank J Prial revs book Chianti–The Land, the People and the Wine by Raymond Flower (M), Ap 4,III,15-1

US Supreme Court to decide whether state-sanctioned system for fixing retail liquor and wine prices violates Sherman Antitrust Act (S), O 2,IV,11:2

Terry Robards on rising wine prices; illus (M), O 3,III,1:5

continued

Terry Robards on wine tasting held under auspices of 'Le Nouveau Guide' of Gault-Millau, France; notes California wines took first, second and fourth of top 10 places in chardonnay section (M), O 17,19:2
Article on impact of wine-barrel inflation; says high cost of French oak wine barrels may force producers of premium California wine to buy American or abandon oak-aging altogether (M), O 17,III,10:4
Richard F Shepard article on wine making in Portuguese enclave of Newark, NJ (M), O 18,II,7:1
Article on 4th Annual Southeastern Homemade Wine competition, Atlanta, Ga (M), O 24,III,18:2
British wines win over French wines in less-than-serious wine competition sponsored by London's Evening Standard and Le Figaro, Paris (M), O 30,II,10:5
Terry Robards on new French vintage for '79; notes prices may not be as expensive as '78 because of good grape crop (M), O 31,III,1:5
Italian wine growers in Chianti region are pleased that harvest was plentiful and wines will be good to excellent (M), N 4:53:1

Figure 4.17: From *The New York Times Index* 1979

Calif Wine Inst ad code prohibits promotions by athletes and other people who are engaged in activities that appeal to persons below legal drinking age; Frank Gifford illus (M), Ap 26,III,13:1
NY Times chart rates vintage wines (M), My 10,III,15:1
Excerpts from Peter Allan Sichel's vintage wine rept (M), My 24,III,16:3
Heublein Inc holds annual wine auction, Atlanta, Ga (S), My 25,IV,2:5
John A Grisanti pays record $18,000 for bottle of 1864 Chateau Lafite; illus (M), My 26,15:2
NYS Assembly passes bill requiring wines and liquors to be referred to in liters rather than in gallons for purposes of imposing excise taxes on distributors and noncommercial importers (S), Je7,II,2:2

Figure 4.18: From *The New York Times Index* 1978

You have obviously hit pay dirt in *The New York Times Index*. Judging by the helpful summaries, you can see that the United States has done a lot of catching up in the wine industry since 1972, the date of the *Encyclopaedia Britannica* edition that claimed there were no great American wines. Already, you see yourself modifying your thesis to something less absolute than "there are *no* great American wines" to maybe "some American wines are being called 'great.' "

Completing Your Working Bibliography on Wine

Your search for secondary sources is complete for now, though you will be uncovering other useful sources as you read. These you will want to track down later. But now you have in front of you two lists on wine—one of books, the other of periodicals. Your next step is to take the book list to the author card catalog and record any missing call numbers in the left margin (Figures 4.19 and 4.20). (Fill in whatever bibliographical information is still lacking as well.) Any books you can't find in the card catalog, your library doesn't have. If your research can get along without it, the loss is minor.

But how do you know whether it can or it cannot? In some cases the titles will tell you. Furthermore, the similarity among the titles of several books suggests duplication of material, so you probably can get along with just one of them. Choose the most recent edition by an author whose name you might have encountered more than once (suggesting the author is an authority in the field) in your exploration of sources. Yet it would obviously help if you could glance through the books. Fortunately, you don't have to have the book in your hands to get a sense of it or of how it was received by reviewers, that is, other experts in the field. There are three indispensable reference works for that. They summarize reviews of books and/or tell you where to find current reviews of current books. Thus you don't have to skim through the book yourself.

Book Review Digest, 1905– . Provides a summary of each review.

Book Review Index, 1965– . Includes three times more periodicals than the *Book Review Digest* but does not provide summaries.

Current Book Review Citations, 1976– . Cites even more journals than the two above but does not provide summaries.

Final Observations on the Working Bibliography on Wine

You can now see the reason for including more titles in your lists than you will probably need. Not all of the titles you find in the reference works are readily available. Of the five books on your list, your library has only one

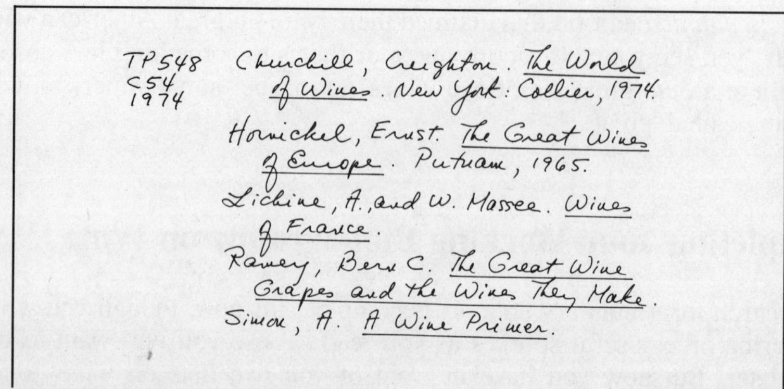

TP548 C54 1974 Churchill, Creighton. The World of Wines. New York: Collier, 1974.

Hornickel, Ernst. The Great Wines of Europe. Putnam, 1965.

Lichine, A., and W. Massee. Wines of France.

Ramey, Bern C. The Great Wine Grapes and the Wines They Make.

Simon, A. A Wine Primer.

Figure 4.19: Sample List of Books on Wine

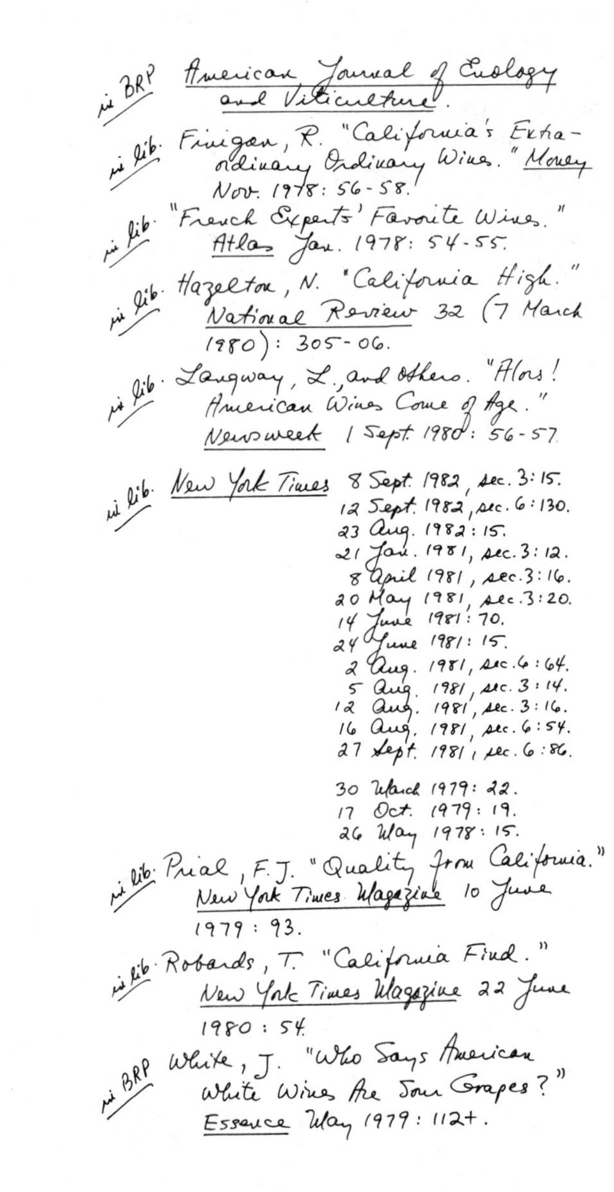

in BRP *American Journal of Enology and Viticulture.*

in lib. Finigan, R. "California's Extra-ordinary Ordinary Wines." *Money* Nov. 1978: 56-58.

in lib. "French Experts' Favorite Wines." *Atlas* Jan. 1978: 54-55.

in lib. Hazelton, N. "California High." *National Review* 32 (7 March 1980): 305-06.

in lib. Langway, L., and others. "Alors! American Wines Come of Age." *Newsweek* 1 Sept. 1980: 56-57.

in lib. *New York Times* 8 Sept. 1982, sec. 3: 15.
12 Sept. 1982, sec. 6: 130.
23 Aug. 1982: 15.
21 Jan. 1981, sec. 3: 12.
8 April 1981, sec. 3: 16.
20 May 1981, sec. 3: 20.
14 June 1981: 70.
24 June 1981: 15.
2 Aug. 1981, sec. 6: 64.
5 Aug. 1981, sec. 3: 14.
12 Aug. 1981, sec. 3: 16.
16 Aug. 1981, sec. 6: 54.
27 Sept. 1981, sec. 6: 86.

30 March 1979: 22.
17 Oct. 1979: 19.
26 May 1978: 15.

in lib. Prial, F. J. "Quality from California." *New York Times Magazine* 10 June 1979: 93.

in lib. Robards, T. "California Find." *New York Times Magazine* 22 June 1980: 54.

in BRP White, J. "Who Says American White Wines Are Sour Grapes?" *Essence* May 1979: 112+.

Figure 4.20: Sample List of Periodicals on Wine

of them. You fared better with the periodicals. Even though your library doesn't subscribe to three of them, two are located in area libraries and are available to you through interlibrary loan.

The question then is how great an effort should you exert to locate the books and the journal? The answer usually depends on the level of the course for which you are writing the research paper. The one book and twenty-two short articles in your library would be adequate for a writing course instructing you in the basics of the research paper, but for one thing. Most of the articles come from predominantly one periodical, the *New York Times*; therefore, you'd be wise to send for the articles in *Essence* and *Money.* Of course, if this were an upper-level course or seminar in anthropology and you were researching the use of intoxicating beverages in primitive societies, for example, you'd be bound by the requirements of thoroughness to use far more than one book and find as many articles as you can, as well as use more learned sources than such popular magazines as *Essence* and *Money.*

ASSIGNMENT

Search through the subject card catalog, bibliographies, and indexes for books and articles relevant to your restricted subject. Compile a working bibliography consisting of two lists–one of books, the other of periodicals. Indicate the availability of the books in your library with a call number and take the necessary steps to locate those books your library does not have but that you think relevant and important. Indicate the availability of the periodicals with appropriate abbreviations and, again, for the ones that you need but your library doesn't have, take the necessary steps to locate them in area libraries.

Do *not* do any reading at this point. Spend your time instead conducting a *thorough* search for pertinent secondary sources.

Should your instructor wish to see your working bibliography, be sure to make a copy of it for yourself before passing it in.

5 Using the Library

Skimming for General Information

You'll probably be surprised to find that the third stage of your research is not the detailed taking of notes but the thoughtful skimming of the readings listed in your working bibliography. Skimming is not just letting your eyes float randomly over words without registering information. Quite the contrary, **skimming** is purposeful reading: You skim to discover whether or not the material is relevant to your paper *and* what the author's central idea is. The only thing you're not reading for when you skim is details.

Stage three should never be skipped in the interest of saving time. To be sure, as you acquire experience in the writing of research papers, stage three can be shortened, modified, and restricted to the skimming of several rather than all of the books and articles you've compiled. But it can *never* be eliminated altogether. The reason is simple. The skimming that you do at this stage initiates the first of the two most challenging phases of your project: processing the information and writing the essay. Unprocessed information that a student hasn't bothered to think about is the major reason that students write poor research papers. It's information that the student hasn't analyzed, interpreted, digested, absorbed, or assimilated; it is information the student mechanically copied out of a book or periodical and then inserted mechanically into the research paper without straining it through the filters of his or her mind. Under such conditions, a research paper becomes a mere collage of notes.

Because you want to avoid such a useless exercise, you should take *no* detailed notes during stage three. Just skim, letting your mind rather than your pencil do the work. Give the ideas you read a chance to slosh around in your head; take the chill off your subject, get a feel for it, see it whole before you take it an article and book at a time. Your paper stands a much better chance of coming together for you if you live with what you read for a while before taking notes. This is known as "processing" information.

Unfortunately, no simple directions on *how* to process information can be given. The guidelines on how to be thoughtful, creative, imaginative in digesting, interpreting, and analyzing your data don't exist. So far, you and your mind have been asked to take things a step at a time—like a computer actually. But during the next stage, your mind will be working more profoundly than any computer. Unlike the computer, when the mind processes information, it leaps creatively from subject to subject and idea to idea. No one can tell your mind how to "leap." It depends on flashes of recognition, intuition, and background experience. It makes connections between what you read in one article and what you read in another one; it detects patterns; it "beeps" you, so to speak, to signal that what you're reading now reinforces or contradicts or repeats what you read earlier; it generalizes from the data in front of you; it makes discoveries, and it feels the thrill of those discoveries.

In short, when it comes to the processing of information, you and your mind are on your own; but then it wouldn't be satisfying if it were any other way.

Some Practical Suggestions

As you skim, look for recurring ideas and facts; they indicate both what is widely known by the experts in the field and what they consider important. Noticing recurrent information when you skim will also save you the trouble of unknowingly recording it a number of times in your notes before catching on to the repetitions. Try to arrange mentally those ideas that seem relevant to your thesis. As time goes on, you will fine tune this mental arrangement of concepts into increasingly clearer focus; but even at this stage you should begin thinking about the general shape of your paper. With that in mind, you wouldn't be violating the whole purpose of skimming, as discussed above, if you kept a piece of paper close at hand when you read and jotted down a few *key* words—no more—to suggest those ideas that advance your thesis. Write them alongside the title and page number of the source you are skimming (Figure 5.1). Use only *one* side of the page.

When you're finished skimming, place your list of periodicals with their titles next to your list of key words and look for patterns: anything to suggest a further restriction of your subject, a modification of your thesis, a particular organization that your paper might, conceivably, follow.

By the time you've completed this phase of your research, you should have a good idea of what your subject is about, some sense of the overall shape of your essay, and a list of key ideas for future reference.

Results of Skimming the Readings on Wine

Taking wine again as an example, examine the two lists in Figure 5.2. What do you see? Should the topic (the inferiority of American wines as compared to European wines) be further restricted? Should the thesis ("There are no great American wines.") be reformulated?

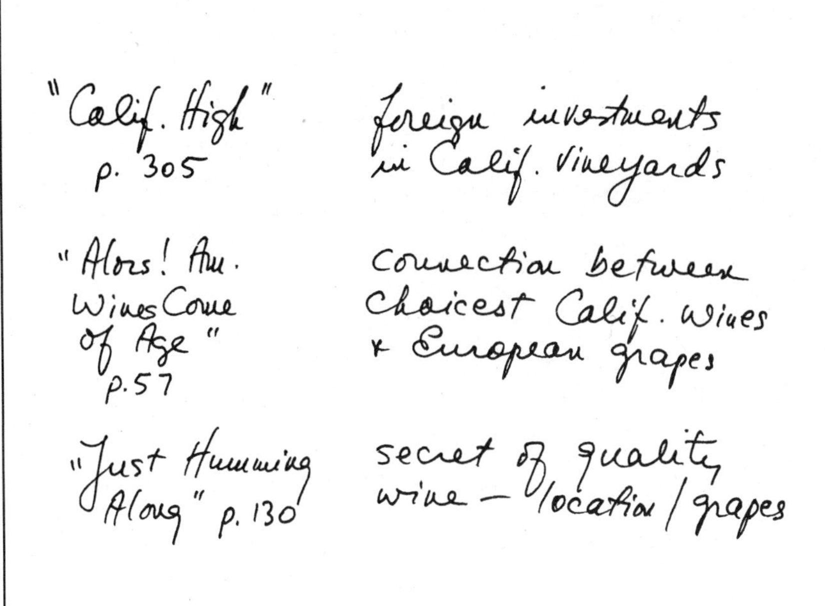

Figure 5.1: Sample from Student's List of Key Words

Judging from the titles and the key words, you can make the following observations: The competition seems to exist primarily between California and French wines; California wines have been winning some wine-tasting competitions; at least one bottle of California wine has outpriced one bottle of French wine in the five-figure market. All this suggests that you should restrict the subject further and change the thesis somewhat: "While French wines still held the title of 'great' as recently as the early seventies, some California wines have been successfully challenging them for the title a decade later."

Preliminary Outline

Indeed, you find that you can do more than just reformulate your thesis. You discover that you can arrange the data into a sketchy, preliminary outline, according to what you see yourself discussing and in what order:

1. What the chief elements in wine making are
   a. grapes
   b. soil
   c. climate
2. What makes the difference between one wine and another

List Of Periodicals	List of Key Words
"Calif. Extraordinary	foreign investments in Calif. vineyards
"French Experts' Favorite	connection bet. best Calif. wines + Europ. grapes
"Calif. High	secret of quality wine — location / grapes
"Alas! Am. Wines Come of Age	Cabernet captures premium wine market
"Quality from Calif.	Calif. — best wines
"Calif. Find	Georgia — high-priced wines
"Who Says Am. White Wine	NY 80's wines — best of century
	great soil = great grapes
	Fr. + Calif. competition
	wine outsells liquor in U.S.
	$24,000 for Calif. wine
	Fr. burgundies — superior
	Calif. cabernets
	Calif. zinfandels
	Calif. — finest reds
	Calif — award-winning wines
	French Cabernets
	Calif. wins competition
	$18,000 for Fr. wine

Figure 5.2: This sample list of periodicals is shorter than the list of key words because *The New York Times Index* did not supply titles.

3. How California wine was being evaluated in the early seventies
4. How California wine is being evaluated now
   a. California wine commanding high prices
   b. California wine winning wine-tasting competitions
   c. heavy foreign investments in California vineyards

Thus without having really worked very hard yet, you have just shaped your material into a research paper—and you're only at stage three. Even if you have to modify this order later, just having one to begin with suggests a firm grip on the subject.

ASSIGNMENT

Thoughtfully skim pertinent chapters in the books and the articles listed in your working bibliography. (If your lists are very long, skim only the most promising titles.)

When you're finished skimming, do one of two things—whichever comes more easily.

1. Place the thesis sentence at the top of the page, and below that arrange the major ideas (no details) you expect to discuss in your paper in outline form. See the preliminary outline above.
2. Write a general and brief (one paragraph only) summary of the major ideas that you have gathered, being sure to include the thesis. Do not give details or facts. Do not be specific. Here's an example:

> The best American wines seem to come from California. The choicest California wines are the Cabernet Sauvignons and the Chardonnays. Ten years ago they were not being called "great." Now some of them are. Their greatest competitors for the title are French wines. It seems that the secret is in the grape, the soil, and the climate.

Notice that the summary above and the preliminary outline above don't coincide; each implies a different approach and a different order. Either is fine for this phase of research since whichever you follow, you will be modifying anyway. What's important is control of the subject, which you demonstrate by arranging key ideas in logical relation to one another.

6 Using the Library

Taking Notes

Taking detailed notes on what you read is the last of the four stages involved in "researching" a library topic. The questions students ask most frequently about note taking concern (1) what notes to take, (2) how many to take, and (3) how to take them. The questions deserve attention since one of the worst consequences of improper note taking is **plagiarism**, the passing off of someone else's words or ideas as your own. (Plagiarism is dealt with in detail in Chapter 7.)

What Notes to Take and How Many

As a student, you can begin to answer the first two questions for yourself with respect to your own assignment if you just remind yourself of the reason for which you are reading the secondary sources in the first place: to find expert opinions, data, and ideas that *explain* your subject and *corroborate* your thesis. Therefore, the answer to the question of "what and how many notes to take" is simply "those notes that show the opinions, data, and ideas that corroborate, elaborate, and explain your thesis."

Remember the research miniatures you wrote (Chapter 2)? The time has come to apply what you learned from that writing experience to the one you're about to undertake. There, too, you were given or asked to devise a thesis statement and were then asked to verify it with the information you found in the *Newsweek* article. If you'd been writing a "real" research paper, whatever data you found in *Newsweek* and in *Nation's Business* to prove your point would have originally appeared in your *notes.*

To be specific, think of the essay you wrote on Sino-American trade. The thesis required that you discuss the obstacles and some of the steps taken to overcome them. In your discussion you had to rely on *Newsweek* for facts regarding Chinese exports and imports, for example, and for observations regarding the red tape American businessmen encounter in China. This is the kind of information that you would have been recording in your notes if you had been doing a real research essay.

It might also be worthwhile at this point to look at the two student research papers in Chapter 15. Notice the sort of material that is documented, the variety of sources used for explanation and corroboration, and the intermeshing of borrowed material and personal observations. In short, both students wrote their own papers and merely *worked in* the corroborating evidence rather than patched the paper together, quilt fashion, from borrowed paragraphs.

Taking Notes on the Subject of Wine

Let's say that you are now ready to start taking notes on wine. Remember your tentative thesis: "While French wines held the title of 'great' as recently as the early seventies, some California wines have been successfully challenging them for the title a decade later." The excerpt below comes from one of the *New York Times* articles that you have found useful in corroborating your thesis. Read it and note the underlined passages. It is the information in these passages that you would be recording in your notes.

WINE TALK

expert opinion

American wines are often challenging French wines in tasting competitions these days, and the results often suggest that certain carefully chosen California wines are superior to the best that France can offer. Such contests are nearly always controversial because of the probability that wines from each country reach maturity at different times and because of the biases of the tasters.

fact

Devotees of the great wines of Bordeaux contend that they need much more time to reach their peaks, that they tend to be far more awkward and coarse in their youth than the fine cabernet sauvignons of California, which are made from the basic grape of Bordeaux and often display great charm and finesse, after only a few years in the bottle.

fact/ expert opinion

Because of Prohibition, which crippled the American wine industry until 1934, and because most American consumers did not begin to take California wines seriously until the early 1970's, there is virtually no supply of older American wines to compare with the fully mature wines of France.

fact

As a result, direct comparisons are made almost entirely among the younger vintages, and the controversy seems never to be resolved. But as time passes and American wines continually defeat French wines in blind tastings, the volume of evidence grows. Now it has happened again, this

expert opinion

time in Canada, where the bias in favor of American wines is probably less pronounced than in the United States.

fact

Saturday, at the Four Seasons Hotel in Ottawa, a group called the Society for American Wines, based there, undertook a blind tasting of some of the best cabernet sauvignons from California against a group of top-rated Bordeaux. The event was organized by Lieut. Col. Donald Kinnan, an American liaison officer attached to NATO in the Canadian capital. He

expert opinion

described the tasters as sophisticated, and I have no reason to doubt him. I was invited to participate, but could not attend. Colonel Kinnan reported the results to me.

fact

Thirteen wines were involved, and California swept the first five places, defeating Chateau Lafite-Rothschild, Mouton-Rothschild, Latour, Margaux and Haut-Brion, all from the excellent Bordeaux vintage of 1970. The best result for a French wine was sixth place for Chateau Ducru-Beaucaillou 1970, suggesting that even within the Bordeaux hierarchy the most celebrated vineyards do not always capture the top prizes.

fact

The outright winner was Sterling Vineyards Reserve cabernet sauvignon 1974, a dark, intensely flavored wine of tremendous character that sold for about $20 a bottle when it was available. It probably still exists in a few stores, but I have not seen it recently. The 1975 Sterling Reserve, not quite as good, can be found for $25.

Second place was taken by the Beaulieu Vineyards Georges de Latour Private Reserve cabernet sauvignon 1970, a wine of great finesse and complexity that is widely recognized as one of the best that this country ever produced. It was especially appropriate to make direct comparisons between this and the Bordeaux because they came from the same vintage.

In third place was the Heitz Cellar Martha's Vineyard 1974 cabernet sauvignon, a wine that has also attracted considerable attention among devotees of the best that California has to offer.

Terry Robards, *New York Times,* January 21, 1981, Sec. 3, p. 12

How to Take Notes

The mechanics of note taking varies with individuals. Eventually, each person develops a personal style and technique often understood by no one else. Even what you choose to write your notes on is a matter of individual choice. Some people use cards; others sheets of paper. What's more, you can take various kinds of notes: you can *summarize* long passages in your own words; you can *paraphrase* passages, that is, put them in your own words, but keep the passage, unlike the summary, roughly the same length as the original; and you can *quote,* that is, record the actual words of the original.

The suggestions that follow on how to take notes do not assume that there is any single best way of taking them. They are made only on the assumption that, as a rule, beginners find it difficult to summarize sources or paraphrase them properly while they are actually in the process of taking notes; and that when it comes to using the notes they've recorded, many beginners find it difficult to avoid quoting excessively. Only about 10 percent of a research paper should be quoted material; a paper in which the quotations exceed 10 percent of its total length indicates inadequate processing of data on the part of the student. Therefore, try the method outlined below.

Use either 3 × 5 note cards or note paper. Note cards are often recommended because they can be shuffled and arranged according to ideas; the intention is to use them to organize information. Needless to say, they do not guard you against treating the organizing process mechanically. In fact, no note-taking method guards against it. For precisely this reason, you have been encouraged (back in Chapter 5) to digest the information and organize *as you skim.* But if you like note cards, use them. Otherwise, blank writing paper is fine. It has the advantage of being cheaper than note cards and, for some people, more manageable than small rectangles of paper.

Step one. Once you've decided between cards and paper, look back at your *List of Key Words* and your *Summary* or *Outline* (Chapter 5). Then do the following: (1) select your essay's main subjects of discussion, that is, the subjects that explain and corroborate your thesis; (2) record them at the tops of your note cards or note paper one subject per page/card. Use one side only. Naturally, in the course of your research, you will discover other relevant subjects. When you do, just make out a page/card for each of them as well. You will also come across information that doesn't quite fit any of your pigeonholes but which you can recognize as probably being useful. By all means, record it too—under appropriate headings. Your note pages/cards will look something like those shown in Figures 6.1–6.4.

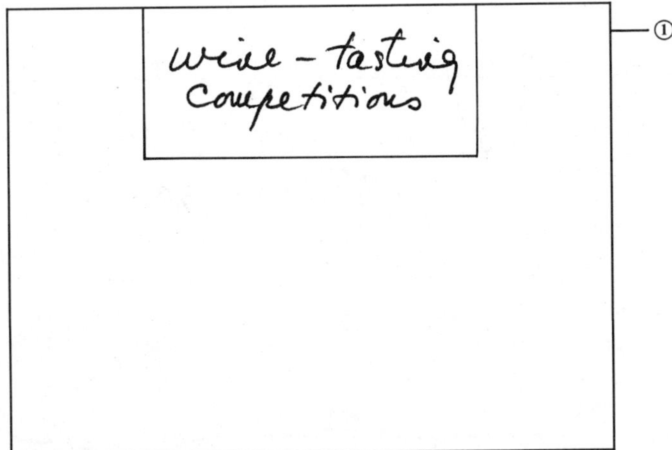

Figure 6.1: 3 × 5 Card 1. Subject of discussion.

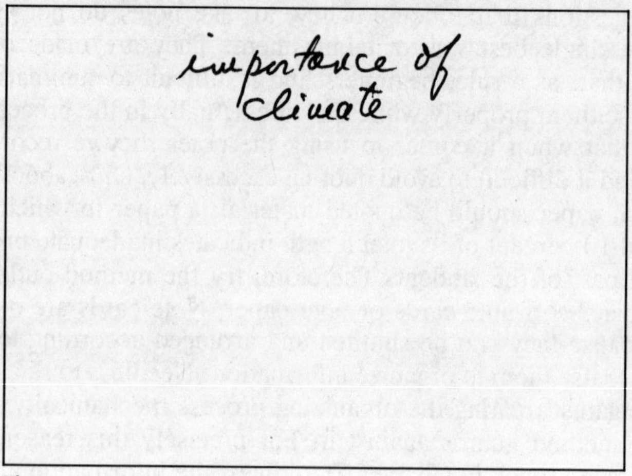

importance of
climate

Figure 6.2: 3 × 5 Card

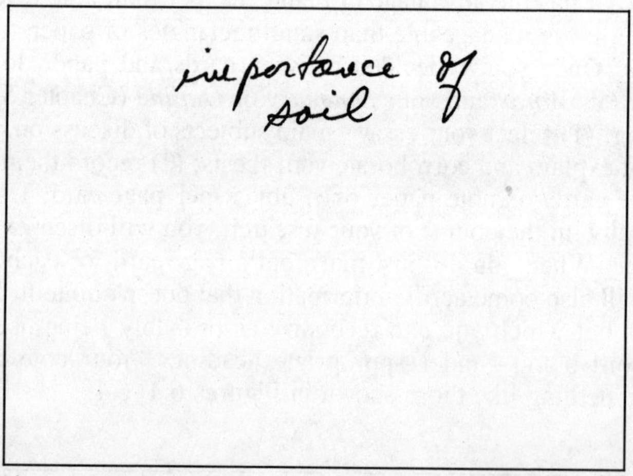

importance of
soil

Figure 6.3: 3 × 5 Card

foreign invest. in
Calif. vineyards

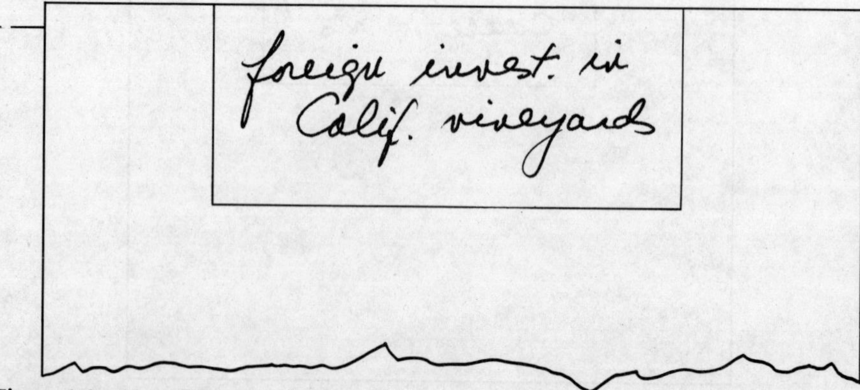

Figure 6.4: Note Paper 1. Subject of discussion.

Step two. Write the author and title of each article and book from which you are taking notes in the left margin of your paper (or on the reverse side of the card). Remember that the rest of your bibliographical data (publisher, date, title of journal, etc.) is in your working bibliography, so you don't have to get it all down here. However, do record the page numbers for the gathered information. Place these also in the left margin.

Step three. When you take notes, do not summarize or paraphrase anything. Just quote. Take down word for word what you find relevant to the needs of your thesis. But do not write down whole passages word for word. Quote entire sentences from beginning to end without leaving out a single word *only* in the following instances: when they summarize or express an idea particularly well or when the information is crucial to verifying your thesis and accuracy is important. Otherwise, quote fragments of sentences, phrases, and single words. Anytime you omit anything—even one single word like "the"—insert three periods (. . .) to mark the omission. (See Chapter 7 for a complete discussion of omissions.) If the omission includes the end of a sentence, or a whole sentence, or more than a sentence, add a fourth period (. . . .). An omission is *never* marked by fewer than three periods or more than four, regardless of how many actual words you omit. Suppose you wished to take notes on the following paragraph from Creighton Churchill's *The World of Wines* (p. 2):

> When the mature grape is crushed (the tradition of using bare feet in ancient times still exists in many parts of the world today) yeasts, which are ever-present in the atmosphere, commence feeding on the natural sugar in the juice, and in turn convert part of this juice to alcohol. This fermentation or chemical conversion can also occur with a peach or a cherry, or even a dandelion blossom—but usually the fruit wines that we know today have had sugar added, and have been fortified with more alcohol than they acquired by natural fermentation. Thus they technically fall into the category of cordials or liqueurs—or what the French call apéritifs—drinks best consumed before or after meals, not during them. Nature's bacteria are only capable of producing a certain amount of alcohol, and natural wine from the wine grape, which rarely contains more than 14 per cent alcohol (and usually less), almost always seems to be best with food. The sole exceptions are wines such as Sherry, Port and Madeira, which are also fortified with extra alcohol, and happen to be delightful and appropriate with certain foods as without them.

This might be the result of your note taking:

"When the mature grape is crushed . . . yeasts . . . ever-present in the atmosphere, commence feeding on the natural sugar in the juice,

```
and . . . convert part of this juice to alcohol. . . . Nature's bac-
teria are only capable of producing a certain amount of alcohol . . .
rarely . . . more than 14 per cent. . . . The sole exceptions are
wines such as Sherry, Port and Madeira . . . fortified with extra
alcohol. . . ."
```

not

```
mature grapes crushed--yeasts in atmosphere feed on natural sugar in
juice and convert part to alcohol.  Bacteria produce only certain
amount alcohol--14% tops--except Sherry, Port, Madeira--fortified
with extra alcohol.
```

The reason for taking such pains with the periods in proper note taking should be obvious when you imagine yourself returning to your notes days or weeks later. In the second example—the improperly jotted notes—you have all the information you need but no idea of which words are Churchill's, which yours, or what you omitted from or added to the passage. In short, you have a problem. If you were simply to reconnect the fragments into sentences and enclose the passage in quotation marks, you'd be misrepresenting Churchill: It may be what he said but *not* how he said it. And if you left the quotation marks off, you'd still be lying: Many of the words are not your own but Churchill's. There is, of course, a solution (see Chapter 7 on paraphrasing): Completely ignore the language in your notes and convey the meaning entirely in your own words. Unfortunately, it is not the solution the beginner resorts to when he or she has been inaccurate in note taking. Therefore, eliminate the temptation to misrepresent the original source, in the first place, by making what you quote and what you omit obvious with quotation marks and periods.

Once you have completed gathering notes, they should resemble the samples shown in Figures 6.5–6.7.

Guidelines on Note Taking

1. *Record two types of data when you're taking notes:*

a. Data for which you can visualize a place in your paper because they obviously corroborate or explain your thesis.

b. Data that are instructive about your topic, that is, data you (and, therefore, probably your reader) need to learn in order to understand your subject.

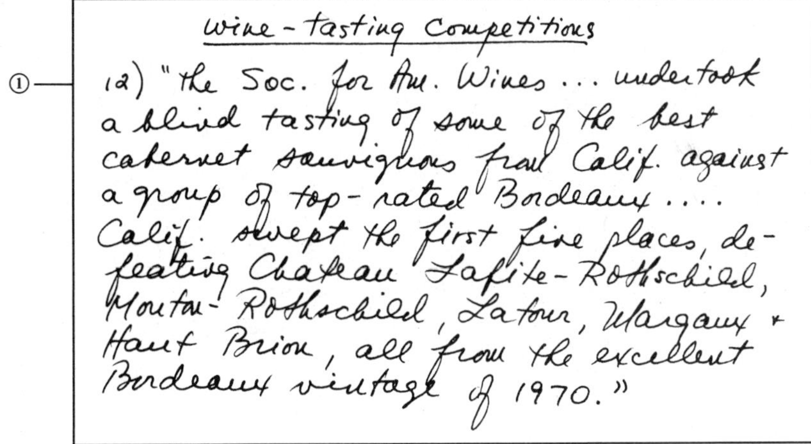
wine-tasting competitions

12) "the Soc. for Am. Wines . . . undertook a blind tasting of some of the best cabernet sauvignons from Calif. against a group of top-rated Bordeaux . . . . Calif. swept the first five places, defeating Chateau Lafite-Rothschild, Mouton-Rothschild, Latour, Margaux + Haut Brion, all from the excellent Bordeaux vintage of 1970."

Figure 6.5: 3 × 5 Card 1. Page.

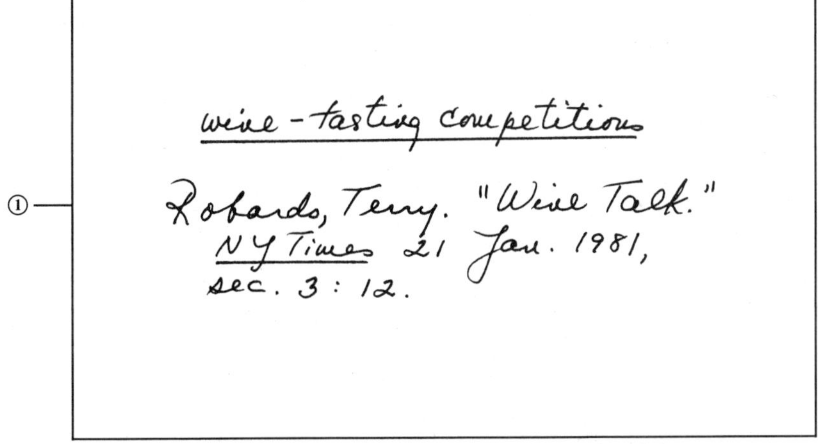
wine-tasting competitions

Robards, Terry. "Wine Talk." NY Times 21 Jan. 1981, sec. 3: 12.

Figure 6.6: 3 × 5 Card (Reverse Side) 1. Bibliographical data.

Suppose that in your research on wine, for example, you continually encountered the term "varietal wine." As far as you could tell, discussion of varietal wine was not relevant to your thesis, but the frequency with which it crops up in the reading suggests that you had better record a definition and perhaps a brief explanation of it in your notes. Just in case you needed to explain it in your paper.

2. *Do not make any effort to summarize or paraphrase at this point. Record* only the *actual words* of the author you're researching. Also place *quotation marks* around anything you quote. Should you want to insert a word or two of your own here and there, the quotation marks will distinguish between your words and the author's.

3. *Be very* accurate *in recording* periods *(and the correct number at*

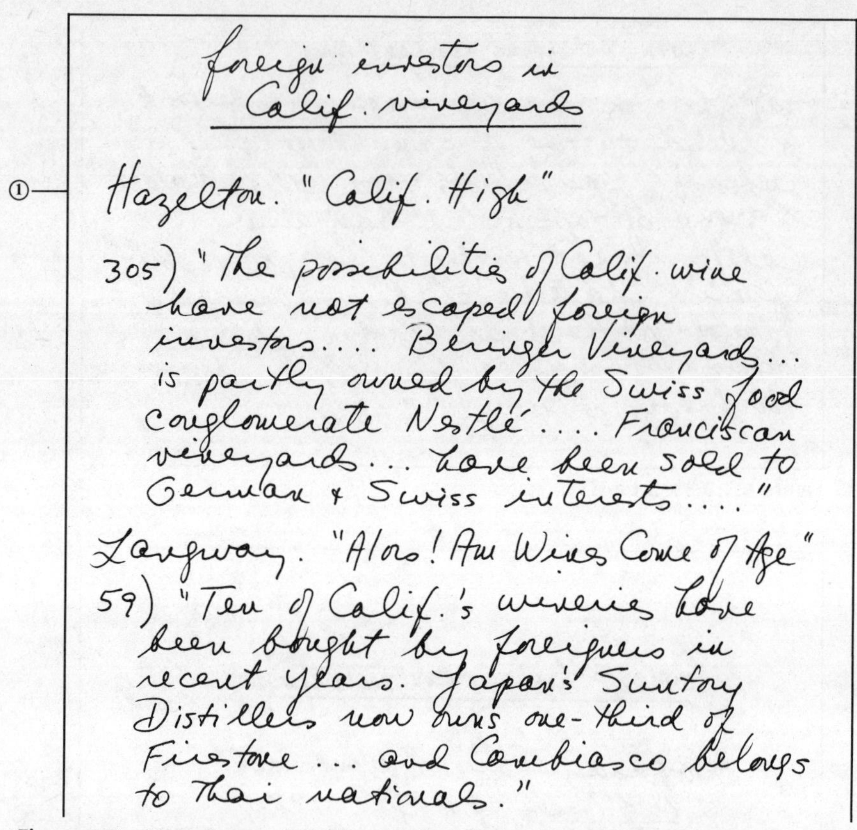

foreign investors in
Calif. vineyards

① Hazelton. "Calif. High"

305) "The possibilities of Calif. wine
have not escaped foreign
investors... Beringer Vineyards...
is partly owned by the Swiss food
conglomerate Nestlé.... Franciscan
vineyards... have been sold to
German & Swiss interests...."

Langway. "Alors! Am Wines Come of Age"

59) "Ten of Calif.'s wineries have
been bought by foreigners in
recent years. Japan's Suntory
Distillers now owns one-third of
Firestone ... and Cambiasco belongs
to Thai nationals."

Figure 6.7: Note Paper 1. Bibliographical data—shortened version when no chance of confusion with other articles.

that) to indicate omissions and capital letters *to show the beginnings of sentences.* When you return to your notes days or weeks later, you must be able to assume correctly that if a sentence of your quoted notes does not begin with a capital letter, it is not the beginning of a sentence and vice versa.

ASSIGNMENT

Having already absorbed some of the major ideas of your project, you are ready to begin taking notes from the sources listed in your working bibliography. Depending on how quickly you work, how much time you have to devote to this stage, and how much library material you have to read, you may be finished by the time your instructor turns to the five prewriting chapters or your note taking may overlap with the next five assignments and, therefore, move at a more leisurely pace. Either way, this stage will obviously take more time than the first three and should be engaged in with care.

However, your note taking should not go on indefinitely, so don't be reluctant to stop. Once you have gathered enough evidence to explain and verify your thesis, the one more book and the one more article you come across may just duplicate what you already have. The scope of a freshman research project does not require that you exhaust all the available sources.

7
Using Your Notes When You Write

Quoting and Paraphrasing

When you're writing your paper—whether in segments, as you will be doing in the next five chapters, or putting it together into a whole at the end—you will have to draw on your notes for some of the ideas and, probably, for all of the facts that you use in it. You will summarize, paraphrase, and quote the material in your notes that advances your thesis.

Acknowledging Sources to Avoid Plagiarism

When you use any kind of material of which you are not the author you are obligated by the principles of honesty and good scholarship to acknowledge your sources. If the *idea of the language* in which it is expressed is not yours, do not mislead the reader into thinking that it is. You are, after all, writing a research paper, so you're expected to use other people's ideas and, occasionally, words. Heaven knows, you've spent enough time in the library looking for them. So acknowledge them.

There's also the matter of good scholarship. Even if it's only in a modest way, your research paper is a contribution to scholarship: It compiles information from a variety of sources; it brings it together in one place; it provides a convenient list of works on the subject. In short, any reader of your paper who is interested in pursuing your topic further should be able to know just where to go for it. That is essentially the way scholarship works: A does research; B picks up from there and does some more or takes it in a different direction; C builds on what A and B have done; and so on.

When C does *not* acknowledge what he or she has borrowed from A and B, C is said to be **plagiarizing**—stealing. To be sure, most students do not do it intentionally. The unintentional kind is often the result of a student's having inadequately processed the information gathered – a problem that prewriting is intended to alleviate. But whether the plagiarism has been intentional or not makes no difference; the result is still theft, passing off someone else's words *or* ideas as your own.

You should, however, have no trouble with plagiarism if you remember to acknowledge the following:

1. *Someone else's exact words.*

2. *Someone else's expert opinions, ideas, or insights that you are presenting in your own words.*

When confronted with these guidelines, students often remark in disbelief that they will have to show their source for *every* sentence in their paper since they didn't know anything about their subject before they began; therefore, *none* of the ideas in the paper can possibly be theirs. Actually, that *is* the case with papers in which the student has done absolutely no thinking of his or her own – put it in neutral, so to speak – and just copied out information wholesale from notes. If that's what you're doing, yes, you *do* have to give the source for every sentence. It will save you from plagiarizing but, unfortunately, not from getting an "F" anyway since, as you have already learned, that is not the way to write a research paper. If, on the other hand, you do process the information you gather, you will find yourself making statements and observations for which you do not have to show a source (see pages 3 and 97).

3. *Facts not regarded as common knowledge.* This rule tends to be a little problematic for beginners, too. What is common knowledge? Simply stated, it is facts and observations that are generally known: the Vikings reached the New World before Columbus; the crash of the stock market was the start of the Great Depression in the thirties; teenage pregnancies are skyrocketing. What is *not* common knowledge? The *interpretation of a fact of common knowledge* is *not* to be considered common knowledge. Everybody knows that teenage pregnancies are on the rise, so you don't document the idea; but if you were to write that "teen pregnancies are rising because family bonds are weakening," you'd have to tell your reader what psychologist or sociologist you were citing. *A fact or idea the reader is likely to question* is *not* to be considered common knowledge either. Although you wouldn't cite the source for the fact that the Vikings reached the Americas before Columbus did, you would have to cite it for the opinion that the Vikings reached the coast of Massachusetts! The reader would want to know what authority has been able to pin the location down so specifically.

4. *Previous knowledge to which you wish to lend authority.* You are always free to use information you already know such as the causes of a stroke or the cut-off point on a breathalizer test that defines a driver as legally drunk. But bear in mind that your reader may not know as much and may question your knowledge and even hesitate to accept conclusions based on information for which you don't give a source. Therefore, don't hesitate to enhance your credibility by indicating in a content note, for example (see Chapter 14 for a discussion of content notes), some chapter in a book that covers the causes of a stroke (and, of course, corresponds with your own memory of the facts); or for information on blood alcohol levels, go ahead and cite Driver Education as the source of your data.

When Not to Document

Once you've acknowledged the four kinds of material that need documenting, you will be left with the material that does not. It, too, falls—more or less—into four categories:

1. *Topic sentences.* Even when they introduce borrowed ideas, they don't need acknowledgment because they're merely *introductions* to ideas you've borrowed and, presumably, will acknowledge in appropriate places within the paragraphs themselves.

2. *Explanations or elaborations of borrowed ideas.* Sometimes a quotation includes technical detail or terminology that isn't going to be clear to the reader, so explain it. In such an event, acknowledge the quotation, but not your own explanation, which might typically begin with the phrase, "in other words." Here's an example: Dr. Turner explains that standard treatment for "cancer that has invaded distant sites is palliative" (38). In other words, unable to cure the patient, doctors will merely try to relieve the pain and the bleeding. (See the discussion below for instructions on how to acknowledge sources.)

3. *Examples.* Obviously, you don't have to document examples you provide. Take the following: Children fed a carbohydrate diet will not thrive (Fuller 56). For example, such meals as canned spaghetti, toast and jam, and donuts and soda will produce health problems.

4. *Original ideas, opinions, and conclusions.* Any concepts you've generated and/or developed on your own will not be documented.

EXERCISE 1

Suppose you were a history major, and the following paragraph from Lionel Casson's "Godliness and Work" were one that you had written in a research paper on tools in the Middle Ages. There are ideas here for which you would have to acknowledge a source; there are also others that you *could* have arrived at yourself (in other words, did not borrow but thought up on your own). Which are which?

> The rise of the windmill was even more dramatic. While the ancients used water power to a limited degree, they scorned wind power except for driving boats. But sometime after A.D. 1140, windmills started making their appearance in northern Europe. By 1300 they dotted all of Europe's great northern plains. Windmills had one important advantage over watermills: They did not stop when rivers froze over. Windmills kept going all year

round. Eventually they made their way to the south of Europe as well—although, for one reason or another, there were pockets of resistance, such as in La Mancha, Spain; even at the end of the 16th century they were still enough of a novelty there to astonish Don Quixote.

Science 81, Sept. 1981

How to Acknowledge Sources

1. *Use quotation marks if you are using someone else's exact words:*

The soil must be gravelly and well drained, "a key factor in nearly every other superior vineyard anywhere in the world" (Robards, "Premium" 54).

2. *Place the documentary information (author; short title, if more than one work by the same author is being cited; page) within parentheses and at the* end *of the sentence or section of the sentence that contains the words* or *idea you are borrowing.* Use a comma between author and title but none between title/author and page. Parenthetical documentation should always *follow* the borrowed material, never precede it; no punctuation should separate the parenthetical matters from borrowed material. Commas, periods, and other punctuation marks should be placed *after* the parentheses—except when using blocked quotations. (See discussion below.) For a complete explanation of the format used in parenthetical documentation, see Chapter 14.

Even today when nobody uses their feet to crush grapes anymore (Waugh 37) and modern technology has introduced temperature-controlled stainless steel storage tanks and mechanical harvesters (Langway 59), wine growing in most places is still an art requiring "judgment, not only as to the time when the grapes should be harvested, but as to how long the wine should ferment, how long it should stay in the barrel, how it should be treated if it gets sick, and when it should be bottled" (Lichine and Massee 10).

If the entire sentence had come from a single page of a single source, one parenthetical reference at the end of the sentence would have been sufficient. As it is, the three ideas (nobody uses feet, technology has introduced modern equipment, wine growing is an art) come from three different sources; therefore, the sentence requires three different references.

3. *Introduce data with the author's name if you foresee the reader having trouble telling where the borrowed material begins.*

There are two reasons for the wine mystique: its history and the skill and knowledge (even love) that it takes to make it. Alec Waugh observes that archaeologists think wine making goes back 10,000 years. Historians confirm its ancient history by pointing to Middle Eastern writings that mention the vineyards of Sennacherib and Nebuchadnezzar existing some 2000 years before Christ (39).

Notice how the framing of the last two sentences with the name of the author at the beginning and a parenthetical reference at the end separates it from the first sentence. If you hadn't identified the author right in your text, you would have left your reader *either* wondering where you got the information about archaeologists and the opinion about the wine mystique *or* assuming incorrectly that the opinion in sentence 1 and the data in sentences 2 and 3 all come from Alex Waugh. But the truth of the matter is that the first sentence expresses your own opinion (that's why it isn't documented), and the next two sentences are the data from Waugh, which you use to substantiate it.

Moreover, when you introduce borrowed material with the author's name, remember to use other verbs besides "says" and "writes": explains, reports, declares, observes, describes, expresses, asserts, states, indicates, confirms, concludes, comments, details, points out.

EXERCISE 2

Which of the two passages is less confusing with regard to where the borrowed material begins and ends? Explain.

1. While foreign car manufacturers were selling vehicles of transportation, Detroit was selling fantasy. Instead of concentrating on getting the American driver safely and efficiently from house to market and beyond, it concentrated, argues Blumberg, on exploiting his aggressive drives by selling illusions of power that come with speed and violence. It designed speedometers that

showed impossible speeds of up to 150 miles per hour and endowed cars with names like Cutlass, Fury, Barracuda, and Cougar (12).

2. While foreign car manufacturers were selling vehicles of transportation, Detroit was selling fantasy. Instead of concentrating on getting the American driver safely and efficiently from house to market and beyond, it concentrated on exploiting his aggressive drives by selling illusions of power that come with speed and violence. It designed speedometers that showed impossible speeds of up to 150 miles per hour and endowed cars with names like Cutlass, Fury, Barracuda, and Cougar (Blumberg 12).

When to Quote

Use quotations, the exact words of the author, whenever they're particularly vivid or summarize a point particularly well or when you wish the idea to appear particularly authoritative. Most of your research paper (approximately 90 percent) is supposed to be in your own words. It should not be a patchwork of quotations.

How to Quote

Anytime you use words that are not your own, you must indicate that fact and cite your source.

Short Quotations

If the passage you're quoting is shorter than about four lines, put quotation marks around it and integrate it into the text of your paper.

California has so many microclimates that it has one suitable for every possible variety of grape (Hannum and Blumberg 36). Adams claims that it is "easier to raise Vinifera grapes in the fabulous climates of California than in any other part of the globe" (222). Therefore, "In the average quality of its wines, it ranks first" (1).

Put quotation marks around even one or two words, if they are significant to your discussion and you want to call attention to them.

The wine produced in the eastern United States has a strange flavor wine lovers, who are used to European wines, consider "foxy" and, according to one California winegrower, "can't stand" (Adams 8).

Normally, of course, you would not put quotation marks around isolated words that you run across in your reading. Nor is your use of quotation marks above required by the principles of honest scholarship. In this case, you're using quotation marks for effect: you're calling attention to the fact that "foxy" isn't your choice of adjective and that the winegrower mentioned was just that blunt and colloquial when he used the expression "can't stand."

Long Quotations

If the passage you're quoting is about four lines or longer, set it apart from the text of your paper by indenting ten spaces from the *left* margin and triple-spacing between quotation and text. The quotation itself should be double-spaced. Do *not* indent the first word of the quotation unless you are quoting more than one paragraph. Do *not* enclose the blocked quotation in quotation marks.

Although it is on a par with the best wines of France, California's zinfandel is difficult to compare with French wines because it is produced from an unidentified grape. Thompson and Johnson explain the problem of the "mystery grape":

> For decades its origins have been lost because records accompanying its importation were destroyed in transit and because the variety acquired new characteristics here. Now there is a spreading belief that it is an acclimated form of a southern Italian variety known there as primitivo. The official word has yet to come down from U.C.-Davis, where Dr. H. P. Olmo and his associates have been sleuthing after zinfandel's origins for fully three decades. (165)

Therefore, zinfandel is not usually included in wine tastings. . . .

Although long quotations are legitimate, use them sparingly. Too many of them will turn your paper into a collage of unassimilated notes. Notice the placement of the parenthetical information. In blocked quotations, documentation (here the page number) is always lined up with the right margin—*outside* the sentence and either at the end of the last line, if there is room, or double-spaced below the line, if there isn't.

Introduce the blocked quotation with a *complete* sentence of your own (which will often include the name of the author and/or work) followed by a colon. The blocked quotation should always consist of *complete* sentences.

As Thompson and Johnson see it, becoming a winegrowing center requires a unique combination of cultural factors:

> It is no coincidence that California is among the intellectual and cultural centers of the world today, and also the place that has revolutionized wine. Californians believe in present pleasure, and they welcome new ideas. The time, the energy, and the resources many Californians are prepared to spend on refining their pleasures can only be compared, historically, with the ways of a tiny class of aristocrats in old monarchical Europe. (9-10)

not

Thompson and Johnson call California one of

> the intellectual and cultural centers of the world today, and also the place . . .

EXERCISE 3

Which of the following three blocked quotations is presented correctly? What is wrong with the other two?

1. Grady describes the physiological effects of a prizefighter's knockout punch:

> "The brain then sloshes around inside the head like the yolk inside a raw egg. Nerve cells and blood vessels

> may be twisted, stretched, ruptured, cut by bony projections in the skull, or bruised from slamming up against it." (22)

2. Grady describes the physiological effects of a prizefighter's knockout punch:

> The brain then sloshes around inside the head like the yolk inside a raw egg. Nerve cells and blood vessels may be twisted, stretched, ruptured, cut by bony projections in the skull, or bruised from slamming up against it. (22)

3. After a prizefighter's knockout punch, according to Grady,

> the brain then sloshes around inside the head like the yolk inside a raw egg. Nerve cells and blood vessels may be twisted, stretched, ruptured, cut by bony projections in the skull, or bruised from slamming up against it (22).

Using Quotations

Always quote accurately. You must not take liberties with the syntax, punctuation, spelling, or capitalization of the original. However, there are times when (1) you don't need the entire quotation; (2) you have to change the grammatical structure of the original to make it fit into your sentence; (3) you have to add a word or two for clarity. Such changes are permitted as long as they don't distort the author's meaning. Whenever you do make any of the above changes, however, you are obligated to show the change you introduced.

How to Show Omissions from a Quotation

1. *If you omit one word or more from the middle of a quotation, use ellipsis (omission) points consisting of three spaced periods (. . .) to indicate the missing word(s).* Note the following example.

Original quotation If a generality must be drawn, one could state that these wines will be pleasantly fresh after a year and a half or two years, and should be fully matured within six years.

Alec Waugh, *In Praise of Wine and Certain Noble Spirits* (New York: William Sloan, 1959), p. 42

Ellipsis "If a generality must be drawn, one could state that these wines . . . should be fully matured within six years."

2. *If you quote a fragment of a sentence, do not use any ellipsis points either at the beginning or end of it.*

Morley insists that last year's vintage "will be pleasantly fresh after a year and a half or two years," despite opinions to the contrary.

Since it's obvious that some of the original sentence has been omitted, ellipsis points are superfluous.

3. *If you omit the last part of a sentence and the omission coincides with the end of your sentence, use four periods (three for the ellipsis and one for the end of the sentence) to indicate the omission.* Leave no space in front of the first period.

Last year's vintage wines should still be "pleasantly fresh after a year and a half or two years. . . ."

If you place anything in parentheses after the omission, use three spaced periods for the ellipsis and a sentence period after the parentheses, to keep the information from floating outside the sentence.

or two years . . ." (Morley 64).

4. *If you omit one sentence or more, or even a paragraph or more, use four periods to indicate the omission.* Double-space after the fourth period, as you would normally at the end of a sentence; be sure that complete sentences precede and follow the omission.

Original quotation In the days of Homer and Herodotus, wine skins were used not only to carry wine but to preserve it. The aperture was at the end of a leg that was tied up with strings. The skins were probably made watertight by a lining of pitch. The same form of preserving wine is much in use today. It is to this type of bottle that reference was made in the Biblical simile of new wine in old bottles. The wine was still effervescent and the old skin could not stretch to meet its liveliness.

Ellipses

```
"In the days of Homer and Herodotus, wine skins were
used . . . to carry wine. . . .  It is to this type of
bottle that reference was made in the Biblical simile
of new wine in old bottles.  The wine was still effer-
vescent and the old skin could not stretch. . . ."
```

not

```
to carry wine. . . ."  "It is to this type
```

5. *If the omissions become excessive, quote only part of the passage and paraphrase the rest.*

Combination quotation/ paraphrase

```
The wine skins carried by men of the ancient world
hardened with age and "could not stretch" to accommo-
date the carbonated bubbles given off by still ferment-
ing wine.  The Biblical reference to "new wine in old
bottles" is an allusion to this phenomenon.
```

See below for more explicit instructions on paraphrasing.

6. *If the omission is long (several pages), use a single line of spaced periods.*

```
"Madeira, I learned from them, is a lucky island, lucky in its loca-
tion, lucky in its history.
. . . . . . . . . . . . . . . . . . . . . . . . . . . . . . . . . . . .
     I venture to prophesy that as soon as the airstrip is completed
Madeira will become one of the most popular of tourist islands."
```

Make this sort of omission the exception rather than the rule in your writing. When two quotations are separated by pages, it is best to end the first quotation and introduce the second with your own words.

```
in its history."  Waugh goes on to observe: "I venture
```

EXERCISE 4

Which of the following statements uses the ellipsis correctly? Correct the ones that do not.

1. Because of a dispute over the agency's findings, the government instructed the Centers for Disease Control to conduct ". . . a more thorough investigation . . ." during the next three years.
2. Some of the current tax protesters have been described as "patriotic and dedicated American constitutional activists."
3. Madison writes that "Mammoth-sized photographs are currently the vogue in museums and galleries . . ."
4. The ancient Greek mathematician, physicist, and inventor, Archimedes, designed "cranes with huge claws that grappled enemy ships whenever they came within range. . . ."

How to Show Additions to a Quotation

If you add anything to the quotation, use brackets (*not* parentheses) to indicate the addition. (Parentheses are not used because they would confuse the reader who would have no way of knowing whether the parentheses were an addition of yours or belonged to the original quotation.) If your typewriter does not have brackets, draw them in with black ink. Use brackets in the following situations:

1. *To change the grammatical structure of the quotation in order to integrate it into your own sentence.*

In his study of towns and squares in antiquity, Zucker wrote that "The earliest planned towns appear[ed] in ancient Indian civilization. . . ."

Or in order to adjust the grammar to accommodate an omission.

"The debate over the situating of the fountain . . . [was] introduced at the first town meeting."

2. *To explain* (usually a reference to a pronoun).

"No one knew what to think of it [sculpture] when it was first erected."

3. *To indicate that you have underlined a word or more for emphasis.*

"It has never [emphasis added] been said that the studies of traffic patterns south of Route 36 were a waste of the taxpayers' money."

4. *To indicate to the reader that the quotation is accurate even though there seems to be an obvious mistake in spelling or sense.*

"Professional city planers [sic] first appeared during the Renaissance."

How to Punctuate Quotations

1. *Place periods and commas inside quotation marks* regardless *of whether you are adding them or they belong in the original quotation.*

Original quotation: The American landscape has never been at one with the white man.

"The American landscape," writes D. H. Lawrence, "has never been at one with the white man."

Original quotation: The essential American soul is hard, isolate, stoic, and a killer.

"The essential American soul is hard, isolate, stoic, and a killer," writes D. H. Lawrence.

2. *Place semicolons and colons* outside *quotation marks.*

Lawrence thought it was "easier to love America passionately, when you look at it through the wrong end of the telescope, across all the Atlantic water"; only in time would it become more lovable.

3. *Place question marks and exclamation points* inside *the quotation marks if the quotation is a question or exclamation; otherwise, outside.*

The student asked, "What makes Lawrence so negative about America?"

Lawrence has called the "American soul . . . hard, isolate, stoic, and a killer"!

4. *Place single quotation marks around a quotation* within *a quotation.*

Original quotation The American hero is usually accompanied by a "protective figure," more popularly known as his "sidekick."

```
"The American hero is usually accompanied by a 'pro-
tective figure,' more popularly known as his
'sidekick.' "
```

Notice the comma and period–both are inside the quotation marks even if there are double quotation marks at the end.

5. *Use a colon at the end of a complete sentence to introduce a long quotation.*

```
D. H. Lawrence writes of James Fenimore Cooper's Leatherstocking tales:

        But I have loved the Leatherstocking books so dearly . . .
```

6. *Do* not *use a comma in front of the word "that" when introducing a quotation.*

```
Lawrence writes that he "loved the Leatherstocking
```

not

```
Lawrence writes, that he "loved
```

Use a comma only when the word "that" is implied.

```
Lawrence writes, "I have loved
```

EXERCISE 5

Which of the following punctuates the quotation correctly? Correct the ones that do not.

1. She described it as having "a staggering effect".
2. "The discoveries", writes Johnson, "are about ten years old".
3. The judge concluded, "The evidence is inadmissible;" he threw the case out of court.
4. The residents insist, that "Love Canal is not a dead issue."
5. "Summertime movies," writes Hartley, "are geared toward the Clearasil set."

How to Paraphrase

When you take quoted material from your notes and put it into your own words, you are said to be paraphrasing. The technique is essential to the writing of any research paper; unfortunately, it creates problems for many students whose paraphrasing is so close to the language of the original as to be plagiarism. The secret of good paraphrasing is *not* to look at the original while doing it. Look at it only long enough to get a grip on its meaning and put it away. Then paraphrase from memory. Examine the following examples.

Original quotation

In the space of a year, Napoleon cleared the Austrians out of Italy and made them sue for peace. In this famous campaign he showed his remarkable ability to strike quickly and surprise the enemy before they could consolidate their defenses. He also demonstrated his flair for what would now be called propaganda and public relations.

Crane Brinton, John B. Christopher, and Robert Lee Wolff, *Modern Civilization: A History of the Last Five Centuries* (Englewood Cliffs, NJ: Prentice-Hall, 1957), p. 343

Plagiarized passage

Within a year, Napoleon had ousted the Austrians from Italy. In one of his best known campaigns he demonstrated a talent for striking quickly and surprising his enemy before they got their defenses together. Napoleon was also good in propaganda and public relations (Brinton, Christopher, and Wolff 343).

This passage is considered plagiarized even though you have a parenthetical reference showing the source of the idea. The plagiarism is in the fact that you have passed off the language as your own when, in fact, it isn't. You have kept it substantially unchanged: You have retained the order and the rhythm of the original and merely replaced some of the words with synonymous expressions. Nor would putting quotation marks around "propaganda and public relations" make any difference. It is still plagiarism.

One of the secrets to writing an acceptable paraphrase is never to try to paraphrase a single sentence; there is simply too little in one sentence to "rearrange" or summarize, which in a sense is what paraphrasing does. Instead, whenever you want to use the data in a particular passage, take a whole block of sentences and paraphrase these.

Another point to remember is not to begin your paraphrase at the same place as the original. Instead, do this: First, try summarizing what the original has said and then elaborate on it to whatever extent your discussion of ideas requires. A paraphrase is under no obligation to be as long as the original.

Finally, when you're revising the first draft of your paper, that is, polishing it up, polish up the paraphrase as well. By then you will have forgotten the words of the original, and the general flow of the language around your paraphrase should influence a completely original choice of words and produce a satisfactory version.

Satisfactory paraphrase

Napoleon proved his abilities as a commander of men and skilled tactician in the Italian campaign. His use of surprise tactics on the Austrians and rhetoric on his own men to keep morale high paid off with victory over Austria (Brinton, Christopher, and Wolff 343).

EXERCISE 6

Read the original quotation. Then decide which of the two passages is plagiarized and which is paraphrased properly.

Original Quotation

The first thing that can be said about the notion of trying to set aside wilderness preserves for solitude is that it doesn't work very well. Environmentalists have discovered this over and over again, much to their chagrin. Every time a new "untouched paradise" is discovered, the first thing everyone wants to do is go and see it.

William Tucker, *Progress and Privilege: America in the Age of Environmentalism* (Garden City, NY: Anchor/Doubleday, 1982), p. 134

1. Wilderness areas tend to remain wild and unspoiled only as long as nobody knows about them. Therefore, designating them as "wilderness preserves" proves counterproductive. The label works like a welcome sign inviting hordes of visitors and turns a wilderness into a park.

2. The point to be made about the idea of setting aside wilderness areas for the enjoyment of solitude is that it's been a failure. Those involved in the environmental movement have repeatedly found that whenever an unspoiled wilderness is discovered, people start coming from everywhere to look at it.

EXERCISE 7

Paraphrase the following passage correctly:

> It is generally agreed that the American frontier closed down in 1890, the year the last Indian Territory of Oklahoma was thrown open for settlement. After that, the Conservation Movement rose quickly to protect the remaining resources and wilderness from heedless stripping and development. Along with this went a significant psychological change in the national character, with an end to the frontier spirit, and a greater national attention to social issues.
>
> William Tucker, *Progress and Privilege: America in the Age of Environmentalism* (Garden City, NY: Anchor/Doubleday, 1982), p. 138

8 Prewriting

Examples

Overview of Chapters 8 Through 12

In each of Chapters 8 through 12, you will be asked to take some aspect of your research paper topic and develop it using one of the rhetorical modes—for reasons that have already been outlined in Chapter 1. The following remarks are addressed to the three questions that will inevitably come up as you work on the assignments in the next five chapters.

1. Don't worry if the assignments overlap or coincide; overlapping is natural since the rhetorical modes are based on mental strategies, which cannot be compartmentalized. If you find yourself "encroaching" on a subsequent assignment, keep writing. For example, in the course of classifying, say, incestuous relationships into least and most detested, you may also find yourself analyzing the reasons for one being more detested than another, thus engaging in causal analysis, a mode you will not yet have formally studied. But go ahead and do the best you can with it anyway. When you finally do study cause and effect, go back and rewrite the assignment and resubmit it.

2. Don't worry if, in the course of writing the research paper, you have to change a section you've prewritten in order to accommodate it in the final paper. Minor changes are inevitable, particularly at the beginning and end of each prewrite, to ensure a "proper fit" in the overall flow of ideas. But even major changes are encouraged; they're part of the adding, deleting, and rethinking that every compositional process undergoes.

3. Don't worry if the prewrite doesn't "fit" even after you've made changes. It's possible for you to have done well on the assignment but for the assignment to be irrelevant to your thesis when you finally get around to developing it in the actual paper. You'll be advised in Chapter 14 on what to do with the segment that you can't integrate into the research essay.

Introducing Examples

An **example** is an illustration, an individual instance of something. Everybody resorts to examples to illustrate what they mean. It's the one intellectual strategy that hardly needs an introduction. In fact, the extent to which people use it testifies to its enormous effectiveness in pinning down meanings that might otherwise be *mis*understood or *not* understood at all. "Gold has been a precious metal since ancient times," announces an ad for the Gold Information Center. It then illustrates with an example: "in the sixth century B.C., when in Italy the Etruscans practiced the art of wiring loose teeth together with strips of gold." Thanks to the example, the reader does not make the mistake of assuming that the ad is speaking of gold *jewelry.*

Furthermore, because an example is so concrete and down to earth, it has enormous reader appeal. It pulls an idea out of the realm of the abstract into the experiences of the day to day and makes it accessible to every reader (or listener). Suppose a professor were lecturing to a class of students on a late Friday afternoon. "Depravity is not a concept limited to the concerns of the Puritans," he intones. His students, however, are not keeping up. So, just before he loses them completely, he shifts gears, "Let me give you a contemporary example. Last week in the personal ads I saw a notice for. . . ." Instantly he's regained his students' attention.

The example is the one rhetorical device that teachers universally demand from their students: "Give examples!" "Be specific!" "Illustrate!" Whatever the phrasing, the instructions all mean the same: Don't just tell your readers what you mean, show them. Convince them of your familiarity with your subject. No instructor wants a list of generalizations such as those given by this student:

France is a country with problems. Limited development of industry has produced economic troubles. Unemployment has created problems for young people who are qualified and educated yet can't find jobs. Centralization of the government has caused political unrest, and the education system is run poorly.

As you can see, the student has made some obvious statements, most of which actually apply to any number of countries—including the United States. How is the teacher to know whether the student really understands the subject? Or is he or she just guessing—or worse, mindlessly rehashing notes? Generalizations need supporting evidence, and one of the most effective is the example. The paragraph above needs examples as evidence of "limited development of industry," "economic troubles," "problems for young people," "can't find jobs," "political unrest," and so on.

Or take the case of the student whose essay on the commercial aspects of Christmas makes the following observations:

For most people the Christmas season arrives with the Christmas mail-order catalogs. Then the local stores begin to advertise their pre-Christmas specials. Radio is also guilty of commercializing Christmas.

Three general assertions; none is supported by examples. Compare them with the partially revised version below in which the student has added examples of mail-order Christmas presents in support of sentence one.

For most people the Christmas season arrives with the Christmas mail-order catalogs. American Express and Diners' Club offer such grandiose gifts as Sony stereo components, "autumn haze" mink jackets, and diamonds that few can afford even with interest-free monthly payments. Neiman Marcus parades an exotic item each year that has ranged from twin giraffes to "his and her" yachts and relaxation tanks with underwater speakers, like the kind used by the Dallas Cowboys, "for the ultimate in floating experience."

The difference between the first and the second version is unmistakable. It's the difference between black and white and color, between a flat and glossy surface. The examples bring the idea in sentence one to life, but they do even more than that. They convince the reader of the writer's familiarity with Christmas catalogs, thus bestowing credibility on the writer. Someone who has never experienced the holidays American style could have written the first version on pure hearsay. But only someone who has thumbed through the catalogs and drooled over the merchandise could have actually provided the examples—hence the drabness of version one and the appeal of authenticity of version two.

EXERCISE 1

All the following statements are vague generalizations without examples. Suggest the kinds of examples that could be used to pin down their meanings, provide evidence for generalizations, and convince the reader of the writer's familiarity with the subject.

1. Alecky Ike is the meanest man in town.
2. Throwing a party is a lot of work.
3. Our beagle, Scooter, thinks he's a member of the family.
4. There are advantages to growing up in a rural area/small town/city.
5. Owning a car/motorcycle is expensive.
6. Being the youngest/middle/oldest child in the family has its disadvantages.

Single and Multiple Examples

In addition to knowing what an example is and why it should be used, there is still the matter of learning how to make the most effective use of it. When a writer decides to illustrate an idea, he or she can choose between several alternatives: a single short example, a single extended example, multiple short examples, multiple longer examples, or the example handled like a story. Which alternative is chosen will usually depend on the writer's intention. If he or she merely wants to give the reader a quick illustration of a point purely for the sake of clarity, the writer uses one short example or if several are used, they should be kept brief. (See 1a, 1b, 3 below.) The writer doesn't want to interrupt the flow of thoughts by distracting the reader with many or elaborate examples. If, on the other hand, the illustration is part of the evidence for the topic idea (as in 4), then he or she will use multiple examples—the more the better.

Sometimes, of course, the writer's intentions are not as straightforward as suggested above, and some of the examples you will encounter in your reading will not fall neatly into the categories given here. When using examples becomes second nature to you, as it should eventually, there will be no need to think in terms of categories—short examples, extended examples, single examples, multiple examples. . . . You'll know instinctively what kind and how many examples to use. But for the time being, make yourself familiar with the types of examples listed below.

1. *The single short example:*

a. Even economists like Michael Carliner of Regional Data Associates are astonished by the new housing boom.

b. Life on the tiny island of Madeira hasn't changed much in the last hundred years. For example, windmills still stone-grind grain into flour.

2. *The single extended example:*

> Indeed, most animals know instinctively how to keep body temperature in the safe range. Emperor penguins, for instance, go into a huddle. After the female lays her egg on an ice floe in the dead of an antarctic winter, she trudges off to find food and leaves her mate to warm the egg—in temperatures that would freeze an unincubated egg solid in about a minute. Left alone, the male's body temperature would fall too low to warm the egg sufficiently. But he joins great circles of huddling

penguins, a formation so effective that it keeps his temperature around 97 degrees, warm enough to incubate his brood.

Sharon Begley and others,
"How Animals Weather Winter," *Newsweek*, Feb. 28, 1983

3. *Multiple short examples:*

By the Fourth of July the shores of the beach are covered with debris such as churned-up eel grass, film cartridges, plastic coffee cups, cigarette packages, and Miller's Lite beer cans.

4. *Multiple longer examples:*

Nantucket has one of the most varied habitats in the world supporting the most diverse kind of vegetation. Thanks to the Gulf Stream, the climate is both warm and dry enough for the cactus and cold enough for the creeping snowberry. The prettiest of the wildflowers, the pink mallow, covers the marshes, and purple and white heather (a rarity elsewhere) blanket the moors. Altar Rock, its highest elevation, is dotted with sassafras, viburnum, and wild indigo. The huckleberry bushes grow to giant heights, and in October they blaze like Oriental rugs. The island is also famous for its wild rose that blooms beside the sweet fern everywhere.

5. *The example handled like a story:*

How, for instance, could the father with the two different sons, one very close to him and the other extremely distant, deal with his problem? Let me give two examples of such a case. The first shows an unproductive way of dealing with such a problem. The second is an example of a creative solution.

In the first case, the executive was sensitive and shy. His son was 12 years old and doing very well at school. He appeared to be happy but he was also shy and seemed to have problems making friends. The executive wanted to have a closer relationship and also wanted to help his son overcome his shyness. One day he proposed that they go camping together. His son agreed, but one week before the camping trip he sprained his ankle while playing tennis. The trip was cancelled. The father waited until the following summer and again proposed a camping trip. Three weeks before the second trip his son broke his leg playing basketball.

What went wrong? It is clear that the camping trip was a bad idea. It meant moving abruptly from great distance to excessive closeness, and the child subconsciously managed to avoid it.

Another father with a similar problem dealt with it more creatively. He noticed that his 13-year-old child was studying botany at school and had a couple of new plants in his room. The father was very proud of the garden he himself tended in the backyard. One day he told his son in passing, "You know, I'm not using all the space in the back. If you want to plant anything, feel free." The son planted melons, and soon he was coming to his father for advice.

In the second case, both the "solution" and the process were right. The father first paid attention to his son's growing interest in plants. Second, he approached his son gently suggesting "in passing," that he plant something; instead of invading his son's territory, the father invited him into his own. Finally, it was their common interest and gradually increasing physical proximity that brought father and child together. It was an elegant solution to a complex problem.

Fernando Bartolomé, "The Work Alibi: When It's Harder to Go Home," *Harvard Business Review,* March–April 1983

Notice in 4 above that examples don't always have to be introduced with the signal words, "for example," "for instance," "like," or "such as." That is particularly true of multiple examples given in a series.

EXERCISE 2

Look at the following examples. Identify the idea that is being illustrated in each and the type of example that is used to illustrate it—single short, single extended, multiple short, or multiple longer.

1. The new welterweight champion has qualities such as constant movement, ring savvy, and generalship (the ability to control the pace of a fight) that are unmatched by any other boxer.
2. Today's kids are much more stylish than they were years ago. Year-old toddlers take their first steps in imported French boots and wear diapers stuffed into Calvin Klein jeans.
3. Laser light can halt bleeding in difficult to reach places like the back of the eye and the innermost recesses of the stomach.
4. All seems well on the island of Nantucket. Hy-Line and Steamship Authority tours unload a steady supply of tourists all summer long. The shops are full; obliging islanders sell scrimshaw to day-trippers and $300 oak-rib lightship

baskets to status-seeking summer people. The boat basin is crowded with yachts. Madaket beach is filled with surfers. Restaurants serve lobster mousse to gourmet diners and fried clams to families. The rose-covered cottages are as quaint as ever, and the elegant tea and cocktail parties go on in Siasconset.

Example Called "Grabber"

There is a particular category of examples called the **grabber** or **lead** that is sometimes used at the beginning of an essay or article to "grab" at the reader's attention and "lead" him into the rest of the writing. Because of its enormous reader appeal, the example as a rhetorical device is particularly suited to arouse the reader's interest in the subject matter. It's a favorite technique of journalistic writing, which is obliged to appeal to a general audience and even to entertain it while providing news. A grabber works like a slide or videotape to arouse interest in the ensuing discussion.

In other words, the grabber is a unique type of example, distinguished from other examples by its prominent location at the beginning of a piece of writing. There is no ideal way of starting an essay. A safe way is to begin with the thesis. You state your purpose and then proceed to fulfill it. The approach is blunt and simple. In some kinds of writing (an exam, for instance), it's an advantage. You impress your teacher instantly with the fact that you're capable of focusing your information on a particular idea rather than just randomly reciting everything you can remember on the subject. But at other times (journalistic prose, the personal essay, the critique, the research paper), you want to present your subject from the most attractive angle possible. Using the grabber is one good way of doing that.

There is as much variety among grabbers as there is among examples. However, most grabbers do fall into one of three categories. And even those that don't—exactly—are more like one type than another.

1. *A single paragraph with a series of sentence-length examples:*

Grabber

Aristotle, an ancient naturalist, announced that every spring the European robin transformed itself into the European redstart. In 1703, an unidentified parson claimed unequivocally that birds flew to the moon every fall on a journey that took 60 days. Linnaeus in 1735 wrote that the house martin spent the winter under roofs of houses and emerged in the spring. Another sixteenth-century naturalist was convinced that swallows hibernated in the mud in the bottoms of lakes.

Topic sentence

Unlike the ancients, we know today that birds migrate. An inherent force causes millions of them to fly twice a year--in the spring and fall--to predetermined locations throughout the world. The routes they take are the same routes their ancestors took thousands of years ago. Even if there is a shorter more convenient pathway, they will take the time-honored one. Migration also includes the movement of some birds from a high elevation in spring to a low elevation in fall. Some birds that seem to stay in one place permanently actually do migrate, although it may be only a mile or two.

Follow-up

2. *Three paragraphs with an example per paragraph:*

Grabber

Coughing and gasping, an L.A. area couple awake before dawn to slam down their bedroom windows and shut out a plume of black smoke that has drifted downward from a nearby hospital chimney.

In an underground parking lot, some 1200 after-concert patrons start their cars almost simultaneously. Fumes fill the air, and dozens of drivers collapse at their wheels. A not-so-quick-thinking parking attendant stops to collect parking charges instead of waving the suffering patrons through.

In New York City a cab driver complains of frequent headaches from the exhaust fumes of the heavy daytime traffic. In order to avert the problem he switches to the night shift, which has a more moderate air pollution content.

Topic sentence

Every day of the year most Americans have to live with some sort of air pollution. The millions of tons

Follow-up

of pollutants come from a variety of sources: automobiles, smoke stacks, fireplaces, wood stoves, even forest fires and volcanoes.

3. *One paragraph or more with a single example:*

Grabber

"Johnny is retarded"--a frightening statement for a mother to hear from a teacher. But not Johnny's mother. She couldn't understand what the fuss was all about. Johnny wasn't any different from any of her other seven children. So what was the problem? Maybe he couldn't read very much, but she couldn't either; at least, he wasn't giving her any trouble as were his older brothers. And Johnny couldn't understand what the fuss was about either.

Johnny had been a healthy baby and seemed alert and bright enough as an infant. He stayed in his crib all day, however, shoved back into the corner away from the window. His mother fed him when he cried, propping his bottle with a folded towel, too tired to want to sit and hold him, and anyway, the other kids were always bothering her. So Johnny stayed there alone. As he grew and his eyes began to focus, he looked around, but there was nothing to see except a drab wall; no people or toys or bright pictures to watch. There was nothing to reach for either, so when the time came to roll over or sit up, as babies do at a certain stage, he didn't try very much and didn't creep until he was over a year old and his mother needed the crib for the next baby. Then he sat on the floor with nothing to play with, no songs or bedtime stories from his unhappy mother, and not quite as healthy any more because he ate mostly sugar-frosted cereal, canned spaghetti, and bread. He didn't give his mother any trouble, so he didn't get any attention from her. Insidiously and inevitably, Johnny gradually became retarded.

Topic sentence

Follow-up

Mental retardation is generally considered by the nonprofessional to be congenital and irreversible--a condition that an infant is born with and cannot improve upon. Before the turn of the century, this was apt to be the case, but with the advent of modern society, a new class of mental retardation that wasn't congenital or irreversible was actually created by lack of attention, lack of stimuli, and poor diet--mild mental retardation.

Topic sentence restated

There are three important observations to be made regarding the grabbers above:

1. Each is followed by a topic sentence that expresses the unifying idea of the grabber. As a rule, the grabber itself does not state the topic idea explicitly, so a follow-up paragraph is provided to introduce the point of the grabber—and the subject of the essay. Thus the follow-up links the grabber with the remainder of the essay. Without it the grabber would remain suspended in a vacuum.

Occasionally, however, a grabber will include a topic sentence, particularly if the grabber is a narrative. Notice example 3 above. Without the topic sentence at the end of the story, the latter would sound unfinished. Despite this minor variation, the function of the follow-up remains the same: to introduce the subject matter of the essay and state (in this case, *re*state) the topic idea of the lead example.

2. Examples that are listed in a series (as in 1 and 2 above) should observe some degree of parallelism in their grammatical structure. Notice how each sentence in paragraph 1 of example 1 begins: Each has as its subject a naturalist who had some gross misconceptions about what happened to birds in the fall and spring: "Aristotle," "an unidentified parson," "Linnaeus," "another sixteenth-century naturalist." In number 2, each of the three examples has as the subject of the first sentence the person or persons suffering from air pollution: "an L.A. couple," "some 1200 after-concert patrons," "a cab driver."

3. Finally, remember that there is no set limit (except as dictated by common sense) to the number of examples you use in the first grabber—the single paragraph with a series of short examples. It's usually no fewer than three (since one or two could hardly be called a "series"). In the bird migration example four are given, but the number could have been higher as long as each example was an example of a *different* kind of error. If Aristotle, the parson, and Linnaeus, for instance, had all believed that birds flew to the moon, giving more than those three examples would have been repetitive.

In the second grabber—three paragraphs with an example per paragraph—convention suggests that three paragraphs is a good number. But even here the number isn't absolute. You will sometimes encounter writers using more than three.

EXERCISE 3

Look at the following examples. In each locate the grabber, the follow-up paragraph, and the topic idea. Then identify the type of grabber each represents: one paragraph/series of examples; three paragraphs/three examples; or one paragraph or more/one example.

1. Every eye is glued to the algebra equations on the blackboard. Eager hands wave in the air. The teacher calls on Jon, and the rest of the students turn their faces toward him in rapt attention.

   Kim is having problems in chemistry. Nancy offers to tutor her lab partner so that her team can be the first to master molecular structure.

   An English Club was the students' idea, so was their latest project—holding bake sales every week for the last ten weeks to raise the money for tickets and a charter bus to New York to attend a performance of *Hamlet* at the New York State Theater.

   Enthusiasm, goals, and first-hand experience are all part of the total learning environment at King's Wood High School. While other schools in the area complain of absenteeism, lack of student motivation, and even vandalism, King's Wood High School has never had a better caliber of student—competitive, enterprising, and capable of sustaining interest in independent projects.

2. On a winter evening in New York City in 1868, a heavy snowfall had left the streets almost impassable. A horse-drawn streetcar filled with people was stuck in a snowdrift; the driver was whipping its two floundering horses, straining frantically to free the unmoving car. Suddenly a tall, well-dressed man bounded into the street. "Stop beating those horses, you fool!" he bellowed.

   Within minutes the stranger, bristling with authority, had made the passengers get out, led the exhausted horses out of the snowdrift, and convinced the intimidated driver that if he flogged the animals again, or allowed the streetcar to become overloaded, he would be arrested. So a number of grumbling people had to walk home that night, two workhorses were spared further beating, and a streetcar driver had met up with Henry Bergh.

   One characteristic of the mid-Victorian period was a mood of moral indignation. *Les Misérables* and *Uncle Tom's Cabin* both left a mark, debtors' prisons were abolished in England, and the Emancipation Proclamation announced to the world that the United States, officially at least, considered human slavery unacceptable. Americans were ready for Henry Bergh.

Patricia Curtis, "Animal Shelters Struggle to Keep Up with Millions of Abandoned Pets," *Smithsonian,* June 1982

3. Spray flying from his heels, a stallion stampedes his retinue of mares, yearlings, and foals through the marsh grass. Behind them, two young stallions rear up suddenly in mock battle, their forehooves flashing. In the morning mist, the tableau of wild horses is stunning.

This scene is played out in isolated places around the world—lonely East Coast barrier islands, the mesas and gulches of the West, Mongolian steppes, the barren extremes of Australia, Mexico, and even Europe. In the past 15 years, a few zoologists have been tempted into these no-man's-lands. They go there to understand the biology and behavior of the horse, an animal that has contributed much to the growth of human civilization in 5000 years of domestication.

David Monagan, "Horse of a Different Culture," *Science 82,* May 1982

4. On August 12, 1978, after failing a lie detector test, Floyd Fay was convicted of murdering Fred Ery, a clerk at Andy's Carry-out in Perrysburg, Ohio. In July 1980, an informer produced evidence implicating other men. One confessed, and Fay was freed.

On August 28, 1964, 15-year-old Edmund Emil Kemper admitted that he murdered his grandparents. He was convicted and sent to an institution for the criminally insane. Five years later he was paroled. In the fall of 1972, psychiatrists declared Kemper "no danger to society." The next spring Kemper murdered his mother and a friend of hers, then gave himself up. He confessed to the murders as well as to those of six young women.

On March 20, 1979, Father Bernard Pagano was indicted after a parade of seven eyewitnesses positively identified him as the armed robber who had held up several small shops and convenience stores near Wilmington, Delaware. On August 23, 1979, in the midst of the trial, Pagano was freed with the apologies of the state after a man named Ronald Clouser confessed to the robberies.

Three cases: three mistakes. Each represents a much larger problem. Each illustrates an area in which new scientific developments challenge common practices in the American legal system. Lie detector tests, increasingly used in courtrooms, are turning out to be less reliable than many of us, including judges and juries, believe. Psychiatric testimony, widely relied upon to protect the public from habitual criminals, is also vastly overrated. And according to memory experts, even eyewitness testimony, the bulwark of Western jurisprudence, can be twisted to obscure rather than reveal what a witness really saw.

"Science Takes the Stand," *Science 82,* June 1982

Writing the Example

Make your examples as vivid and concrete as possible. Don't be afraid of resorting to personal experiences and imagination for examples, if you can't come up with any or enough examples from your reading–especially in the case of the grabber. Say that you're writing a paper on the decline of the American railroads. Based on some western movies you have seen and hints you have picked up in your reading, you could write an effective grabber using *one* example in *one* paragraph to describe the posh interior of the typical train (sleeping compartments, dining car, etc.), as it existed before the advent of the automobile and airplane. At the end, you'd follow it up with a topic sentence that went something like "The days of the luxurious train ride are gone. Today. . . ."

Length

Examples can be of varying lengths–phrase, sentence, paragraph, several paragraphs. Even a whole story can function as a single illustration of a single example, like George Orwell's well-known essay, "The Shooting of an Elephant." However, you should think in terms of, at least, a paragraph for your example(s).

Discovering Use for the Example

Every conceivable thesis can make use of both a grabber and internally placed examples–regardless of the phrasing of the thesis. However, a thesis *can* make greater or lesser demands on illustration. Therefore, observe the following guidelines.

1. *Check your thesis statement for the expression of an abstract concept to which the question* What kind? *can be applied.* For example, take the following two thesis statements: (a) " Manú National Park in Peru supports one of the greatest abundances of tropical forest wildlife found anywhere in the world"; (b) "Unlike the early Japanese geisha who were in the vanguard of the latest styles, contemporary geisha are curators of Japanese tradition." As you read thesis (a), you ask, *what kind* of "tropical forest wildlife"? As you read thesis (b), you ask, *what kind* of "latest styles"? and *what kind* of "Japanese tradition"? In each case, the thesis needs illustrating.

2. *Check your topic for the possibility of using examples elsewhere than in the illustration of the thesis.* For example, the following thesis statement doesn't require any specific examples: "A gasoline-driven car can be converted to an electric car for roughly $1500." The reader is not inclined to ask what kind of "gasoline-driven car"? what kind of "electric car"? what kind of "$1500"? what kind of "conversion"? The reader, of course, needs an explanation but *not* exactly an illustration. Nevertheless, all sorts of extended illustrations are desirable: example(s) of individuals, businesses, government agencies that may have already made the conversions from gas to electric; examples of the savings in cost that a conversion brings about; examples of the expenses involved in the maintenance of a gas-driven car.

Introducing the Example

Remember to introduce all examples *except* the grabber with a statement that explains what you are illustrating.

Organizing the Grabber

If you are using a grabber, the first thing in your research paper will not be the thesis statement. Nevertheless, the thesis ought to appear early in the essay. Therefore, give some thought to its location. A conventional spot for it is in the follow-up paragraph *after* the topic sentence of the grabber.

Paragraph 1	Grabber
Paragraph 2	Topic sentence of grabber Thesis of essay General discussion of topic

Here's an example from an essay entitled "Reagan's War on Drugs" by Mark Starr and others:

Grabber

U.S. Customs Service officers in Miami spotted the "mule" the moment he stepped off Avianca Flight 6 from Bogotá: Gabriel Antonio Pino, 27, was simply too nervous to be an ordinary tourist. An intense search of Pino's suitcase and clothing uncovered no drugs, but X-rays revealed more than lunch in the Colombian's stomach. Under guard over the next 12 hours, Pino defecated 85 condoms stuffed with cocaine, then underwent major surgery to extract another 35 condoms from his stomach. In all, Pino had ingested 944 grams, more than two pounds, of high-grade cocaine worth almost $60,000 on the U.S. wholesale market.

Topic sentence of grabber / Thesis of essay / General discussion of topic

Pino was only a pawn in the federal war against international drug traders. Since early this year, when the Reagan administration created a Federal South Florida Task Force under the auspices of Vice President George Bush, the war has grown fiercer than ever before—and the very use of body carriers like Pino suggests that the Feds may be winning. More efficient smuggling techniques, such as the small planes that used to carry contraband with virtual impunity, are getting tougher and tougher to use. "I think the body carriers reflect the desperation of these people to get their product in," says Al Pringle, a task-force member from the Drug Enforcement Administration (DEA).

Newsweek, Aug. 9, 1982

Sometimes it is possible for the topic idea of the grabber and the thesis statement of the essay to be one and the same. For instance, suppose that like *Newsweek* (November 15, 1982), you conceived an essay with the thesis: "English has become the universal language of the world." What could you use as a grabber? How about three separate examples in three separate paragraphs of English being used all over the world: by diplomats in Geneva, Switzerland; by rock musicians in Poland; by Japanese businessmen building oil refineries in Kuwait. And for a topic sentence to unify all three examples you can use your thesis. Thus you would have a thesis serving two functions simultaneously—topic sentence for the grabber and thesis statement for the essay.

Paragraph 1 Grabber	Example 1:	Diplomats speaking English in Switzerland
	Example 2:	Rock musicians singing in English in Poland
	Example 3:	Japanese businessmen speaking English in Kuwait
Paragraph 2 Topic sentence of grabber and thesis of essay	Sentence 1:	English has become the universal language of the world.

Finding Location for the Example

1. If you are using a grabber, you have no choice as to location. It is always the first segment of your essay.

2. If you are not using a grabber, the location of your example will be determined by the location of the idea you have chosen to illustrate. That means an example can go anywhere.

WRITING ASSIGNMENT

Using the Example in the Research Paper

Write a solid paragraph or more using the example as a rhetorical strategy to develop some idea that is relevant to your research paper thesis or overall topic. Although you're encouraged to use as many examples as necessary and as often as possible in your final paper, avoid, for the purposes of this assignment, the single and multiple short examples. Concentrate on one of the following only: single extended example, multiple longer examples, or grabber (any of the three types).

Remember to provide documentary references (author, page) in parentheses for any words or ideas you might borrow in writing this and the next four assignments. If more than one work by a given author is cited in your working bibliography, add a title to the reference in order to distinguish between sources with an identical author. (See Chapter 7 for instruction on documenting your sources.)

Prose Models

DO AS I SAY, NOT AS I DO

Progressive educators are keenly aware that preaching ethics in the 1
classroom is not likely to meet with much success. They also know that assigning "morals" readings in textbooks, the way children are taught, say, geography, is not likely to be anywhere near as productive for character building as such techniques are for developing factual understanding. In the search for an appropriate way to get moral value across, a variety of approaches are being tried.

In 1970, Jane Elliott, a teacher at Community Elementary school 2
in Riceville, Iowa, wanted to teach her third-grade students the injustice of discrimination, but sensing that just talking about the arbitrariness and unfairness of race prejudice would be too academic to have much impact, her inspiration was to appeal directly to the children's capacity for emotional experience and empathetic insight by declaring a day of discrimination against the blue-eyed. She began by "explaining" the innate superiority of the "cleaner, more civilized, smarter" brown-eyed. When the children were, at first, disbelieving, she snapped sarcastically at a blue-eyed child, "Is that the way we've been taught to sit in class?" and then moved all the blue-eyed to the back of the room. To snickers from the brown-eyed, she then informed the blue-eyed that they would not be permitted to play in the big playground at recess and could only play at all if invited by a brown-eyed child. Throughout the day she was conspicuously more tolerant of mistakes made by brown-eyed children. The brown-eyed quickly started to enjoy lording it over the blue-eyed, who soon showed signs of growing insecurity and loss of confidence.

After reversing the roles for a day, Mrs. Elliott had every child write 3
about how it felt to be discriminated against. Though to many adults her procedure may sound heavy-handed, as far as her students were

concerned the experience "took." That it made a profound impression is apparent from such comments as "I felt dirty, left out, thought of quitting school." The children were not shy about saying how "rotten" it felt to be labeled inferior and how relieved they were to be equal again.

Amitai Etzioni, "Do As I Say, Not As I Do,"
The New York Times Magazine, Sept. 26, 1976

DISCUSSION QUESTIONS

1. Is the example in this passage a grabber? Explain.
2. What topic idea is the example illustrating?
3. What is the purpose of paragraph 3? Could it have been omitted?

TRIGGER CONTROL

Donna Brugnoli (Student)

The 1861 Shiloh, a .177-ca. CO_2-powered single-action revolver, popular with youngsters, topples tin cans and easily dispatches field mice, fox squirrels, and Texas scrub jays. The Perazzi can pick out a grouse that is flying incredibly fast over the brow of a hill and with a single pull of the trigger can slam it against a rock wall. The Weatherby Mark V Magnum is designed to drop a magnificently antlered buck, its matted coat steaming in the morning air, with one shot at 100 yards. And "Saturday night specials" maim and kill human victims daily in the living rooms, parks, stores, highways, and streets of America. 1

A gun is a weapon whose sole purpose is to destroy. Whether he is shooting at animals, tin cans in a junkyard, clay pigeons, or people, the marksman's goal is to hit and destroy or maim that object. In the United States today there are an estimated 90 million guns in private hands; about half of America's families admit to owning at least one firearm (Diener and Kerber 227, 228). 2

DISCUSSION QUESTIONS

The thesis of Brugnoli's research paper: The mere presence of a gun can have an aggressive effect on behavior because of a phenomenon called "the weapons effect."

1. Where is the grabber and what type has Brugnoli used?

2. What is the topic idea of the grabber? Where is it expressed?
3. How effective is Brugnoli's use of the names of the guns she mentions? If you were writing this lead example and knew nothing about guns, where could you go to pick up enough terminology and some idea of what kinds of guns kill what kind of game in order to write a grabber like this?
4. Has the writer observed parallel structure in her series of examples? That is, has she begun each sentence with the same kind of subject?
5. Turn to page 249 where this grabber has been incorporated into the research essay. Notice the location of the thesis idea: paragraph 3. What is the progression of ideas from paragraph 1 to 3? In other words, what is the topic idea of each paragraph?
6. Turn to pages 254–256 for other uses of the example.

CALIFORNIA WINES ARE ALIVE AND WELL

Ned Hawkins (Student)

Terry Robards, wine critic for the <u>New York Times</u>, chooses the 1
five wines he serves at a Thanksgiving dinner with the care of an
artist blending his colors (Robards, "Giving Thanks" 148).

In preparation for a wine-tasting ceremony in New York, the 2
Barons Elie and Eric de Rothschild ship their wines from France
three months ahead of the event to "give them time to rest" and
then "stood [them] on end" for three weeks prior to the tasting to
give the sediment a chance to settle (Prial, "Rare Tasting" 22).

Gerald Asher writes in what sounds like poetry of a 1951 3
Cabernet Sauvignon from the Louis W. Martini Vineyard of California:
"But as we talked, sniffing, sipping, and wondering aloud, the wine
changed, its strangeness clearing like morning fog to reveal a youthful berrylike bouquet that contradicts its 28 years" (Asher 6).

These are people who take their wine seriously and believe, 4
like Edward VII, that " 'Not only does one drink wine, but one
inhales it, one looks at it, one tastes it, one swallows it . . .
and one talks about it' " (Lichine and Massee 11). They're oenophiles, connoisseurs, wine experts, and they don't treat wine like
an ordinary beverage.

DISCUSSION QUESTIONS

The thesis of Hawkins' research paper: The finest California wines are now challenging the finest French wines and sometimes winning.

1. Which of the three types of grabbers has Hawkins used? Since there are only three sentences in the grabber, can you explain why he did not arrange them all in one paragraph?
2. What is the subject of each grabber sentence? Is Hawkins using parallel structure?
3. What is the topic sentence of the grabber?
4. Look at the thesis statement, which focuses on the competition between California and French wines. The grabber, on the other hand, does *not* focus on competition at all. In other words, they seem to have nothing to do with one another. Yet somewhere along the line, Hawkins will have to make a connection. Turn to Hawkins' research paper in Chapter 15 and starting with paragraph 4 on page 263 read the first few sentences of each paragraph until you come to the paragraph containing the thesis sentence. Identify it. Can you explain the connection between the grabber and the thesis? In other words, give the progression of ideas as they move from the grabber in the direction of the thesis.
5. Notice that each example in the grabber has been taken from a different secondary source. What does that suggest about the source of Hawkins' idea for his grabber? Do you think Robards, Prial, and Asher themselves used grabbers? Explain.
6. Notice that like any good writer, Hawkins does not begin any of his paragraphs with quotations. Even when a quotation dominates a paragraph (as in 3 and 4), he introduces it with his own words.

9 Prewriting

Division and Classification

To **divide** is to separate a class of things or an idea into smaller subclasses. To **classify** is to proceed in the opposite direction; it is to collect separate things or small subclasses that are tied together by a common property into a larger class. In other words, **division** generates new classes out of existing ones. **Classification** brings existing classes together to form new ones.

The following is a schematic diagram of a division:

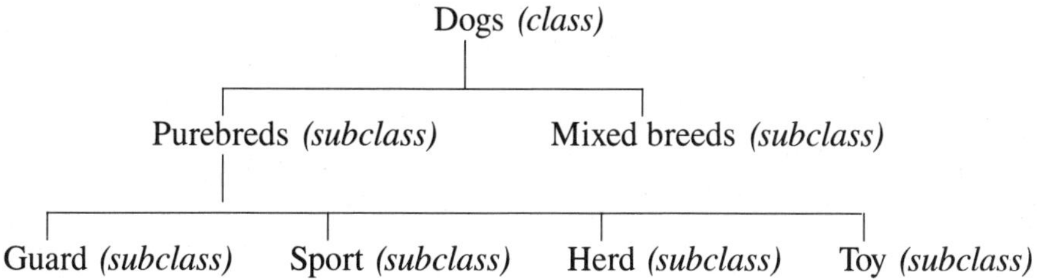

This diagram demonstrates that the class, dogs, is divided into two smaller subclasses (purebreds and mixed breeds) and that the subclass purebreds is divided even further to generate four more subclasses. (Since there are no subclasses of mixed breeds, no further division of mixed breeds is given.)

The following is a schematic diagram of a classification:

Guard *(subclass)* Sport *(subclass)* Herd *(subclass)* Toy *(subclass)*

Purebreds *(subclass)* Mixed breeds *(subclass)*

Dogs *(class)*

The diagram above inverts the order of the first diagram. It exhibits the fact that four subclasses of dogs (guard, sport, herd, and toy) have been collected to form one larger subclass (purebreds) and that the two subclasses, purebreds and mixed breeds, have been collected to form one large class (dogs).

You can also think of division as moving *down* through the various levels of classes from the largest and most general to the smallest and most specific; and classification as moving *up* through the levels from the smallest and most specific to the largest and most general.

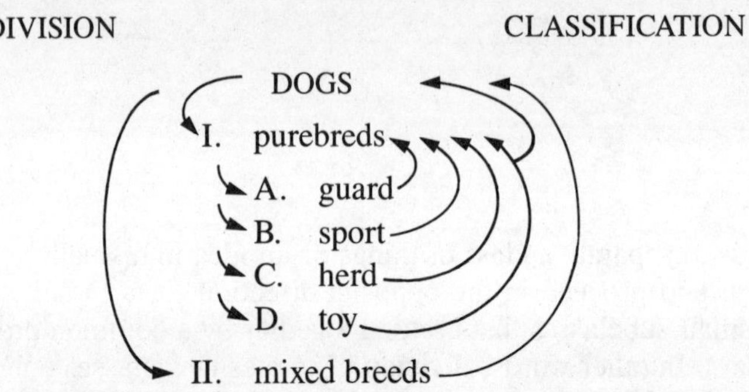

The fact that one diagram can be used to exhibit *both* strategies simultaneously demonstrates how mirrorlike the two mental processes are. They're twin strategies in a single system. Each is a sorting process; each can sort the same things; it just sorts them in reverse directions. In division the intention is always to finish up with *more* classes of things than you started out with. Imagine toys (class) scattered over the floor. You decide to sort them into some kind of order: you put games (subclass) in one section of the room, dolls (subclass) in another, cars and trucks (subclass) in a third, stuffed animals (subclass) in a fourth, dollhouses (subclass) in a fifth, trains (subclass) in a sixth, balls (subclass) in a seventh, sporting gear (subclass) in an eighth, and so on. When you first looked at the toys on the floor, you had just one pile (class) of things, toys. Now when you look around the room, you have, at least, eight piles (subclasses). In other words, you've divided; you've gone from the larger, more general class, toys, to the smaller, more specific subclasses.

But let's say you don't stop there. In your passion for order you notice that some of the piles could be combined because they contain similar kinds of toys: the dolls and the dollhouses could go in the same pile; the balls and the sporting gear could go into another pile, and so on. Besides, with eight piles of toys, the room looks only slightly less disorderly than it did before. So you begin to consolidate the piles; everything that has to do with dolls you place in one pile; all the sporting gear including balls in another pile; all the vehicles, that is, cars, trucks, and trains, in a third; stuffed animals in a fourth; games in a fifth. You've thus reduced eight piles to five. You have classified. In classification, the intention is to finish up with *fewer* classes of things than you started out with.

In other words, both division and classification are devices for bringing order to a subject. Because division reduces a large class to smaller subclasses, it renders a large subject manageable. Thus a writer couldn't possibly begin a discussion of water pollution, for example, without clarifying what *kind* of water he had in mind (lakes, rivers, oceans, wells, ground water, drinking water, aquifers, reservoirs, etc.) and what *kind* of pollution (bacterial, chemical, radioactive, thermal, etc.). Even if the division never reaches paper, that is, even if the writer simply runs through the subclasses in his mind before zeroing in on one (or more), as a mental strategy, the division is essential and invaluable in revealing the scope of a subject and a way of limiting it.

By the same token, because classification brings existing classes together to form new ones, it can provide a larger frame for the subject a writer is discussing. For example, if the subject is windmills as an energy source, classifying them as an energy source of the "inexhaustible" as opposed to the "exhaustible" variety is a means of establishing perspective.

The subjects that can be divided and classified are unlimited. Since just about everything can be sorted (pigeonholed), just about everything can be divided and classified: small things (computer chips, cells, dust particles); large things (planets, countries, space); animate things (actors, bats, sea anemones); inanimate things (clouds, asphalt, tennis serves); serious subjects (war, child abuse, unemployment); frivolous ones (gum drops, girl watchers, sneezing); concepts such as immigration, body language, and navigation; and concepts such as love, violence, and immortality.

Division and Classification as Tandem Operations

The two sorting processes can also be thought of as operating in tandem. Take a final example, this time from James W. Clarke's *American Assassins.* In it he divides American assassins into four subclasses:

- **I.** "Rational extremists" with a political motive, e.g., John Wilkes Booth, Sirhan Sirhan
- **II.** Frustrated and alienated "neurotics" without a political motive, e.g., Lee Harvey Oswald, Lynette Fromme
- **III.** "Sociopathic killers" without a political motive, whose targets represent a society they hate, e.g., Arthur Bremer
- **IV.** Insane "psychotics" who are not aware of what they are doing

What you see above is the division of one large class, assassins, into four smaller subclasses. Next, notice the examples. Providing them is an act of classification; in fact, giving examples during the sorting process is always an act of classification because it is the taking of something specific (which an example always is) and placing it into a larger class of things. Classifying Arthur Bremer as a "sociopathic killer" is moving up from the most specific (the example) to the more general (a subclass).

In other words, you can be sure that when you're sorting, you'll be engaged in *both* dividing *and* classifying simply because the whole system of division–classification operates in tandem. Just how tandem can best be demonstrated by reconstructing the steps Clarke had to take in sorting his subject. He first had to classify, then divide, then classify again. Here's an imagined replay. In the early stages of his research (before he wrote his book), he might have drawn up a complete list of American assassins. With his list in front of him, he probably began noting the ways in which some of the assassins were alike by jotting down some key words next to each name:

- Lee Harvey Oswald: feelings of rejection and frustration
- Sirhan Sirhan: political convictions
- Arthur Bremer: hatred of society
- John Wilkes Booth: political convictions
- Lynette Fromme: frustrated neurotic

Then to help him visualize the pattern that had begun to emerge, he might have grouped the assassins together:

I. Sirhan
Booth

II. Oswald
Fromme

III. Bremer

What he's done is classified, that is, consolidated his list of names into several piles, groupings.

Classifying the assassins, therefore, was step one. Step two follows with the simple act of asserting that "there are four subclasses of American assassins" and then naming them. The naming of categories, in other words, is division (step two). Notice that given the uncharted territory of his subject, Clarke couldn't divide before he'd classified because he was identifying subclasses that had not previously been identified. But as a mental process, classification doesn't always have to precede division. (Depending on a person's familiarity with dogs, for example, he or she may or may not have to make a list of all the breeds and classify them before division can take place. If the writer is familiar with canine breeds, the subclasses might come to mind without the need to classify first. Without prolonged thought he or she might be able to say, "there are two subclasses of dogs—purebreds and mongrels," and then, after some momentary thought, observe, "and there are four subclasses of purebreds.")

But getting back to Clarke, you'll notice that there is still one more step to go. After we've imagined Clarke dividing, we can still imagine his feeling obligated to provide examples of each subclass. And that, as you already know, is classification, step three. It is also worth noticing that in his book, Clarke engages only in division and then classification in that order. He gives the reader the finished product of his research, which includes step two (division) and step three (classification) but not the preliminary first step of classification, which remains in his notes.

EXERCISE 1

The following is an exercise in the process of division and classification. Imagine a large, well-furnished living room; it contains every sort of furniture that could possibly be found in a living room. Like Clarke, make a list of all the conceivable pieces of furnishings (including things like curtains, etc.) that an actual living room might have. Next classify the furnishings into subclasses. When you're finished you should have about seven. Next see whether you can further consolidate the seven or so subclasses into larger subclasses so that you've reduced them to only two or three.

You should now be prepared to express the mental process you've engaged in as division and draw an appropriate diagram:

```
Living Room Furnishings
 I.
     A.
         E.g.,
         E.g., etc.
     B. etc.
 II.
     A. etc.
```

Terminology

To prevent confusion, only one term, *subclass,* was used up to this point when referring to the ranks below the level of class. But other terms can be used: *type, kind, category,* and *variety.* In division your sentences are likely to sound like this: There are two types of diamonds . . . , three kinds of rock music . . . , four categories of neighbors . . . , five varieties of salads . . . , and so on.

In classification the terms will remain the same but will be expressed differently; you will first refer to something specific (subclass or example) and then to something general (class or larger subclass): punk is one *type* of rock music (meaning there are other types); Mrs. Jones can be classified as the *kind* of neighbor that keeps to herself (meaning there are other kinds of neighbors); cole slaw falls into the *category* of foods known as salads.

Sometimes, if it's otherwise obvious to the reader that you're classifying, the terms *type, kind, category, variety* are omitted and merely implied: the liquid diet is a fad diet (meaning that the liquid diet is one type of fad diet); alfalfa, comfrey, and aloe vera are medicinal herbs (meaning alfalfa, comfrey, and aloe vera all fall into the category known as medicinal herbs).

Being familiar with the terminology of division and classification is particularly important because of its use as a test or criterion for making sure that you are indeed dividing and not engaging in some other mental process. You can only be said to be dividing when you are sorting things into types, categories, varieties, and so on: types of fabrics, categories of motors, varieties of yawns. If you cannot apply any of those terms to what you're dividing, you are not dividing. (See page 139 for further explanation.)

Flexibility of Categories

You will find that, regardless of what you're dividing or classifying, the categories (subclasses) aren't inflexible or predetermined by some outside authority. There is no such thing as one set of subclasses being more "correct" than another set. There are only two requirements. First, they must be *logical,* meaning that only one basis of division should be used per rank per breakdown. Thus dogs that were divided in the first rank according to purity of breed (purebred and mixed breed) and then at the second rank according to purpose (guard, sport, herd, toy) could have been divided according to other bases of division: for example, according to familiarity with the breed (ordinary breeds, exotic breeds) or according to hair length (short hair, long hair) or according to temperament (even-tempered, high-strung), and so on. (See pages 137–139 for discussion of errors in division logic.) Second, the categories of the division must be *significant.* Sorting the living room furnishings into small things and large things is indeed dividing them into categories, but it isn't saying very much.

You will get the ideas for categories from your reading and from some good, hard thinking that is based on logic, intuition, and experience. Take the subject of laughter as an example. The following diagrams of laughter, though each is different, are all valid.

A. Laughter

I. Makes you feel like an insider

II. Makes you feel like an outsider

B.

Laughter

I. Good-natured

II. "Sick"

III. Devious

IV. Mocking

V. Nervous

C.

Laughter

I. Polite

II. Genuine

A. Mild and brief

B. Convulsive and unstoppable

None of the divisions is better than the others. Each is tailored to fit a particular purpose—usually to organize a subject, aid in analyzing it, and advance a particular thesis. The division in diagram A, for example, may be used to explain that not all laughter makes one feel good. B may be used in examining the thesis that laughter is a complex matter that expresses a whole range of emotional and psychological states and attitudes. C may be used in an analysis of laughter's physiological aspects.

Notice that when you divide into only two categories (as in A and C above), the two categories will usually express opposing ideas. Other examples are shrubs that shed leaves in the fall *and* those that don't; pollution that is reversible *and* pollution that isn't; renewable natural resources *and* nonrenewable ones. This is division at its simplest and most straightforward. It doesn't usually cause students difficulty. The difficulties arise when there are more than two categories and they are not neat opposites. If this happens, you must guard against problems.

EXERCISE 2

As you have learned, there is more than one way to divide or classify anything. Look at the three diagramed divisions of laughter above as examples of the assignment. Then divide and diagram one or more of the following subjects in, at least, two ways: lies, fast-food restaurants, salads, roommates, pets, vacations, neighbors, procrastinators, parties, junk food, rock music, cafeterias, Sundays, divorces, sports, blind dates, shoes, student dress.

Common Faults of Dividing

1. *Confusion.* When you use more than one basis of division at a time, you are not being logical. The result is confusion and the error of cross-ranking.

2. *Failing to be exhaustive.* When you don't provide enough categories, your division will not be complete. The result is that your reader will not have a pigeonhole for some of the things that come to mind while reading your division. Remember that no category can be left out at whim or for lack of space or thought. (However, it is perfectly acceptable to be less than thorough in your *discussion* of the categories; that is, you must be thorough when you divide, but you may want to focus on only one of your categories in your actual discussion. "There are two types of birds," you write, "those that migrate and those that don't." Then you dismiss the birds that don't migrate as being outside the concern of your essay and concentrate only on the ones that do.)

What follows is a division that demonstrates both problems: confusion and failure to be exhaustive.

```
Abusers of Alcohol

  I. Heavy social drinkers
 II. Binge drinkers
III. Teen-agers
 IV. Businesspeople
  V. Winos
```

First, the matter of confusion. A logical division should use only one basis of division at a time. A basis of division refers to the principle held in common by all the categories in the division. If you look at the diagram above, you'll see that there is no single basis; in fact, there are three. In I and II the basis of division is how much and when an abuser drinks (a lot on social occasions and a lot once in a while). In III and IV the basis of division is the kind of person who abuses alcohol. In V the basis of division is the kind of alcohol that is abused (wine) as well as the type of person (derelict).

Furthermore, one error leads to another. Whenever more than one basis of division is used, **cross-ranking** is inevitable. Simply stated, that means that the different categories in the division overlap. Look at the diagram again: heavy social drinkers and binge drinkers can be both teen-agers and businesspeople. In other words, the distinction between categories isn't sharp. The result is confusion!

The other problem that needs guarding against is failure to be exhaustive. The basis of division in I and II brings to mind two other categories that aren't mentioned: all-day drinkers and bar drinkers. The basis of division in III and IV suggests many other stereotypes: housewives, house painters, actors, and others. In fact, so many types of people abuse alcohol as to make that particular basis meaningless as a principle for categorizing alcohol abusers. In short, the division of abusers of alcohol into the four categories above is both confused and incomplete.

3. *Mistaking lists for division.* Another pitfall is the inclination to mistake several other kinds of mental activities for division. Remember that division is *not* simply a list of things: "There are nine plants on the patio" is not a division; neither is "two effects," "six factors," "three problems," "four causes," and so on. Nine plants is not the same as nine *types* of plants. Nine plants on the patio is simply an exact count of the plants, say, three roses, two ferns, and four cacti. Types would have to refer to the categories in which specific plants can be placed such as "flowering" and "nonflowering," for example. For the same reason, seven causes is not the same as seven types of causes. The following, for example, are seven causes of injuries sustained by runners: improper warm-up, fatigue, improper training schedule, temperature change, poor terrain, poorly fitted shoes. Only if you were to group similar causes together into categories would you have types of causes: for example, causes within the control of the athlete, causes arising from outside influences and outside agencies.

4. *Mistaking components for division.* Division is not a breakdown of something into its component parts. None of the following statements shows division:

(a) There are three major phases in a person's life: childhood, adolescence, and adulthood.

(b) A football team is composed of three different smaller teams.

(c) A college is made up of the administration, the faculty, the students, and the custodial help.

Only when you talk about types of phases, types of childhoods, types of teams, types of colleges, types of administrations, and so on, are you said to be dividing.

EXERCISE 3

The division of college students below is both confused (illogical) and incomplete. Therefore, straighten out the diagram. First, sort out the categories according to the various bases involved; next, diagram each new division that you have generated; finally, add categories wherever they are missing in any of the diagrams in order to make the division exhaustive.

College Students

I. Career oriented
II. Keep up with their studies
III. Do not participate in class discussions because of timidity
IV. Do not participate in class discussions because of lack of interest
V. Over 21

VI. Commuters
VII. Residents
VIII. Attend classes regularly
IX. Work part time to help pay for their education
X. Do assigned reading
XI. Do additional reading
XII. Sit in the front row
XIII. Socially oriented

EXERCISE 4

Look at the following statements and identify the ones that (a) express division; (b) express a list of things rather than a division of things; and (c) express the component parts of something.

1. The Hybrid-Electric car will have two sources of power: a battery system and a small gas engine.
2. Americans protested the draft in two ways—violently and nonviolently.
3. Courts of law recognize three categories of privileged communication: doctor and patient, lawyer and client, and priest and penitent.
4. The rock group touring the Soviet Union consists of a lead singer and four instrumentalists.
5. There are three types of performers in a rock group: lead singers, instrumentalists, and vocalists.
6. Some of the claims that promoters of fad diets make are harmful; others are harmless.
7. There are three reasons for running—fun, fitness, and competition.

Writing Division and Classification

Length

Division and classification can be any length: for example, an informal and self-explanatory sentence: "There are two kinds of people in the world—those who slipcover their couches when they're new and those who slipcover them only after they've become worn." Division and classification can also be a paragraph, several paragraphs, or even provide the organizational strategy for an entire essay. You will concentrate on writing divisions and classifications that are at least a paragraph in length.

Discovering Use for Division and Classification

1. *Check your thesis sentence for an* outright statement *of division or classification.* Take the following thesis as an example: "For birds, migration is often a life-threatening obstacle course that is composed of five types of hindrances." The discussion of these hindrances would obviously constitute the bulk of the essay, as you can see from the diagram below.

```
Hindrances Encountered by Migrating Birds

  I. Bad weather conditions
     E.g., snow
     E.g., wind
     E.g., extreme temperatures
 II. Inadequate food supplies
III. Physical obstacles
     E.g., towers
     E.g., airplanes
     E.g., lights
 IV. Predators
     E.g., birds
     E.g., animals
     E.g., people
```

Caution: A division is not an outline, and the diagram of a division is not the same thing as the outline of an essay. However, division and outline will coincide in one particular instance: when division is expressed in the thesis.

2. *Check your thesis for division and classification that is not actually expressed but implied by the way that the thesis is phrased.* Look at the following set of thesis statements. Thesis 1 expresses classification, while thesis 2 does not. Yet thesis 2 implies it.

Thesis 1 The women who settled the early frontier fell into three categories: educated and refined women from the East; immigrant women; women born and bred in the West.

Thesis 2 Of all the different kinds of women who settled the early frontier, the educated and refined women from the East experienced the greatest psychological hardships.

The classification expressed in thesis 1 provides the essay with its overall organization—a discussion of each of the three categories of women. Thesis 2, however, implies a possible division. While the bulk of the essay would be devoted to the "educated and refined women from the East," the beginning might be devoted to categorizing the different kinds of women that settled the frontier. The writer would thus start by framing the subject for the reader and then concentrate the rest of the essay only on the women from the East.

3. *Check your thesis and topic for the possibility of using division and classification as background information.* For example:

The victims of anorexia display symptoms of starvation, but the basis of the disease is psychological.

The thesis does not imply a division or classification, but both are possible as background information. The writer would, first, classify anorexia as an eating disorder; second, divide eating disorders into two categories—obesity and anorexia—thus effectively framing the subject against a larger background. Having done so, the writer would then move on to his or her primary objective: discussion of the thesis. Such an overview would probably take no more than a paragraph at the beginning of the essay and might begin something like this:

Anorexia nervosa is classified as an eating disorder. In fact, there are two types of eating disorders that are on the rise in our society--obesity and anorexia. Obesity. . . .

The writer would then go on to discuss obesity briefly in the paragraph. Only then would he or she turn to the main subject of the essay—anorexia.

4. *Check back in your secondary sources for ideas.* Say that your thesis is the idea that the glorification of sport played an important role in Nazi Germany. A look through your sources might reveal the following idea, which you'd overlooked before: namely, that public ceremonies had great appeal in the Germany of the thirties and forties. What you're suddenly struck by is the fact that sport is one of the "ceremonies" that the source is talking about; and that a classification of sport as one type of ceremony (with perhaps a brief overview of the other types) is in order.

EXERCISE 5

Look at the sample thesis statements below. Which statement expresses a division? Explain. Which statements require or imply a division–classification without expressly stating it? Explain.

1. Mining conditions have improved very little over the years.
2. Gunpowder was not used as an instrument of destruction in China as it was in Europe because the Chinese had a different attitude to death, battle, and personal honor than did the Europeans.

3. Expensive cosmetics are essentially no different from cheap ones.
4. Juvenile delinquency in the middle and upper classes is different from lower-class juvenile delinquency.
5. The three types of seating arrangements that can be found in places of worship express the three types of relationships commonly found between worshippers and their deity.

Introducing Division and Classification

Remember to introduce your division or classification with a statement that spells out what is being divided or classified. The only time you want to avoid such a statement is in the thesis. "There are two kinds of child abuse" is fine as a topic sentence but flat as a thesis statement. With a change in focus, the thesis can be rendered more appealing: "While there are several types of child abuse, they are not all equally damaging." Thesis statements of division are interesting only when the division itself is unusual or interpretive in nature: "While most people do not realize it, there are actually two kinds of graffiti—graffiti as vandalism and graffiti as art."

Organizing Division and Classification

Discuss the ranks of your division in *exactly* the same order in which you list them in your statement. If, in the course of writing your essay, you discover a more logical order (for whatever reason) than the one in your statement, change the order in the statement to reflect the order in the essay. The point is that the order of your discussion and the order expressed in your statement of division should always coincide. In short, if the following is your thesis—"The federal crackdown on drugs is resorting to three kinds of approaches: commonsense reforms, military resources, and legal investigations of laundering practices in banks"—the following should be the order of discussion: (1) commonsense reforms, (2) military resources, (3) legal investigations.

Finding Location for Division and Classification

1. If the division is expressed in your thesis, it's crucial to the corroboration and explanation of your thesis. Therefore, it will provide the organizational structure for your whole essay or constitute its climax. In the latter instance, you will use the essay to build up to it, in which case the division may take up the last one, two, three, whatever, pages of your paper.

2. If the division or classification is not expressed in the thesis but constitutes background data, place it early in the essay before zeroing in on the most essential part of your discussion.

3. If the division or classification is not expressed in the thesis and is not background information, use division to organize some localized section of your essay.

WRITING ASSIGNMENT

Using Division and Classification

Write a solid paragraph or more on a subject dealing with your research paper that is in need of sorting. Look at your thesis. If it doesn't express division or classification, see whether it implies it or whether your subject doesn't have to be classified just to provide a background for the essay. If nothing suggests itself, do a little more reading and a little more thinking to find a way of working division–classification into your research paper.

Before you write anything in prose, however, diagram it. The schematic will help you catch any faults in your division. Then use the diagram to organize your discussion.

If your particular thesis statement expresses division, you are not expected to submit the entire essay now. If you have more than two categories and, particularly, if you have subdivided as well as divided, turn in only the schematic diagram to your instructor. However, if your division or classification is fairly simple (two categories only, for example), then do more than diagram the division: write the paragraph that you are going to use to introduce the division–classification and a partial discussion of it. How partial depends on you and on how much research you've done to date. Try to submit enough to enable your instructor to examine the division–classification for its logic and significance and make comments.

Prose Models

NAME-CALLING

The insults spoken by adults are usually more subtle than the simple name-calling used by children, but children's insults make obvious some of the verbal strategies people carry into adult life. Most parents engage in wishful thinking when they regard name-calling as good-natured fun which their children will soon grow out of. Name-calling is not good-natured and children do not grow out of it; as adults they merely become more expert in its use. Nor is it true that "sticks and stones may break my bones, but names will never hurt me." Names can hurt very much because children seek out the victim's true weakness, then jab exactly where the skin is thinnest. Name-calling can have major impact on a child's feelings about his identity, and it can sometimes be devastating to his psychological development. 1

Almost all examples of name-calling by children fall into four categories: 2

1. Names based on physical peculiarities, such as deformities, use of eyeglasses, racial characteristics, and so forth. A child may be called *Flattop* because he was born with a misshapen skull —or, for obvious reasons, *Fat Lips, Gimpy, Four Eyes, Peanuts, Fatso, Kinky,* and so on.
2. Names based on a pun or parody of the child's own name. Children with last names like Fitts, McClure, Duckworth, and Farb usually find them converted to *Shits, Manure, Fuckworth,* and *Fart.*
3. Names based on social relationships. Examples are *Baby* used by a sibling rival or *Chicken Shit* for someone whose courage is questioned by his social group.
4. Names based on mental traits—such as *Clunkhead, Dummy, Jerk,* and *Smartass.*

These four categories were listed in order of decreasing offensiveness to the victims. Children regard names based on physical peculiarities as the most cutting, whereas names based on mental traits are, surprisingly, not usually regarded as very offensive. Most children are very vulnerable to names that play upon the child's rightful name—no doubt because one's name is a precious possession, the mark of a unique identity and one's masculinity or femininity. Those American Indian tribes that had the custom of never revealing true names undoubtedly avoided considerable psychological damage.

Peter Farb, *Word Play: What Happens When People Talk,* 1973

DISCUSSION QUESTIONS

1. What is Farb dividing? How many categories?
2. How does he explain the order in which he lists them? Why does the explanation follow rather than precede the division?
3. What topic sentence introduces the division? How else might Farb have phrased that sentence to express the same division?
4. What is the purpose of the division? In other words, is the division an end in itself or is Farb using the division to explain another idea? If so, which?

THE THEORY OF LOVE

What matters is that we know what kind of union we are talking about when we speak of love. Do we refer to love as the mature answer to the problem of existence, or do we speak of those immature forms of love which may be called *symbiotic union*? In the following pages I shall call love only the former. I shall begin the discussion of "love" with the latter. 1

Symbiotic union has its biological pattern in the relationship between 2
the pregnant mother and the foetus. They are two, and yet one. They live "together," (*sym-biosis*), they need each other. The foetus is a part of the mother, it receives everything it needs from her; mother is its world, as it were; she feeds it, she protects it, but also her own life is enhanced by it. In the *psychic* symbiotic union, the two bodies are independent, but the same kind of attachment exists psychologically.

The *passive* form of the symbiotic union is that of submission, 3
or if we use a clinical term, of *masochism.* The masochistic person escapes from the unbearable feeling of isolation and separateness by making himself part and parcel of another person who directs him, guides him, protects him; who is his life and his oxygen, as it were. The power of the one to whom one submits is inflated, may he be a person or a god; he is everything, I am nothing, except inasmuch as I am part of him. As a part, I am part of greatness, of power, of certainty. The masochistic person does not have to make decisions, does not have to take any risks; he is never alone—but he is not independent; he has no integrity; he is not yet fully born. In a religious context the object of worship is called an idol; in a secular context of a masochistic love relationship the essential mechanism, that of idolatry, is the same. The masochistic relationship can be blended with physical, sexual desire; in this case it is not only a submission in which one's mind participates, but also one's whole body. There can be masochistic submission to fate, to sickness, to rhythmic music, to the orgiastic state produced by drugs or under hypnotic trance—in all these instances the person renounces his integrity, makes himself the instrument of somebody or something outside of himself; he need not solve the problem of living by productive activity.

The *active* form of symbiotic fusion is domination or, to use the 4
psychological term corresponding to masochism, *sadism.* The sadistic person wants to escape from his aloneness and his sense of imprisonment by making another person part and parcel of himself. He inflates and enhances himself by incorporating another person, who worships him.

The sadistic person is as dependent on the submissive person as the 5
latter is on the former; neither can live without the other. The difference is only that the sadistic person commands, exploits, hurts, humiliates, and that the masochistic person is commanded, exploited, hurt, humiliated. This is a considerable difference in a realistic sense; in a deeper emotional sense, the difference is not so great as that which they both have in common: fusion without integrity. If one understands this, it is also not surprising to find that usually a person reacts in both the

sadistic and the masochistic manner, usually toward different objects. Hitler reacted primarily in a sadistic fashion toward people, but masochistically toward fate, history, the "higher power" of nature. His end—suicide among general destruction—is as characteristic as was his dream of success—total domination.

In contrast to symbiotic union, mature *love* is *union under the condition of preserving one's integrity,* one's individuality. *Love is an active power in man;* a power which breaks through the walls which separate man from his fellow men, which unites him with others; love makes him overcome the sense of isolation and separateness, yet it permits him to be himself, to retain his integrity. In love the paradox occurs that two beings become one and yet remain two. 6

Erich Fromm, *The Art of Loving,* 1956

DISCUSSION QUESTIONS

1. What exactly is Fromm dividing? Subdividing? In fact, this is the most elaborate division you have encountered so far. It begins in paragraph 1 and runs right through paragraph 6. Write out a schematic diagram of the division or plot it in the margins of the essay (whichever your instructor prefers).
2. Does Fromm give equal weight to each category and subcategory in this passage? Where is his emphasis and why? Explain.
3. Look at the opening sentences of paragraphs 2 through 4 and 6. Is Fromm's introduction of categories clear and easy to follow? Where does paragraph 5 fit in? Why does Fromm make it a separate paragraph rather than just attach it to 4? After all, he didn't break up his discussion of the *passive* form of symbiotic union into two paragraphs. Explain.
4. Notice the word *love* in quotation marks in paragraph 1. Why are quotation marks used? Explain.

TRIGGER CONTROL

Donna Brugnoli (Student)

Gun owners can be divided into two main categories—ordinary citizens and criminals. Ordinary citizens include hunters, sportsmen, security personnel, collectors, and individuals who purchase guns for protection against antisocial elements. These people register their weapons and customarily abide by the law. Criminals buy or steal firearms with the express purpose of committing illegal actions. Numerous statistics and studies prove that strict gun control laws will not save ordinary citizens from criminals because they do not deter criminals from obtaining weapons (Murray 90), but, as Leonard Berkowitz explains, gun control laws may "save some ordinary citizens from other ordinary citizens" because of a phenomenon called "the weapons effect." Research in recent years suggests that "the mere presence of guns can have an aggressive effect on behavior. . . . The weapon itself becomes a stimulant to violence" ("Control" 11). This one factor is the strongest argument for strict gun control.

DISCUSSION QUESTIONS

The thesis of Brugnoli's research paper is found in the second and third to the last sentences. The following is a succinct expression of it: The mere presence of a gun can have an aggressive effect on behavior because of a phenomenon called "the weapons effect."

1. What is being divided?
2. Number the categories and explain why Brugnoli does not discuss them in separate paragraphs.
3. Why does she offer examples of only one of the categories? Why are they brief? Do you expect her to discuss gun-owning criminals in her research paper? Explain.
4. Does the thesis imply a division? Or is Brugnoli using division merely as background information? Could her essay have gotten along without this division? Explain.
5. Turn to page 249 where you will find this passage incorporated into the research paper. Is the beginning a good location for it? Explain.

CALIFORNIA WINES ARE ALIVE AND WELL

Ned Hawkins (Student)

In any comparison of French and California wines, it's necessary to take into account the fact that there are basically *two* kinds of grapes: those that produce the premier wines (which are the dinner wines that connoisseurs get ecstatic about and that show up in wine-tasting competitions) and those that produce all the rest (which are the inexpensive wines that are served with home-cooked daily meals in France or the $5 per gallon bulk wines sold in the United States). Any comparison of French and California wines is usually between the premier wines; it's always a comparison of the best of California with the best of France. 1

Two of the grapes in the first category that produce premier 2
wines are the cabernet sauvignon grape and the chardonnay grape. The cabernet sauvignon is the grape that produces a dry red wine, called Bordeaux in France and just Cabernet Sauvignon in the United States. This wine is considered one of the finest in the world; such French wines as Chateau Lafite-Rothschild, Chateau Mouton Rothschild, Chateau Latour, Chateau Margaux, and Chateau Haut-Briton are the most celebrated examples of it. The chardonnay grape is the famous white grape that produces a white wine; it is also responsible for some of the best and most expensive wines, called Burgundies in France and, again, just Chardonnay in America. The intriguing question is obviously how these two wines, produced from the same two grapes but on different sides of the Atlantic, compare with each other.

DISCUSSION QUESTIONS

The thesis of Hawkins' research paper: The finest California wines are now challenging the finest French wines and sometimes winning.

1. What is being divided? Why? Look at the thesis. How has the division served to bring order to the subject of wine, making it easy to handle in a research paper?
2. The first category of grapes is discussed at length in the second paragraph. Why isn't the second category also discussed at length in a separate paragraph?
3. Turn to page 270 for the location of the division in the research essay.
4. Notice the changes in the final version: (a) several sentences have been added at the beginning; (b) the parenthetical explanations have been condensed and somewhat modified; and (c) the order in which the two grapes are discussed has been reversed. Explain the reasons for the changes. In the case of (b) is the change an improvement over the original?

10 Prewriting

Definition

To **define** is to give the meaning of a word or term. The definitions that this chapter is concerned with, however, cannot be found in a dictionary, or, at the very least, exceed those provided by the dictionary. This chapter is not concerned with the "According-to-Webster-love-is . . . " kind of definition that beginners sometimes think of as clever. In fact, you'd better think twice about giving your readers a definition they can find on their own. This sentence from David Monagan's "Horse of a Different Culture," for example, contains a word unfamiliar to most people: "Nearly all the world's free-ranging horses are not wild but feral, because their ancestors—decades and in many places centuries ago—were domesticated." The unfamiliar word is *feral.* But even a pocket-sized dictionary will contain a definition of *feral:* "having reverted to the wild state, as from domestication." So the writer of the sentence should not and does not bother defining it.

Sentence Definition and Extended Definition

The only definitions that a reader wants to see on the printed page are usually either those that aren't in most dictionaries; those that comment on, criticize, or disagree with the dictionary; or those that have little to do with the dictionary meaning. Such definitions fall into two categories:

1. The sentence definition of specialized words (jargon).
2. The extended definition of any word.

First, the **sentence definition**. Sometimes a writer will use a word, or an expression made up of familiar words but foreign to most people, that isn't in Webster's or any standard desk dictionary because it represents language (jargon) peculiar to a particular trade, profession, or group: like the language of biomedicine (e.g., endorphins), sociology (e.g., urban gentrification), technology (e.g., real-world control interface), politics (e.g., truth squad), meteorology (e.g., hurricane hunters), regional language (e.g., laning), slang (e.g., clearance creeps), and so on. When a writer uses words like the above, he or she is obligated (if writing for nonspecialists) to define terms that the reader will not understand and—more importantly—cannot look up. As you would expect, the definitions are short (usually a sentence) and to the point: *endorphins* are hormonal substances that supply the typical "high" experienced by athletes; *real-world control interfaces* are computer components that allow control of such devices as furnaces, thermostats, burglar alarms, or robots; *laning* is what residents of Nantucket do when they stroll in the evening along the island's secluded lanes; and so on.

These definitions, while they are important, are not a very significant part of the essay. They're primarily important to the reader's comprehension rather than to the writer's thesis. Indeed their chief characteristic (which distinguishes them from the extended definition) is the fact that they're dispensable. In other words, if the writer could assume that readers knew the meaning of, say, *endorphins,* he or she could just lift the sentence definition out, and no one would miss it. The sentence definition is a favor the writer does the reader since the definition is more important to the reader than it is to the development of the writer's ideas or the organization of the essay. That is not to say that the definition should always be omitted; not at all. But the point is that the writer does not need the sentence definition to get from idea A to idea B in the essay. And this distinguishes the sentence definition from the second type of definition, which is not just a sentence and not dispensable—even when the reader thinks he or she knows the meaning of the word being defined.

It is the second type, the extended definition, with which this chapter is primarily concerned; it is the kind of definition that will call upon the powers of your thought and imagination to write. An extended definition is not found in the dictionary, and it is not a standard definition. When Karl Marx defined religion, for example, as "the opiate of the people," he did not supply a definition that applies to every and any context. Thus an extended definition is always tailored to fit a particular thesis, a certain kind of discussion.

Furthermore, unlike the sentence definition, an extended definition is longer than a sentence; it's usually a paragraph or more. The part of the extended definition that gives the actual meaning of the word (its formal definition) will often be only a sentence long; but the whole passage in which the single-sentence formal definition is contained is called an **extended definition** because the writer extends the discussion of the word beyond the sentence and calls attention to it in a very unmistakable and pronounced way.

Notice how the example of an extended definition below calls attention to itself as a definition in two ways. First, the passage constantly refers to the "word" and the "term." (Both have been *underlined* to emphasize the frequency of their occurrence.) Second, the passage constantly refers back to the phrasing and terminology of the formal sentence(s) that actually defines the word. (These words and phrases have been *circled* to call your attention to the way in which the writer of an extended definition "plays" with the key words of the definition by referring to them several times.) In other words, an extended definition is a definition that "talks about itself," recognizes itself as a definition, and calls attention to itself as a definition. Notice, particularly, that unlike the sentence definition, the formal definition cannot be "lifted out" without upsetting the flow of ideas. The extended definition is like a house of cards: Remove the sentence with the formal definition in it, and the entire structure topples.

Remember this tight relationship between formal definition and surrounding sentences as the most prominent feature of the extended definition: It will help you determine whether the extended definition you will write is extended, in fact, or just a simple sentence (or dictionary) definition with some other ideas thrown in to make it longer.

Now that we are well past the season of vacations and 1
fully settled into another year of the "rat-race" of the human race, it may be appropriate to consider the concept of stress—a term that has become the banner designation for our human condition in the latter part of this decade. Stress is one of those words we all think we understand—until we are forced to become precise about its meaning and implications. It is, therefore, a word around which all kinds of myths and misunderstandings have gathered. The goal of this essay is to sort out some of the fact from the fiction concerning stress.

Definition 1

It *is* possible to define stress rather precisely in *physio-* 2
logical terms as a collection of predictable body responses—increased heart rate, soaring blood pressure, rapid breathing and increased muscle tension. Indeed, the famous description . . . of this arousal as the "fight or flight" response points to the exquisite ability of a living organism to prepare itself almost instantaneously for an appropriate response to physical threat. Years later (1946), Dr. Hans Selye of Montreal first popularized the word "stress" while describing this adaptational response of the human body.

Since then, of course, the word has become widely used 3
to cover not only predictable physical threats but a whole range of reactions. Indeed, we now use the word as a synonym for less precise terms—such as anxiety or tension—

Definition 2

> to indicate our feeling that stress, far from being constructive, is potentially damaging to a person who is "under stress."
>
> Definition 3 In short, the word stress in current usage no longer refers 4
> to an appropriate body response—as experienced by a runner at the starting blocks—but to the whole range of modern psychological devils which trigger our bodies into a state of arousal for which no appropriate release can be found. It is not often acceptable to fight physically against or flee from the enemies of our time; the nasty office memo, instead, arouses a state of smoldering frustration that we instinctively sense does us no good. What happens next may be a translation of mental suffering into physical expression, the term "psychosomatic"—meaning "mind-body"—hides a fair amount of ignorance concerning how this happens.
>
> "A Leisurely Look at Stress," *The Harvard Medical School Health Letter,* October 1979

In the passage above, you will notice that the definition of the word *stress* is an ongoing process. The word is defined and redefined three times; what's more, all three definitions and paragraphs are tied together. It's paragraph 1 that says the word *stress* ought to be defined; and it's paragraphs 2 and 3 that say the first definition is inadequate because it doesn't cover the current meanings of the word. In short, the three sentences that actually define the word are *extended* into the passage and are inextricably embedded in its whole network of meanings. Unlike the simple sentence definition, the three definitions cannot be removed without rendering the rest of the passage meaningless.

EXERCISE 1

The following paragraphs either contain a sentence definition or constitute an extended definition. Identify each paragraph in terms of the kind of definition involved by, first, locating the word or term that is being defined and the sentence that formally defines it and, second, by determining how relevant the definition is to the rest of the paragraph.

1. The Dense Pack plan is a $26.4 billion proposal to place 100 MX missiles 1800 feet apart in a narrow strip of land. It drew mixed reactions from the area residents. Businessmen welcomed it; some antinuclear church groups, ranchers, and farmers opposed it. The rest of the citizens didn't care one way or the other.
2. Man is a creature attached to things. By definition, he's the only creature whose survival has depended on things since he made his appearance on planet Earth. Without things, he's ill-suited for survival: he has no claws, no sharp teeth, no fur, can't run or swim very fast, and can't fly at all. His skin is a poor example of adaptation; he can't change his colors like the chameleon or

resemble a twig like the praying mantis. Without the brilliant plumage of the macaw, he'll never be mistaken for a tropical flower. His first instruments of survival were rocks, clubs, and fire. Later, arrows, plows, and guns. Later still, refrigerators, supermarkets, and security systems—and microwave ovens, jogging suits, cable TV, portable smoke alarms, computerized exercisers, Minuteman missiles, space satellite-borne nuclear reactors. Destined to depend on things for survival by his very nature, man has so overcompensated that his *things* are pushing him to the edge of annihilation.

3. Unless the jury was convinced "beyond a reasonable doubt" that John W. Hinckley, Jr., was sane, it had to return a verdict of not guilty by reason of insanity. According to U.S. District Judge Barrington Parker, reasonable doubt is doubt that is "based on reason and a doubt for which you can give a reason." As everyone knows, the jury did return a not-guilty-by-reason-of-insanity verdict that brought criticism from many parts of the country. Some of the most important criticism came from legislators who offered proposals for reforming the federal insanity laws.
4. You may perhaps wish to hear from me exactly what is meant by those words "reasonable doubt." They mean, just so much doubt as you might have in everyday life about an ordinary matter of business. This is a case of murder, and it might be natural for you to think that, in such a case, the words mean more than this. But that is not so. They do not mean that you must cast about for fantastical solutions of what seems to you plain and simple. They do not mean those nightmare doubts which sometimes torment us at four o'clock in the morning when we have not slept very well. They only mean that the proof must be such as you would accept about a plain matter of buying and selling, or some such commonplace transaction. You must not strain your belief in favour of the prisoner any more, of course, than you must accept proof of her guilt without the most careful scrutiny.

Dorothy L. Sayers, *Strong Poison* (Harper & Row, 1930)

Reasons for Using an Extended Definition

What will make writing extended definitions easier is understanding the reasons for using them. The one overriding reason that covers and includes all the others given below is the fact that the word to be defined is so central to your thesis that it needs much more attention than a mere sentence can supply. Here's an example: the issue of man's fear of the increasing sophistication of the computer. What if you wanted to write an essay claiming that the computer poses no threat to man, that man should not be in any fear of being overtaken by it because the computer can't think. Wouldn't such a thesis require that you define *thinking*? After all, what kind of reassurance could you give your reader unless you defined human "thinking" as more sophisticated, more complex, or more far-ranging than computer "thinking"? Roger Rosenblatt is confronted with just this kind of need for definition in "Mind in the Machine." His extended definition is excerpted below:

Essentially, what one wants to know in sorting out this relationship is the answers to two questions: Can computers think (a technical problem)? And, should they think (a moral one)? In order to get at both, it is necessary to agree on what thinking itself is—what thought means—and that is no quick step. Every period in history has had to deal with at least two main definitions of thought, which mirror the prevailing philosophies of that particular time and are usually in opposition. . . .

Definition of human thinking

At the same time, certain aspects of thinking can be identified without encompassing the entire process. The ability to comprehend, to conceptualize, to organize and reorganize, to manipulate, to adjust—these are all parts of thought. So are the acts of pondering, rationalizing, worrying, brooding, theorizing, contemplating, criticizing. One thinks when one imagines, hopes, loves, doubts, fantasizes, vacillates, regrets. To experience greed, pride, joy, spite, amusement, shame, suspicion, envy, grief—all these require thought; as do the decisions to take command, or umbrage; to feel loyalty or inhibitions; to ponder ethics, self-sacrifice, cowardice, ambition. So vast is the mind's business that even as one makes such a list, its inadequacy is self-evident—the recognition of inadequacy being but another part of an enormous and varied instrument.

Definition of computer thinking

The answer to the first question, then—Can a machine think?—is yes and no. A computer can certainly do some of the above. It can (or will soon be able to) transmit and receive messages, "read" typescript, recognize voices, shapes and patterns, retain facts, send reminders, "talk" or mimic speech, adjust, correct, strategize, make decisions, translate languages. And, of course, it can calculate, that being its specialty. Yet there are hundreds of kinds of thinking that computers cannot come close to. And for those merely intent on regarding the relationship of man to machine as a head-to-artificial-head competition, this fact offers some solace—if not much progress.

Time, May 3, 1982

The specific reasons for writing an extended definition are summarized below:

1. To clarify the meaning of an unfamiliar word or term: for example, weapons effect,* orphan drug, latchkey children, silver storm.

*Defined in the prose models at the end of the chapter.

2. To establish a mutual understanding of a familiar word or term crucial to the discussion of your thesis: for example, invent,* wine.*
3. To restore precision to a familiar word or term the meaning of which has become vague or confused through popular usage: for example, love, obscenity, happiness.
4. To apply a rather unorthodox or simply different meaning to a familiar word or term for reasons the thesis of the essay or topic idea of the paragraph makes clear: for example, squirrel,* wine.*
5. To be amusing, witty, clever: for example, get into a beef.†

Formal Definition: Etymological, Basic, and Connotative

Just how you extend the formal definition of a word will depend on how much and what needs to be said to advance your thesis. There are no rules on how to extend a definition. What's required is imagination and a grasp of your subject, which you'll be getting from your research. As you will see in the prose models by the differences between, say, Kinkead's definition of *squirrel* and Sutherland's of *invent,* there is no single approach or iron-clad format. But there *are* guidelines.

There are *three* ways to handle the formal definition: etymologically, basically, or connotatively. None is exclusive of the others; in fact, it's possible to make use of all three ways within the same extended definition.

1. Etymological definition explains the derivation of a word; that is, it gives its original meaning. If you looked up the word *schizophrenia* in an unabridged dictionary, here is what you'd find: shizo- Gr. *schizein* to split; -phrenia Gr. *phren* mind + *ia* -ia. Translated this means that schizophrenia is derived from two Greek words: *schizein* meaning "to split" and *phren* meaning "mind" plus the suffix *ia.* For example, Joann E. Rodgers uses this derivation in handling her extended definition of *schizophrenia* in "Roots of Madness."**

*Defined in the prose models at the end of the chapter.

†Incidentally, if two players disagreed on the rules, we might say they "got into a beef." This term goes back to the Renaissance when a man would court a woman by stroking the side of her head with a slab of meat. If she pulled away, it meant she was spoken for. If, however, she assisted by clamping the meat to her face and pushing it all over her head, it meant she would marry him. The meat was kept by the bride's parents and worn as a hat on special occasions. If, however, the husband took another lover, the wife could dissolve the marriage by running with the meat to the town square and yelling, "With thine own beef, I do reject thee. Aroo! Aroo!" If a couple "took to the beef" or "had a beef" it meant they were quarreling (Woody Allen, *Without Feathers,* New York: Random House, 1975).

**But most will never recover. At least no one ever has since the disease was described in great detail, in 1906, by a Swiss doctor named Eugen Blueler. Blueler coined the word *schizophrenia* from the Greek, meaning split mind, to suggest the breakup of the mind's unity. He recognized that the minds of schizophrenics operate not as integrated systems but in bits and pieces that distort reality, muddy perceptions, and loosen the links between thoughts. As time goes on, the afflicted confuse fantasy with reality for longer and longer periods. They make peculiar movements. Some giggle at tragedy, others go for decades without speaking (*Science 82,* July–August 1982).

2. Basic definition is a term that applies to (a) definition by *denotation* (putting the word or term you're defining into a class and then identifying the characteristics that distinguish it from all other members of that class):

Cottage	small, modest house (class), as at a resort, used as a vacation home (distinguishing characteristic) (*The Random House College Dictionary*);
Urban gentrification	innercity phenomenon (class) which has urban pioneers renovating old buildings and displacing the poor (distinguishing characteristic);
Happiness	the pleasure (class) of taking pains (distinguishing characteristic) (Robert Frost).

(b) Definition by *synonym:*

Cottage	cabin
Happiness	bliss
Afraid	alarmed, frightened
Injure	damage, hurt, harm

Definitions by synonym are obviously going to be much shorter than definitions by denotation and might often be inadequate by themselves. Therefore, you'll sometimes find them used in combination with each other.

3. The **connotative definition** gives the associations the word or term has for the writer and, most likely (though not necessarily), for the reader:

Corsage	proms, graduations, Mother's Day;
Happiness	standing still for hours knee-deep in the swift current of a trout stream;
Tacky	travel stickers on luggage, curtains on vans, mascara on the beach, artificial flowers on graves, alligators on shirts;
Quality	"serving freshly grated horseradish with roast beef, having a ripened goat-cheese selection and offering a perfect Forelle pear with it" (George Lang, "A Food Lover's Quest for Quality," *Travel and Leisure,* Jan. 1982).

EXERCISE 2

What crucial word would need defining in the essays arguing the following?

1. That genetic screening of job applicants for susceptibility to certain occupational diseases is discrimination/not discrimination?
2. That the film *Caligula* is pornographic/not pornographic?
3. That abortion is murder/not murder?

EXERCISE 3

1. How would you define the following words denotatively?
automobile, gun, chaos, poem, concert
2. How would you define the following words by synonym?
automobile, poem, concert, gun, diminish, chaos
3. How would you define the following words connotatively?
automobile, poem, concert, gun, ice cream, shopping mall

EXERCISE 4

The following are formal definitions, each of which is part of an extended definition. In each case, identify the type of formal definition it is (i.e., etymological, basic—denotative or synonym—or connotative). If it is set up as a denotative definition, identify its class and distinguishing characteristics.

1. Positive reinforcement is a bribe, a payoff.
2. Generally speaking, Indian lands are those territories that have been designated as reservations for tribal living and those designated as sacred for religious rites, not those properties owned privately by urban Indians.
3. The barrio is a refuge from the harshness and the coldness of the Anglo world (Robert Ramirez, "The Barrio").
4. A superhero is a superperson, an individual who is more than what he appears to be on the surface.
5. A silver storm is freezing rain that covers everything with ice, dazzling the world with diamonds in the sun.

Common Faults of Defining

1. *Using verbs other than* is/are, means/mean, *or* defines as/is defined as. Any other verb will make your sentence sound like a *description* rather than a definition. The following, for example, isn't a definition because it uses the wrong verb: "A shield law *protects* a reporter's source of information." The sentence describes what a shield law does rather than what it is. The following is the corrected version: "A shield law is legislation that protects a reporter's source of information."

2. *Using* is when, is where, is how. None of these combinations is grammatically correct and should not be used in a definition. The following, therefore, is incorrect: "Ballooning is when you use a lighter-than-air craft to ascend into the atmosphere and float and ride in it." The word that follows the verb in basic definitions (though not necessarily in etymological or connotative ones) should always be the same part of speech as the word or phrase that is being defined:

Noun = noun	*Clearance creeps* are *people* who exhibit nasty behavior during storewide sales. *Politics* is a blood *sport.*

Verb = verb	*To cultivate* is *to stir up* the soil.
Adjective = adjective	*Luminous* means *radiant.*
	Tacky means *cheap.*

3. *Unrestricted definitions.* When you define by denotation, don't stop after class. "A cottage is a small, modest house" is too unrestricted as a definition because it doesn't distinguish the cottage from other "small, modest houses," like bungalows, for example. Similarly, defining urban gentrification as an "innercity phenomenon" is too inclusive; the definition fails to distinguish it from crime and other innercity phenomena. Furthermore, make sure that the distinguishing characteristic you do give restricts the class sufficiently. Notice that the following definition is set up properly with a class and distinguishing characteristic, but the definition still fails to be narrow enough: "A belt is an accessory [class] worn around the waist [distinguishing characteristic]." So is a sash, rope, ribbon, cord, and scarf. Notice how the following revised version excludes the concepts of sash, rope, ribbon, cord, and scarf: "A belt is an accessory worn around the waist and contains some sort of buckle or clasp by which one end is attached to the other."

4. *Circularity.* Do not use the same words in your definition that are found in the word you are defining. The following is an example of circularity: "*Greenbelt legislation* is *legislation* preventing development of the *greenbelt* along the highway."

5. *Failing to explain the point of an etymological definition.* After you have presented the derivation of a word, be sure to put it all together for the reader; tell the reader what you're getting at. The following statement is incomplete: "Marshal is derived from the Old High German *marah* 'horse' and *scalh* 'servant.' " What the reader is still waiting to be told is that "Marshal, therefore, originally meant "servant on a horse." Notice how the following etymological definition pulls the entire definition together with the final statement:

> Architecture comes from the Greek prefix *archi* (which when applied to modern words means "chief," "principal," or "superior") and *tecture* ("construction" or "building"); therefore, architecture is something superior to ordinary construction.

6. *Failing to indicate that you are using a word or term semantically.* When you call attention to a word *as a word,* underline it or put it in quotation marks; when you call attention to its meaning, put that in quotation marks too:

- The word *fantastic* originally meant "existing only in the imagination, unreal."

- The word "democracy" is a word that is familiar to relatively few people in the world.
- Democracy is government by the people. (No attention being called to the word or its meaning; therefore, no underlining or quotation marks used.)

7. *Failing to indicate that you are using a foreign word.* When you use a foreign word (in etymological definition), *underline* it and put its English meaning in *quotation marks:*

- Marshal is derived from the Old High German *marah* "horse" and *scalh* "servant." or
- Marshal is derived from the Old High German *marah* ("horse") and *scalh* ("servant"). or
- Marshal is derived from the Old High German *marah* meaning "horse" and *scalh* meaning "servant."

Writing the Extended Definition

Length

The extended definition must obviously be longer than a sentence, but it can be as short as a paragraph or as long as an essay, in which case it would provide its basic structure.

Discovering Use for Extended Definition

1. Check your thesis sentence for an *outright statement* that says the following: that the understanding of a particular word or term is important for whatever reason the thesis gives. The following is an example of such a thesis: "The concept of 'wilderness' is being manipulated by environmentalists to serve their own tastes in recreation."

2. Check your thesis for its use of a word or term that is either unfamiliar or vital to the verification or explanation of the thesis. Whether the definition should be extended will depend on the term, the thesis, and your judgment. If the definition is required merely for the sake of basic comprehension, then a sentence definition may be enough; in fact, it may not even be possible to extend it. Say, for example, that your thesis is the following: "The 'wind shear' phenomenon is a factor that has been overlooked in the past in both the design of aircraft as well as in the explanation of airplane crashes." Obviously the reader needs a definition of *wind shear:* powerful changes of wind direction that can affect both horizontal and vertical air currents. But once you get that defined, you can probably go on to discuss "faulty" designs and "inadequate" accounts of previous plane crashes without referring to the definition again. On the other hand, say you had the following as a thesis: "Terrorism thrives today in less, not more, repressive societies because of what sociologists refer to as 'value-stretch' morality." Because *value-stretch morality* is sociological jargon and unfamiliar to most people, you define it as the "just-this-once approach." The definition is helpful but not enough. You need to say more; you need an extended definition.

3. Check your thesis for its use of a word or term that implies the need for a definition by virtue of the way the thesis is phrased. Such a definition will serve a key function in the essay. For example, look at the following thesis: "El Salvador has made little progress in human rights and reforms in the last two years." The key word in the thesis is "progress." You will not be able to verify your thesis without defining *progress.* And since the word is a familiar one, a simple sentence definition will not be enough.

4. Check back in your secondary sources for ideas, and use your imagination. Do not ignore familiar words that you may want to redefine for the purposes of the thesis or topic. The following thesis, for example, requires no immediate definition: "Fire was the most important tool in the management of the economy of the American Indian." However, since one of the uses of fire by the Indian was ceremonial, that is, ritualistic, an extended definition of *ritual* would be very enlightening.

Introducing the Extended Definition

Remember to provide a statement expressing the point of the extended definition. Generally, such a controlling idea is expressed in one of two ways:

1. *In the formal sentence definition itself, which can be used to unify the entire discussion:* "The workaholic is a person who, like the alcoholic from which the word is derived, uses his addiction as an avenue of escape."

2. *In a statement introducing the formal definition along with the other ideas in the discussion.* For example:

Introductory statement

Definition

America's response to her government's feeble call to honor the Vietnam veterans upon their return home fell pitifully short of the traditional meaning of the word honor. Instead of being "hailed," the veterans were detached from their fighting units, sent on a lonely airplane ride from Southeast Asia and set down again a day later in a California airport, often empty of anyone to meet them (frequently there wasn't even time to

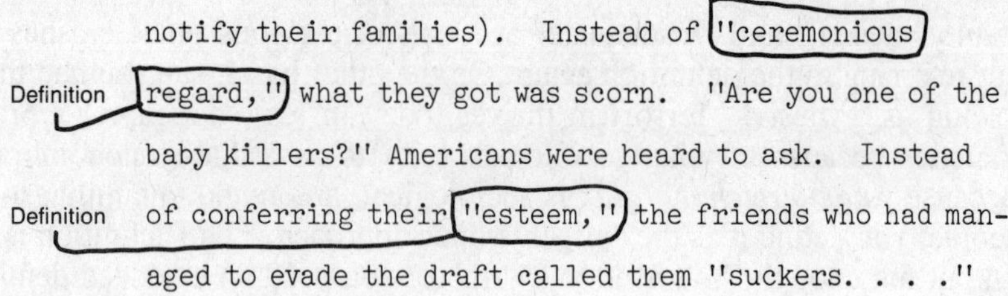

notify their families). Instead of "ceremonious regard," what they got was scorn. "Are you one of the baby killers?" Americans were heard to ask. Instead of conferring their "esteem," the friends who had managed to evade the draft called them "suckers. . . ."

EXERCISE 5

Which *one* of the following denotative definitions is set up correctly? What's wrong with the rest? Try to correct them based on the information given and your own general knowledge.

1. A computer chip is an electronic component.
2. A personality is a complex system of behavioral patterns such as actions, beliefs, habits, attitudes, and values.
3. Lethal means something that kills.
4. Organic gardening is gardening that uses organic fertilizers and pesticides.
5. Positive reinforcement means to motivate someone to do a certain action by giving him an immediate reward if he does it.

EXERCISE 6

The following are student attempts at etymological definitions. They begin well but then encounter problems. None "puts it all together" for the reader. As a result, the derivation seems superfluous; what's more, there's a gap between the derivation and the statement(s) that follows. Using the information provided and your imagination, supply the missing links. The first is provided as a model.

First version: An osprey is a large hawk. The word "osprey" is derived from the Latin *ossifraga,* which literally means "bone breaker." The osprey feeds on fish.

Revised version: An osprey is a large hawk. The word "osprey" is derived from the Latin *ossifraga,* which literally means "bone breaker." The bird is aptly named since it crushes the bones of the fish it feeds on.

1. The word *restaurant* comes from the Latin *restaurare* "to restore." There are many kinds of restaurants.
2. Vivisection, a term used to describe animal experiments, comes from the Latin words *vivus* "life" and *section,* which means "a cutting." Crucial to any argument over vivisection is the matter of pain.
3. The word "charm" is derived from the Latin *carmen* meaning "song" or "magical formula." Charming people make friends easily.

EXERCISE 7

Which *one* of the following definitions does not require underlining or quotation marks? Supply underlining and quotation marks for the ones that do.

1. The word love is overused.

2. Orangutan is a Malayan word that means man of the woods.
3. In politics the word crunch means a period of high pressure and tension.
4. Transhumance is the seasonal movement of herds of animals between lowland and mountain pastures.

EXERCISE 8

Both of the following are intended to be connotative definitions. One of them, however, contains an error in the part of speech used for the word(s) that follows the verb. Identify and correct.

1. To a dyslexic child dyslexia means failure marked by frustration and shame.
2. A nurse is kind, gentle, sympathetic, efficient, and competent.

EXERCISE 9

Which of the following paragraphs, both of which are intended to be extended definitions, contains a sentence(s) that defines its word and which does not? Underline the denotative definition(s) in the one that does and construct a denotative definition out of the information given in the one that doesn't.

1. A learning environment encompasses more than four walls, a desk, and a chair. Environment is everything (conditions, circumstances, and influences) that surrounds and affects that aspect of a child's development that is *not* controlled by heredity. Therefore, a learning environment is an atmosphere that fosters education.
2. The term *discipline* is not limited to punishment only. Children also need to be taught self-discipline and responsible behavior. They need help in learning how to face the challenge and obligations of living in their world. They must learn self-control and personal strength needed to meet the demands they will face in their schools and their friendships. Some people believe these characteristics cannot be taught, that children should be allowed to follow the least resistant path. These same people would advocate letting a child fail in school if he or she pleases, letting the bedroom look like a pigpen, or letting the pet go hungry.

WRITING ASSIGNMENT

Using Definition

Write an extended definition of at least one paragraph in length that discusses the meaning of some word or term that is crucial or, simply, relevant to your topic.

Before you begin, check the unabridged dictionary for a possibly useful etymology of the word. If the word you look up does not give a derivation, or the derivation is not particularly different from the current meaning of the word, and, therefore, not very revealing, don't give up immediately. First, follow any suggestions the dictionary might make, like "See *megrim*" (a cross-reference that the dictionary gives in its entry under *migraine,* for example). If this doesn't help, look up all the synonyms of the word; one of them might carry a derivation that you can use. You might then be able to replace the word you were planning to define with its synonym and instead use that as the word you define etymologically. Needless to say, even if you do find an etymological derivation for your word, you're not obligated to use it. The point of looking it up is simply to check out all the possibilities. Once you've done that, you can choose whatever alternative best serves your thesis.

After you've written your first draft of the extended definition, check it over for the following essentials: see that it has a sentence(s) that actually defines the word; and see that the rest of the passage is dependent on the definition for the discussion of its ideas. Test for the latter by removing the sentence that contains the definition. If the rest of the paragraph makes no sense without it, your definition is indeed extended and you have fulfilled the assignment.

Prose Models

CENTRAL PARK SQUIRRELS

Squirrels, found widely in the Old and New Worlds, constitute the 1
family Sciuridae. The species in Central Park is the eastern gray, whose range covers the entire eastern United States. The scientific name is *Sciurus carolinensis* as the species was first described from the Carolinas. The word "squirrel" itself comes from the Old French noun *esquireul,* created from the diminutive of the Vulgar Latin *scurius,* a distortion of formal Latin's *sciurus.* That, in turn, derived from the earlier Greek term *skiourous* (formed of the roots *skia,* shade, and *oura,* tail), the translation of which is "he who sits in the shadow of his tail."

The description, bestowed more than 2,000 years ago, especially 2
fits the eastern gray. Of all the quadrupeds inhabiting eastern North America, none has a tail so splendid, dramatic, and useful. The nine-inch plume is roughly half the body length of the adult, a measurement that varies from seventeen inches in the southern part of the range to twenty in the northerly. Much time is spent fluffing and grooming it, an indication of its importance, the owner being particularly careful to comb out all bits of foreign matter. One of the unhappiest squirrels I ever saw was sitting on a low limb of a tree near Summit Rock, the Park's highest point just in from Central Park at Eighty-third Street, trying with claws and teeth to remove some chewing gum that had become embedded in its tail.

The eastern gray depends on its tail for many vital functions. It 3
serves as a sunshade, a blanket in cold or stormy weather, a foil and a shield in the fierce fights that often develop between males in the mating season, a counterbalance to effect marvellously quick turns, an aquatic rudder on the rare occasions the animal takes to the water, an aerial rudder on its customary leaps from branch to branch, and, lastly, as a parachute to soften the impact of occasional falls.

On sunlit summer noons, it arches the tail over the head like a parasol; in the dead of winter, when squirrels do not hibernate (except briefly when the temperature drops so low that it threatens life, a situation which does not occur in Central Park), the tail is wrapped around the curled-up form in the nest like a comforter, preserving body heat. Males can be seen flicking it at their foes in mating skirmishes that interrupt their pursuit of females over the bare limbs of the park trees in late February or early March; sometimes, if the skirmish becomes a battle, the tail may be brought directly into the path of an oncoming bite. 4

Eugene Kinkead, *A Concrete Look at Nature: Central Park (and Other) Glimpses,* 1974

DISCUSSION QUESTIONS

1. Which sentence brings the etymological derivation to a point, that is, summarizes it?
2. At which point does Kinkead begin extending his definition? Is there an actual sentence that links the derivation with the rest of the passage? Identify it.
3. An extended definition is characterized by the fact that the formal definition is so integrated in the flow of ideas that it cannot be removed from the passage without damaging the latter's coherence or its point. How dependent are paragraphs 2 through 4 on the definition in paragraph 1? Explain by identifying the topic ideas in paragraphs 2 through 4 and point out their relationship to the formal definition.
4. What other rhetorical mode, already studied, is used in paragraph 2?

THE OFFICE OF YESTERDAY

So who invented this paragon? Depending upon how you choose to define the terms "invent" and "typewriter," the "typewriter" was "invented" by between 52 and 112 different people, working at different times and in different parts of the world. 1

If "invent" is defined as conception in the abstract, the "typewriter" was "invented" in 1714 by one Henry Mill, an Englishman to whom Queen Anne granted patent no. 395 for "an artificial machine or method for the impressing or transcribing of letters singly or progressively one after another, as in writing, whereby all writings whatsoever may be engrossed in paper or parchment so neat and exact as not to be distinguished from print." Though the language certainly describes a typewriter, there is no indication that Mill actually built his creation or even worked out its mechanical particulars. 2

If "invent" means to devise a contrivance that performs a function, the "typewriter" was "invented" by an Italian named Pelligrino Turri, 3 who apparently hand-built one for a blind ladyfriend to correspond with; her letters commencing in 1808 have been unearthed.

If "invent" means to mass-produce with intent to sell, then the "type- 4
writer" was "invented" by an American named John Jones, who in 1852 manufactured about 130 of his writing machines, all but a couple perishing when the factory burned down.

All manner of definitions have been advanced, their respective sup- 5
porters insisting that theirs is the proper definition of the "invention of the typewriter." Their accolades are bestowed with unwavering conviction upon Peter Mitterhofer, Giuseppe Ravizza, Xavier Progin, and hordes of others. Whether their efforts were applied to drawings, working models, or appliances that received actual use, the technical literature of the middle nineteenth century virtually crawled with Plume Kryptographiques and Mechanical Typographers and Mechanical Chirographers and Literary Pianos and Writing Harpsichords.

But if "invention" refers not only to concept, not only to production 6
of one or a few workable samples, but also to the continued evolution of a particular product over an extensive period, during which concerned personnel spin off their own variations that become the foundation of "an industry," then the "typewriter" was "invented" by Christopher Latham Sholes, a citizen of Milwaukee. It is he who is most widely accorded the title of "father of the typewriter." Yet even here, the definition is arbitrary or subjective to a degree. Sholes was inspired to sit down and "invent a typewriter" by articles he read in *Scientific American* about a device called the Pterotype, produced (and apparently sold in limited numbers) in England by an American named John Pratt. Sholes was a local politician and publisher by profession, but during the bloom of the Mechanical Age with its vast possibilities, he was by avocation an amateur inventor. Working with cronies in Kleinstuber's Machine Shop in Milwaukee, he began his writing-machine experiments in 1867. By 1873 he considered himself done, and yet the factory had to rework many of his invention's principles. In short, the Sholes device was a harbinger of another institution of the modern age: invention by committee.

Donald Sutherland, "The Office of Yesterday,"
The Wharton Magazine, Winter 1981–82

DISCUSSION QUESTIONS

1. How many definitions of "invent" does Sutherland give? Is "invent" the only word defined in paragraph 2? Why has he provided that many definitions of "invent"? Why only one of "typewriter"?
2. For which of the five reasons does Sutherland seem to define "invent"? Which of the three types does he use in each case?

3. Notice that paragraph 5 interrupts the pattern he's established by the end of paragraph 4. Paragraphs 2 and 3 begin with the phrase "If 'invent.' . . ." Do you approve of the interruption or would you prefer Sutherland to have reversed the order of paragraphs 5 and 6 so as not to disturb the pattern? In short, what does Sutherland gain in the way of clarity by repeating "If 'invent' "? What does he gain by interrupting it once?
4. Look at the first sentence of paragraph 6. How does it pull together the definitions given in paragraphs 2 through 4? What parts of the sentence summarize the preceding definitions? Which part points to the remainder of paragraph 6? Why didn't Sutherland introduce paragraph 6 with the same phrase he used in paragraphs 2, 3, and 4?
5. Notice that except for the definition in paragraph 2, sentence 1, the definitions in paragraphs 3, 4, and 6 are consistent with the guidelines given for using the same part of speech in the formal definition. Which verb does Sutherland use to define the verb "invent" and which nouns does he use for the definition of "invention" and "typewriter"? In which of these definitions does he take liberties with the rule? Any reason?
6. Why does the author keep placing "typewriter" and "invented" in quotation marks in paragraphs 2, 3, and 4?

TRIGGER CONTROL

Donna Brugnoli (Student)

The weapons effect is an unconscious aggressive reaction to the sight of a weapon. In other words, the weapon itself functions as a "conditioned stimulus," provoking violent behavior (Berkowitz, "Control" 12). People associate guns with violence and behave accordingly. Wanting to kill someone, getting a gun, and shooting isn't necessarily the "normal" sequence of events. In the case of "ordinary citizens," the following is the more likely sequence: having a gun, getting depressed, angry, or frustrated, then shooting. This kind of killing isn't planned; it's triggered by the gun; it's "impulsive" violence (Berkowitz, "Impulse" 19). Nor can the weapons effect be related to other instruments of aggression such as knives and axes, because these weapons have other uses. For example, the knife is primarily associated with food and the axe with such innocent outdoor activities as chopping trees. The link between the weapon and aggression is strongest when the weapon's only purpose is killing.

DISCUSSION QUESTIONS

The thesis of Brugnoli's research paper: The mere presence of a gun can have an aggressive effect on behavior because of a phenomenon called the "weapons effect."

1. Locate Brugnoli's definition.
2. Consider the way in which Brugnoli extends her definition. Does she refer back to key words or key concepts used in her formal definition? Where? Explain.
3. How is the definition of "weapons effect" related to the thesis? Is it an unfamiliar term? Vital term? Both?
4. Does the topic idea of her paragraph coincide with her definition? Or is there a separate controlling idea for the paragraph of which the definition is a part? Explain.
5. Without looking to see where Brugnoli inserts the extended definition, would you say that, given the thesis, it would come at the beginning, middle, or end? See page 250 for its actual location.

CALIFORNIA WINES ARE ALIVE AND WELL

Ned Hawkins (Student)

For the wine connoisseur, wine isn't simply a beverage. It's not like a bottle of Coke or a glass of Scotch on the rocks. It's not something to quench your thirst with after a football game or hold onto for hours at a cocktail party. It's certainly not something to get drunk on. It's the aristocrat of alcoholic beverages to be served in crystal goblets and golden chalices. Everything associated with it is regal. The vineyards that grow the wine have mansions and chateaus as their centerpieces. Their visitors include "heads of state, Hollywood celebrities, [and] corporate moguls" (Robards, "Premium Red" 54), who wouldn't think of visiting a Coca-Cola plant or the Scotch distilleries in Scotland. Notables like Prince Charles, Henry Kissinger, Gen. Douglas MacArthur, and ten American presidents, who wouldn't dream of phoning Seagram's for a case of whiskey, find it perfectly appropriate to call the Beaulieu Vineyard in California's Napa Valley, so the story goes, to order a Private Reserve Cabernet (Robards, "Premium Red" 54). Clearly, wine is in a class by itself.

DISCUSSION QUESTIONS

The thesis of Hawkins' research paper: The finest California wines are now challenging the finest French wines and sometimes winning.

1. Where does Hawkins state his formal sentence definition? How does he express it—etymologically, denotatively, or by synonym? Explain.
2. How are the first four sentences connected to the formal definition? In what sense are they also definitions? How are the sentences that follow the formal definition connected to it? What concept in the definition does the rest of the paragraph develop? In what sense is sentence 6 pivotal (linking everything that precedes it to everything that follows it)? What is the key word in sentence 6?
3. What keeps the last sentence from being a definition?
4. Do you think the thesis suggested an idea for a definition to Hawkins? Look at his research paper in Chapter 15. Observe paragraphs 1 through 4 on page 263. If the thesis didn't suggest an idea, as it probably didn't, do you think the grabber did? Explain.
5. Turn back to Hawkins' grabber in Chapter 8. Notice how his extended definition ended up changing the grabber's follow-up paragraph. Although the original follow-up paragraph sounded fine, notice that the change in it permitted Hawkins to work in his definition very smoothly.

11 Prewriting

Cause and Effect

Whenever you answer the question *why,* you're analyzing **cause**; if the question you're answering is *what happened when* or *what are the results of,* you're analyzing **effect**. Together the two processes constitute the rhetorical strategy called **causal analysis**. They can appear together but do not have to. An essay analyzing the effects that working mothers have had on family life does not automatically require that the writer also analyze the reasons why mothers have left the home and gone to work. The analysis may examine both, but it does not have to.

Causal analysis is so basic to human thinking that a child probably asks "why" before he asks anything else—and, what is more, usually follows every answer he gets with another question. "Why do I have to eat my spinach?" "Why do I have to be strong?" "Why do I have to grow up?" And so on to the chagrin of the parent. What's more, not only does he want to know why, he wants to know what happens if—if he pulls his sister's hair? if he catches a snowflake on his tongue? if he runs barefoot in the rain? Without being aware of it, the child wastes no time in asserting his humanness—his capacity to ponder the laws of his world—the why's and the what if's.

Yet causal analysis is perhaps the most sophisticated of intellectual strategies; it requires a careful observation of the world, reflection on it, and logical thinking. What makes causal analysis particularly demanding as an intellectual strategy is the fact that not all causal analyses deal with easily demonstrable facts or, at least, irrefutable ones. Only some do. For example, when the aviation industry traces the effects inflation and economic hard times have had on it, it has facts and figures to prove that (1) corporate jets were eliminated; (2) aircraft sales disrupted; (3) jobs cut back. But other causal analyses, either because they deal with essentially unverifiable facts or because they deal with human behavior, are speculative. Thus economists speculate on the causes of inflation and, unfortunately, can't agree among themselves on how to bring it down. Similarly, behavioral psychologists speculate on the various effects that using computers as a teaching device is going to have on a child's psychological development. All they can do is speculate, based on observation and common sense, because computers haven't been around long enough for them to be able to verify long-range effects. The validity of their answers will depend simply on how logical and how true to observable phenomena they are.

But verifiable or not, speculation about cause and effect is a valid intellectual enterprise through which humans seek to make sense of the world. And because the world is complex, so are the answers to the questions. Especially in the matter of human behavior. Since people were not born attached to a manual that explains how they operate, they have to analyze themselves. So you shouldn't be surprised to hear more than one explanation for any single phenomenon. In fact, you should anticipate more than one. Have you ever considered why people are squeamish at the sight of blood, for instance, especially a lot of it that isn't their own? Psychologists attribute it to the instinctive avoidance of emotional arousal that the sight of mutilation evokes; anthropologists attribute it to civilized people's fear of pollution that blood, along with vomit and excreta, represents; mythologists attribute it to a subconscious response to taboos on mutilation and death. Three different answers to the question why; all seemingly valid.

Immediate and Remote Causes and Effects

When you choose a topic for causal analysis, you should bear in mind that there are two types of causes and two types of effects: immediate and remote. An **immediate cause** immediately precedes an event making it happen; it's the obvious cause, the one that's immediately apparent. An **immediate effect** is the first thing to happen as a result of the event. Take the following example. Paul fails his Math 200 course. The immediate cause is his failing the final exam; an immediate effect is having to repeat the course.

But there are also remote causes and remote effects. A **remote cause** is the underlying reason for which an event took place, the underlying factor that explains the more apparent reason for the event having occurred. Similarly, a **remote effect** is a consequence that occurs down the line from the event. Taking Paul again as an example, the immediate cause for his failing the course may have been his failing the exam, but the remote cause might be any number of factors: he didn't study; he was involved in too many extracurricular activities; he had a part-time job. All these factors are the remote causes of his failing Math 200. There are also remote effects: having to spend more hours on homework; being pressured by his parents to give up some of his extracurricular activities and quit his part-time job.

As you can see, the immediate cause and effect of an event is usually the easiest to spot, and of all causes and effects, often the least important, interesting, or insightful. Paul could be accused of ignoring the problem if he never saw beyond the immediate reason for his F in math or the immediate effect of it. Therefore, when you're engaged in causal analysis, you're always obliged to get past the immediate reasons or results of something and examine their remote causes or effects. Sometimes that will mean digging even more deeply into the matter than we've done with Paul's failing the course. After all, there are causes and effects of his failure that are even more remote than the ones already described. Consider the unanswered questions that suggest further remote causes: Why didn't Paul fail his other courses? Why didn't some of his classmates who are also involved in extracurricular activities and hold part-time jobs fail the math exam? Why did Paul do so poorly on an exam for which he'd been given some of the questions a week ahead of time?

Remote Causes	**Remote Causes**	**Immediate Cause**	**Immediate Effect**
Poor study habits	Doesn't study	Fails exam	Repeats math
Misconceptions about college	Extracurricular activities		
	Part-time job		
Math–demanding course			

Consider also the questions that suggest even more remote effects than those mentioned above. What effect is hitting the books and quitting his job and maybe the tennis team going to have on his new friendships with his former teammates, his car (which he won't be able to afford any more), and his girl (who likes his car almost as much as she does him)? In short, an event as simple as failing a course may have very complex and far-ranging consequences.

Immediate Cause	**Immediate Effects**	**Remote Effects**	**Remote Effects**
Fails math	Repeats course	Does more homework	Loses touch with former friends
		Drops some activities	Sells car
		Quits part-time job	Loses girlfriend

EXERCISE 1

First, identify the causes and effects in the following statements; then identify those sentences that state only immediate causes or immediate effects rather than reaching beyond them for the remote causes or effects.

1. Teen pregnancies are caused by the failure to use contraceptives.
2. The United States found itself in an energy crisis because it was wasteful and because some of the energy sources had run dry.
3. Juveniles burglarize homes because they need money.

4. Fancy shoelaces designed with rainbows, hearts, and stars are a big sale item with kids because they want to dress up their sneakers and jogging shoes.

The Causal Chain

Sometimes a cause has an effect that turns out to be the cause of the next effect. Then you have a causal chain. The example of Paul above demonstrates such a chain.

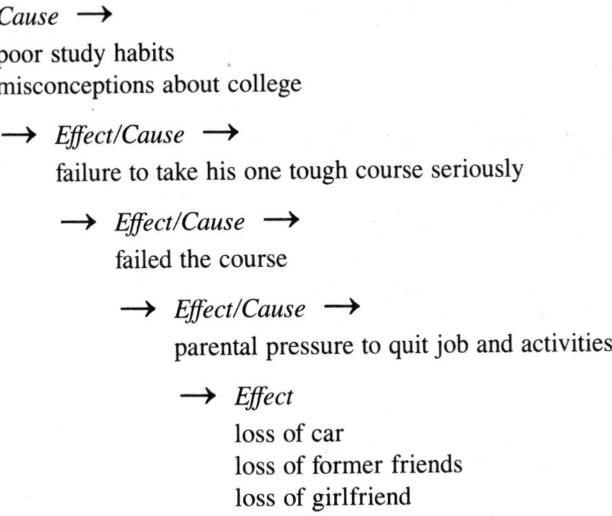

If your causal analysis involves tracing the causes and effects of an event chain-link style, remember that your analysis may begin and stop at any of the links. Where it begins and stops depends on the purpose of the analysis and your personal judgment.

Furthermore, as the diagram above shows, a cause can have more than one effect and an effect can stem from more than one cause. Cause and effect are complex phenomena, and it's the exception rather than the rule when one cause has only one effect and vice versa. In other words, be prepared to examine casuality in some depth.

Main and Contributory Causes

Another way of labeling causes besides immediate and remote is main and contributory. Both main and contributory causes are responsible for causing the event, but a **main cause** is a primary factor without which the event could not have happened, while **contributory causes** are the additional factors that bolster the main cause but by themselves are not enough to cause the event.

For example, the cause of any heart attack is a blood clot in one of the coronary arteries. But there are usually one or more contributing factors to heart attacks, such as obesity, smoking, and overexertion.

Contributing Causes	Main Cause	Effect
Obesity	Blood clot	Heart attack
Excessive smoking		
Overexertion		

However, don't confuse main and contributory causes with immediate and remote causes. The two categories are two distinctly different ways of looking at causes. A contributory cause cannot bring about the effect (it isn't the three packs of cigarettes a day or the ten-mile jog that causes the heart attack), nor does a contributory cause bring about the main cause (a blood clot is *not* caused by obesity or smoking or overexertion). On the other hand, a remote cause can bring about the immediate cause, as you can see in the example below, and can be considered to cause the effect.

Remote Causes	Main Cause	Effect
Elevated cholesterol	Blood clot	Heart attack
Hardening of arteries		
Diabetes		

What's more, there are two reasons for stressing the differences between the two sets of labels. Immediate causes are being distinguished from remote ones in this discussion to get you to see that remote – not immediate – causes are the ones that deserve your attention. However, the purpose of distinguishing between main and contributory is to keep you from always giving equal weight and emphasis to all causes.

EXERCISE 2

Identify what you would regard as the main and contributory causes in the following statements.

1. Flight 139 out of Kennedy Airport crashed because of bad weather conditions and pilot error.
2. Some parents push young children into competitive sports because they believe competitive games are good for their children's social development and physical coordination and because they get a vicarious pleasure out of their children's successes.

3. Cults are able to exert a great deal of power over adolescents because they have effective brainwashing techniques and because the adolescents that join cults are lonely and looking for meaning.
4. Habitat destruction through lumbering and mining operations and the introduction of shotguns pose major threats to the wild birds of paradise in Papua, New Guinea.

Common Faults of Causal Reasoning

1. *Mistaking coincidence for cause.* Do not assume that just because two events happened in a sequence, the first caused the second. The fact that it rains every time you wash the car does not mean a car wash causes rain any more than wearing socks inside out causes a home run.

2. *Oversimplifying.* Do not look only at immediate causes and effects. Do not attribute only one cause or effect when there is obviously more than one. If you were to attribute the grass-roots antinuclear movement to nothing but communist agitation you'd be ignoring the complexity of the issue and fail to give your reader the complete picture. It is perfectly appropriate to run through a number of causes (or effects) quickly just to show that you are not oversimplifying the matter and that you are familiar with the territory. Then stop at one of the causes (or effects) for a thorough analysis if your subject requires that kind of concentration on a single cause (or effect). For example, let's say that you are writing on the causes of the hardships during the Great Depression, but you do not want to discuss all of them; in fact, there's really just one that is *apropos* of your thesis. You might, therefore, handle it this way:

Several factors contributed to the poor's inability to raise themselves out of their poverty during the Great Depression: high unemployment; strain in the normal channels of relief caused by several short-lived financial panics on top of a major depression; the government's refusal to give assistance in the form of cash; inadequate immigration laws to deal with soaring numbers of immigrants in the 1930s. But equally damaging was a factor that is only now being recognized as an important reason for the crippling hardships that some of the poor endured needlessly: namely, society's failure to understand the poor and their circumstances. Poverty was seen as a result of some sort of personal failure; as a result, unfair laws were designed to discriminate between the "worthy" poor and the "unworthy" poor. The discussion that follows will concentrate on these psychological and political factors rather than the economic ones.

3. *Overstating your case.* Do not make assertions that sound like absolute statements of incontestable fact when you're only speculating. The following statement, for example, is simply too strong: "The effects of television viewing are negative." Yes, some effects of some programs on some people. But TV has also had some good effects: brought the world to shut-ins, provided cheap entertainment, eliminated provincial attitudes by exposing viewers to great varieties of issues and people; taken the glamor out of war by bringing it into people's living rooms on the six o'clock news, and so on. To keep from overstating your case, use qualifiers (words that modify or tone down other words). The assertion above would sound less overstated if you limited the sweeping statement with one or several of the following modifiers: "*Some* of the effects" or "*Excessive* television viewing" or "*Certain* types of programs" or "*can* have negative influences" or "on *children and adolescents.*"

EXERCISE 3

Which of the faults in causal reasoning can you identify in the following statements? Which of the statements are free of errors?

1. The Olympic Games cause friction rather than harmony between countries.
2. Because John didn't eat his breakfast, he did poorly on his history quiz.
3. The reason for the internment of Japanese-Americans in camps during World War II was U.S. fear that they might be enemy agents.
4. Karen has a good figure because she drinks Pepsi.

Writing Cause and Effect

Length

Some causal analyses are very informal and no more than a sentence in length like the one written by Paul Blumberg in "Snarling Cars": "Japanese companies are selling cars in this country primarily because they have the product, and they have the product because they've had long experience making it. American companies don't." Others can be a paragraph or longer. Finally, there are those in which the causal analysis constitutes the entire essay, as you can see by the title of Carollyn James' article in *Science 83:* "Why Do Warts Disappear?"

Discovering Use for Cause and Effect

1. *Check your thesis sentence for an* outright statement *of cause and effect.* Here's an example of a thesis that expresses causality: "The main cause of urban suicide is the alienation and lack of communication brought on by urban living conditions." Given a thesis like that, the possibility—in fact, necessity—for a causal analysis is obvious.

2. *Check your thesis for causality that is not actually expressed but implied by the way that the thesis is phrased.* The following is an example: "The only two times that the film industry has portrayed nurse characters realistically and sympathetically as professionals rather than as sexual mascots of the health care world were in the thirties during the Great Depression and recently in the eighties." No cause-and-effect relationship is expressed here. But consider this: How could this particular essay discuss the two different portrayals of nurses without speculating on the *reasons* for the difference in portrayal? Is it only coincidence that economic hard times bring on more realistic and sympathetic portrayals of nurses? Is there a connection? The thesis implicitly raises a question, and the writer is obligated to pursue it or risk superficial treatment of the subject.

3. *Check your topic for the possibilities of using cause and effect as* background information. For example: "Skyscrapers are not an efficient use of natural resources." The thesis neither expresses nor implies causal analysis. Yet a student researching the topic would enhance the essay a great deal by explaining, by way of background, for example, what led to the building of increasingly higher vertical structures.

4. *Check back in your secondary sources for ideas.* If your thesis argues, for example, that gorillas are the gentlest of primates, including man, then a look through your sources might reveal studies that had been done of gorillas in zoos and the negative effect of a caged environment on their behavior.

Introducing Cause and Effect

Remember to introduce your causal analysis with a statement of cause or effect. Tell your reader what you're about to discuss: causes or effects and, if possible, what causes or what effects. If there are too many to list, then summarize or generalize.

If the statement of cause or effect is the thesis, avoid flat assertion like "The Mt. St. Helens eruption had many effects." Notice how thesis statements A and B below improve as the student gets increasingly more specific; and notice how the last example in B also tells the reader which effects are more and which are less important.

Thesis A `People become dentists rather than doctors for various reasons.`

People become dentists rather than doctors for various pragmatic and artistic reasons.

Thesis B The Mt. St. Helens eruption had many effects.

The Mt. St. Helens eruption produced short-term as well as long-term effects.

Although the Mt. St. Helens eruption produced some devastating and costly short-term effects, it's the long-term effects that will do the most harm.

Although the Mt. St. Helens eruption produced some devastating and costly short-term effects on lakes, soil texture, landscape, and the lumber industry, it's the possible climactic changes that will have the most long-lasting and harmful effect.

Organizing Cause and Effect

1. If you're discussing a causal chain, you would obviously discuss causes and effects in the order of causation—from the least to the most recent.

2. If you're dividing your causes into main and contributory you would discuss the main cause first and then the contributory or vice versa (depending on what makes more sense given your thesis).

3. If you simply have a list of causes (or effects), discuss them in the order of increasing importance (from the least to the most important) or increasing interest, decreasing familiarity, and so on. The general rule is to build up to a climactic effect.

Finding Location for Cause and Effect

1. If cause or effect is expressed in your thesis, it is crucial to your essay. Its discussion constitutes the explanation and verification of your thesis. Therefore, the essay must either (1) be organized by it or (2) emphasize it. In the first case, the entire essay will be organized by causal analysis; in the second, causal analysis should be saved for last since the key location is the end of the paper—the last two, three, four, whatever, pages.

2. If cause or effect is not expressed in the thesis but constitutes ideas necessary for establishing a background for your thesis, place it toward the beginning of the essay, where you can cover it, dismiss it, and move on to more important matters.

3. If cause or effect is not expressed in the thesis and can't be considered background, use the causal mode to organize some localized section of your paper.

EXERCISE 4

Which of the following statements need rewriting to make them more specific and more interesting as thesis statements?

1. There are various causes of juvenile diabetes.
2. The two factors that are changing the appearance of zoos are layout and purpose.
3. One of the reasons that English has become the dominant language in the world is the fact that it is the language of rock music and pop culture, which reaches every corner of the globe.
4. Advertising has a profound effect on shoppers.
5. The effect of free legal aid for the poor has been the overburdening of lawyers and the inadequate representation of clients.

EXERCISE 5

The causes and effects listed in the following thesis statements are arranged in no particular order. Rearrange them in each statement according to some principle: increasing importance or least to most dramatic, and so on.

1. The effect of the polar explorer Robert Peary's brutal treatment of his sled dogs was that some died, some went mad, and some got sick.
2. There are three factors that combine to make Willow Wood Park the most popular park in the area: the diversity of its vegetation and wildlife, its size, and its undeveloped state.
3. Torrential downpours and very high tides destroyed several bridges, washed away beachfront houses, killed dozens of people, and caused mudslides and flash floods.
4. A sharp cut in the price of crude oil would choke off further oil exploration, all but kill off the synthetic-fuels industry, unnerve the oil industry, and weaken the domestic coal and nuclear power industries.

EXERCISE 6

The following thesis statements have been drawn from various student research papers. (a) Which of the statements express a causal analysis? (b) Which imply a causal analysis?

1. The Jonestown massacre was preventable.
2. Contrary to popular belief, Napoleon did not die of natural causes but was murdered on the island of St. Helena.
3. Industrial diamonds are more valuable than gem diamonds.
4. The public attitude to Prohibition changed from the time it began in 1919 to the time it ended in 1933.

WRITING ASSIGNMENT

Using Cause and Effect

Write a solid paragraph or more developing a cause–effect relationship that is in some way relevant to your research paper thesis or your overall topic.

If you have a thesis that expresses a causal relationship, you are not expected at this point to write the entire essay. In that case, do the following in fulfillment of the assignment:

1. Submit the thesis statement.
2. Submit the topic sentences that name each cause or effect.
3. Develop *one* of the topic sentences.

Here's an example of how to do the assignment should you have the sort of thesis that explicitly states a causal relationship.

Thesis — Censorship groups have been successful in banning books from schools because (1) they're organized while (2) the school systems aren't and because (3) censorship laws are vague.

Topic Sentence 1 — Censorship groups have a strong organization for distributing propaganda.

Topic Sentence 2 — Schools do not have formal channels for complaints about books.

Topic Sentence 3 — The law is not explicit about the legality of banning books.

You would then go on to develop, say, topic sentence 3 in a paragraph or more.

Prose Models

THE GAY BAR

Occasionally, "fruit flies," i.e., women who like to associate with male homosexuals, are found in gay bars, although they are not a very prominent part of any gay bar scene. Why a woman who is not a lesbian would like to associate with male homosexuals is a question which cannot be altogether answered in general, except to say that some of these women obviously find homosexual men a lot less threatening than heterosexual men, since the former are not interested in them sexually. Since these women are not potential sexual partners for the males, they are not potential sources of rejection for them either, and thereby they find themselves the subject of much attention by the male clientele. Consequently, they are the beneficiaries of a great deal of sociability without being objects of seduction. Some women find this a very appealing position.

Martin Hoffman, *The Gay World* (New York: Basic Books, 1968)

DISCUSSION QUESTIONS

1. What cause or effect is Hoffman analyzing?
2. Is he dealing with a causal chain? What causes and effects are involved? Explain.
3. What signal words does Hoffman use to show cause and effect?

WHAT TV DOES TO KIDS

Even more worrisome is what television has done to, rather than denied, the tube-weaned population. A series of studies has shown that addiction to TV stifles creative imagination. For example, a University of Southern California research team exposed 250 elementary students —who had been judged mentally gifted—to three weeks of intensive viewing. Tests conducted before and after the experiment found a marked drop in all forms of creative abilities except verbal skill. Some teachers are encountering children who cannot understand a simple story without visual illustrations. "TV has taken away the child's ability to form pictures in his mind," says child-development expert Dorothy Cohen at New York City's Bank Street College of Education. 1

Parenthetically, nursery-school teachers who have observed the pre-TV generation contend that juvenile play is far less imaginative and spontaneous than in the past. The vidkids' toys come with built-in fantasies while their playground games have been programed by last night's shows. "You don't see kids making their own toys out of crummy things like we used to," says University of Virginia psychology professor Stephen Worchel, who is the father of a 6-year-old. "You don't see them playing hopscotch, or making up their own games. Everything is suggested to them by television." 2

Too much TV too early also instills an attitude of spectatorship, a withdrawal from direct involvement in real-life experiences. "What television basically teaches children is passivity," says Stanford University 3 researcher Paul Kaufman. "It creates the illusion of having been somewhere and done something and seen something, when in fact you've been sitting at home," New York Times writer Joyce Maynard, 23, a perceptive member of the first TV generation, concludes: "We grew up to be observers, not participants, to respond to action, not initiate it."

Conditioned to see all problems resolved in 30 or 60 minutes, the offspring of TV exhibit a low tolerance for the frustration of learning. Elementary-school educators complain that their charges are quickly turned off by any activity that promises less than instant gratification. "You introduce a new skill, and right away, if it looks hard, they dissolve into tears," laments Maryland first-grade teacher Eleanor Berman. "They want everything to be easy—like watching the tube." Even such acclaimed educational series as "Sesame Street," "The Electric Company" and "Zoom" have had some dubious effects. Because such shows sugar-coat their lessons with flashy showbiz techniques, they are forcing real-life instructors into the role of entertainers in order to hold their pupils' attention. "I can't turn my body into shapes or flashlights," sighs a Connecticut teacher. "Kids today are accustomed to learning through gimmicks." 4

For the majority of American children, television has become the principal socializing agent. It shapes their view of what the world is like and what roles they should play in it. As the University of Pennsylvania's Gerbner puts it: "The socialization of children has largely been transferred from the home and school to TV programmers who are unelected, unnamed and unknown, and who are not subject to collective—not to mention democratic—review." 5

What does TV's most impressionable constituency learn from prime-time entertainment? No one can really be sure, but psychologists like Robert Liebert of the State University of New York, one of the most respected observers of child behavior, don't hesitate to express sweeping indictments. "It teaches them that might makes right," Liebert says flatly. "The lesson of most TV series is that the rich, the powerful and the conniving are the most successful." 6

Harry F. Waters, "What TV Does to Kids,"
Newsweek, February 21, 1977

DISCUSSION QUESTIONS

1. How many effects does Waters discuss? What are they?
2. How does he paragraph them? One or more than one per paragraph? Explain.
3. How does Waters discuss each effect? That is, what does he use to explain or corroborate it?
4. Identify the thesis sentence for the entire passage. Identify the sentences that

introduce each individual effect. What pattern do you find regarding the location of the topic sentences? Can you see a reason for Waters' interrupting the pattern in the last paragraph? Is the last paragraph a discussion of a new effect or the continuation of a previous discussion? Explain.
5. Can you detect any principle by which Waters arranges the effects?

TRIGGER CONTROL

Donna Brugnoli (Student)

The main reason that a gun acts as such a powerful stimulant to violence is the ease with which a gun can be used as opposed to any other weapon. It takes less effort to use a gun than a knife on a person. Using a knife involves muscle, force, and physical contact with the victim. It requires confronting the victim in person and, therefore, risking counterattack, since the victim isn't guaranteed to stand still if he can help it. A gun, on the other hand, can be fired from a distance; by making the killer "invisible," it protects him from any counterviolence by the victim. One quick, light pull of the trigger and the damage is done. 1

The same restraining principle that applies to the knife also applies to any other object that can be used as a weapon, such as a club or even bare fists. The aggressor cannot detach himself from his actions. He has to make bodily, auditory, and eye contact with the victim. As he approaches the victim, he has time for second thoughts. A gun is impersonal. It can shoot its victim as mechanically as it would an object on a practice range. The offender does not have to see, hear, or feel the victim's suffering; he can sever himself totally after pulling the trigger. In fact, he may even feel that it wasn't he that has killed, but the bullet. 2

DISCUSSION QUESTIONS

The thesis of Brugnoli's research paper: The mere presence of a gun can have an aggressive effect on behavior because of a phenomenon called "the weapons effect."

1. What cause or effect is Brugnoli analyzing?
2. How is her causal analysis related to the thesis? Is it stated in the thesis? Implied? Explain.

3. Which sentence introduces the causal analysis? What is the key word in the sentence which the rest of the paragraph concentrates on explaining?
4. Brugnoli has incorporated the passage into her research paper on page 251. Why is the passage fairly close to the beginning? In other words, explain her reason for putting it there rather than at the very end.

CALIFORNIA WINES ARE ALIVE AND WELL

Ned Hawkins (Student)

There are two reasons for the wine mystique: its history and the skill and knowledge (even love) that it takes to make it. Alec Waugh points out that archaeologists have determined that making wine from grapes goes back 10,000 years, and that historians have learned from Middle Eastern writings that Sennacherib and Nebuchadnezzar were drinking wine from their own vineyards some 2000 years before Christ (Waugh 39). In the popular imagination wine is associated with aristocratic wine drinkers who live in moated castles, own hereditary wine cellars, and serve wine after first dusting it of cobwebs. It is also associated with wine festivals in which sultry Italian girls crush grapes with their bare feet to the rhythms of the tarantella. 1

But it is not only the ancient and colorful history of wine that gives it a special aura. It's also the artistry it takes to create it. Even today when nobody uses their feet to crush grapes anymore (Waugh 37) and modern technology has introduced temperature-controlled stainless steel storage tanks and mechanical harvesters (Langway 59), winegrowing in most places is still a craft that involves an artisan. It is still "a matter of judgment, not only as to the time when the grapes should be harvested, but as to how long the wine should ferment, how long it should stay in the barrel, how it should be treated if it gets sick, when it should be bottled" (Lichine and Massee 10). If a cellar-master begins the harvest even a day too late, for example, the sugar-acid relationship will be out of balance in the wine (Lichine and Massee 49). A 2 good example of just how important a role the winegrower plays is Clos de Vougeot, a vineyard in Burgundy, France, "where fifty owners divide forty acres, to produce an astonishing range of character and quality in wines called Clos de Vougeot" (Thompson and Johnson 165). No two winemakers end up producing identical wines; each wine is stamped with the personality of the winemaker (Thompson and Johnson 166).

DISCUSSION QUESTIONS

The thesis of Hawkins' research paper: The finest California wines are now challenging the finest French wines and sometimes winning.

1. What is the cause or effect that is being discussed by Hawkins? Which sentence introduces the causal analysis? Why is "even love" in parentheses? Why doesn't he discuss love? Why then mention it?
2. How does Hawkins paragraph his causal analysis? Along the lines of the ideas in his first sentence? Explain. Which sentence(s) connects the discussion in paragraph 2 to the discussion in paragraph 1?
3. Do you think Hawkins got his idea for a causal analysis from his thesis? Is it implied in it? Is he using causal analysis as background? Without having read his research paper yet, explain (as you see it) the relationship the causal analysis has with the rest of the essay.
4. Turn to Hawkins' research paper and the incorporation of this passage on page 264. Notice how close it is to the beginning of the essay. Why does he want to get the discussion of the wine mystique out of the way before going on to discuss the contest between California and French wines?
5. Turn to pages 266 and 268–270 for additional causal analyses found in the essay. Identify them.

12 Prewriting

Comparison and Contrast

Comparison shows the similarities between things or ideas; **contrast** shows the differences. (However, the term "comparison" is often used in the general sense to include both techniques.)

The inclination to compare is everywhere; in living rooms where television viewers compare their coffees with Maxwell's; on college campuses where freshmen compare their current feelings of alienation with the self-esteem and security they felt as high school seniors; at a dying man's bedside in Evelyn Waugh's *Brideshead Revisited* where a doctor compares fearing death to not having the will to live.

Comparison is frequently used as a strategy for shedding light on the unfamiliar in terms of the familiar. To someone who has never heard of a rutabaga, much less eaten one, you say it's "like a turnip." To all those friends back home who'd like to know what college is like, you say it's nothing like high school–more freedom and more work. A researcher introducing the techniques of laser surgery for the first time to a team of surgeons describes the advantages of a laser beam by comparing it to a scalpel.

What is more, comparison is an immensely effective strategy for making discoveries about things or ideas that otherwise would be less apparent. You've undoubtedly noticed, to give an example, how difficult it is sometimes to tell navy blue from black–except by setting the colored objects side by side. The effect of throwing one thing into sharp relief against another is to spotlight instantly those features that make the two things unique (as well, of course, as those that make them alike). The results are bound to be revealing. Thus consider the insights, for example, that would be possible as a consequence of comparing marijuana with alcohol; or comparing the recession of the eighties with the Great Depression of the thirties; or comparing America's military involvement in the Caribbean with its military involvement in Vietnam.

Comparison and Contrast as a Joint Operation

Comparison and contrast are separate strategies, but each implies existence of the other. They operate together for reasons that may not be immediately obvious but make perfect sense if you just think about them. The sorts of things you are usually inclined to compare and contrast are *never* so completely different as to have nothing in common *nor* so alike as to be identical. Logical comparison and contrast show the similarities and differences between two or more things of a *kind:* two parties, two wars, two coffees, not window shades and Mack trucks nor two exactly identical Paper-Mate ballpoint pens. (There is another special form of comparison, called analogy, that shows the similarities between two things not of a kind; but it is used for very different purposes than the logical comparison and will not be discussed here.)

There's no sense in contrasting the obviously different that have nothing in common nor in comparing the obviously similar and indistinguishable. Therefore, when you compare and contrast two things that belong to the same class, there will always be facts/qualities that they have in common—just because they belong to the same class—and there will always be facts/qualities that make them different—just because they are not identical: horns and antlers; internment and imprisonment; knowledge and intelligence.

When you're writing a comparison, therefore, you will always be doing *one* of the following:

1. Discussing similarities and differences equally (thus saying to your reader, "A and B have a lot in common, but they're also different" or vice versa).
2. Taking similarities for granted or skipping over them quickly and zeroing in on the differences (thus saying to your reader, "you've probably always thought that A and B are similar; well, let me tell you, they're not") or vice versa.

In other words, a comparison does not require that you give equal weight to the similarities and differences, even though both are always implied. It all depends on what you're trying to say and how much your audience already knows. For example, if you were planning to contrast mopeds and motorcycles and your reader was the average American, you would not have to belabor the similarities. Or you might just give the similarities a sentence or two before focusing on the differences. For example:

```
Mopeds and motorcycles may both be motor bikes that consume a lot less
fuel than a car.  But the similarities end there.  Mopeds are dif-
ferent from. . . .
```

On the other hand, if the similarities or differences aren't obvious or if they're particularly important, they should not be dismissed in a clause or a sentence but explained before you go on to do the reverse. For instance, if you were planning to compare two of your teachers, you would have to give some similarities as well as differences since the reader is unlikely to be familiar with either one of the instructors. For example, you would have to establish the fact that both are teachers, perhaps of the same subject and equally knowledgeable and effective; and only then would you go on to show the differences in their teaching styles.

EXERCISE 1

Look at the following sets of subjects and indicate what similarities and/or differences you would discuss and how much weight you would give each.

1. Resident and commuting student
2. Airplane and bird
3. Knowledge and intelligence
4. Prison and jail
5. Calvin Kleins and Levis
6. Private and public schools
7. Private parochial schools and private Christian academies

Informational and Judgmental Comparisons

The first, and most important, rule to remember when you write a comparison is *never* simply to list similarities and differences. Lists are for grocery shopping not essays. That was the mistake of the student who wrote the following comparison of soccer and football.

On the regulation soccer team there are eleven players whose uniforms consist of jerseys, shorts, knee-length stockings, shin guards, and light cleated shoes. On a regulation football team there are eleven players whose uniforms consist of helmets, shoulder pads, waist pads, leg pads, knee pads, jerseys, knee-length pants, regular socks, and either spike-soled shoes or sneakers, depending on the type of playing surface. Soccer games are played on rectangular fields of natural grass or artificial turf, of which the dimensions range from 100 to 120 yards in length by 55 to 75 yards in width. Football games are played on rectangular fields of natural grass or artificial turf, of

```
which the regulation dimensions are 100 yards from goal line to goal

line and. . . .
```

Not only is the passage dull, it's pointless. You read and shrug, "so what?"

A paragraph or an essay developed by means of comparison and contrast is subject to the same regulations as any other kind of paragraph or essay: It must have a point. It must have a thesis sentence or controlling idea that explains *why* the writer has taken the pains to distinguish A from B or insist that A and B are alike.

Generally speaking, therefore, your comparison must be either informational or judgmental.

Informational comparisons supply significant information for a significant reason. In other words, do not bore your reader with the obvious: that winter is cold and summer is hot. Instead inform the reader of similarities and/or differences he or she might be unaware of, have overlooked, or be confused about: for example, between workaholics and "prisoners of success"; unexplored caverns and tourist caverns; the old cut-rate Laker Airways and the new cut-rate People Express Airlines.

Furthermore, make it clear that that is what you're doing. For example, you would not begin with the flat and dull assertion that "charge cards are different from credit cards" and then go on to show the differences; instead you would begin by pointing out perhaps that people mistakenly assume, to their later regret, that the two are synonymous, when, in fact, they differ in the kinds of terms and expenses they impose on a borrower. In other words, establish a kind of platform for your comparison, introduce it, get an angle on it, give the reader a reason for it. Here's another example. A writer wanting to discuss the similarities between basketball and ballet, for example, would begin by admitting that the comparison seems improbable on the surface and that basketball fans no less than balletomanes would doubtless be outraged by the claim that one activity is anything like the other. Only after having staged the comparison in this way would the writer present the discussion of the similarities: the comparable demands each makes on physical endurance, the fluid and graceful movements of each, and so on.

In other words, an informational comparison points out the fact that A is like B and/or different from B; but it always does so for reasons that the writer presents as being significant and interesting.

Judgmental comparisons evaluate or pass judgment on the things that are being contrasted. (The emphasis is always on differences.) Furthermore, because one thing is being judged relative to the other, the emphasis is always on one of the subjects rather than on both. Such a contrast either states or implies an adjective(s) or adverb(s) in the comparative degree: bigger, better, more difficult, less difficult, more versatile, less versatile, more painfully, less painfully, and so on. For example, oil is easier to paint with than water color (emphasis on oil); winter mountaineering is a more dangerous sport than summer mountaineering (emphasis on winter); the ninth international economic summit conference was less productive than preceding ones (emphasis on ninth).

EXERCISE 2

Look at the following sets of subjects and provide each with two separate and interesting statements: one introducing an informational comparison; another introducing a judgmental comparison:

1. Resident and commuting student
2. Knowledge and intelligence
3. Internment and imprisonment
4. Calvin Kleins and Levis
5. Water skiing and snow skiing
6. Home-grown vegetables and store-bought ones
7. Soccer and football

Terminology

Because comparing and contrasting require particular discipline to keep the alternating patterns straight, it is the richest of the five strategies in words that are used to signal the writer's intentions. They are not always essential to use; they can be omitted when the writing is lucid and the patterns are clear without them. But they're always helpful and should be learned. The following terms signal the fact that a *similarity* is about to follow: both, like, also, too, similarly. The following signal a *difference:* but, however, unlike, by contrast, on the other hand, whereas, while.

Two words of caution, however. Say, you find yourself making a long series of observations about similarities: "Religion has its disciples and heretics; psychoanalysis also has its disciples and heretics. Religion has a dogma that stresses original sin; psychoanalysis, too, has a dogma that stresses an original 'sin.' Religion believes in the possibility of redemption; psychoanalysis also believes in the possibility of redemption. Religion proposes the salutary effect of confession; similarly, psychoanalysis proposes the salutary effects of confessional analysis." While such a discussion of similarities is admirably systematic, it is also repetitive and mechanical. To relieve the monotony, consider dealing with religion and psychoanalysis together in one of two ways. Either use the word "both": "Both religion and psychoanalysis have a dogma that stresses original sin; both believe in the possibility of redemption," and so on. Or follow Peter S. Prescott's approach, which is to list the similarities and introduce the list with a sentence: "If psychoanalysis is a religion uniquely suited to the 20th century, it shares with its sister faiths in the West numerous indispensable elements: disciples, heretics and an early history of persecution; a dogma that stresses original sin, the possibility of redemption and the salutary effect of confession . . ." ("Restoring Freud," *Newsweek,* January 10, 1983).

The second word of caution: the signal words "whereas" and "while" are, grammatically speaking, subordinating conjunctions (words used to connect sentence parts of unequal rank). Therefore, a "sentence" that begins with either word is not actually a complete sentence and cannot stand by itself. For example, the following clause is grammatically incomplete: "Whereas video games stimulate activity." It can be corrected in one of two ways: (1) either attach the clause to the preceding sentence ("Television encourages passive enjoyment, *whereas video games stimulate activity*"); or (2) substitute "on the other hand" for "whereas" ("Television encourages passive enjoyment. *On the other hand, video games stimulate activity*").

EXERCISE 3

Supply the appropriate signal words in the following sentences.

1. ________________ ordinary blue cheese, Roquefort is made with ewe's milk not cow's, and, therefore, has a juicier texture.
2. Knowledge is information, ________________ intelligence is the ability to judge and synthesize it.
3. Gas engines have literally hundreds of moving parts that are subject to wear and tear. Electric motors, ________________, have only one part that moves, thus reducing the cost of repairs due to excessive wear.
4. Randle "Tex" Cobb wins fights by leaning on his opponents and by constantly giving chase. Because he can withstand extraordinary punishment without going down, he takes advantage of his foe's fatigue and is able to score heavily with his own punches, which lead to knockouts and wins. ________________, Alexis Arguello brings skill to the role of challenger. He is quick, the classic "stand-up" craftsman. His lightning movements make him hard to hit, and few can parry his punches.
5. Downhill skiing requires a certain outlay of money for clothes and equipment. ________________, cross-country involves spending money on special clothing as well as skis and poles. ________________ the overall expenses are considerably less in cross-country than in downhill.

Writing Comparison and Contrast

Length

Informal comparisons can be very brief, as you can see in Roger Rosenblatt's statement: "The difference between us and any machine we create is that a machine is an answer, and we are a question." However, a formal, logical, and full-scale comparison, such as you will be writing, must be, at least, a solid paragraph in length. Furthermore, like most of the other strategies, it can go the full length of an essay.

Discovering Use for Comparison

1. *Check your thesis sentence for an* outright statement *of comparison or contrast.* For example: "The ancient world had an entirely different attitude toward work than did the Middle Ages."

2. *Check your thesis for comparison or contrast that is not actually expressed but implied because of the way the thesis is phrased.* Say your thesis is the following: "Bright colors and elaborate costuming are staging a comeback in men's fashions in the West." While your thesis makes no explicit reference either to similarities or differences, it's obvious that you must be thinking in terms of both. What you obviously have in mind are similarities between the flashy contemporary trends and those that were evident several hundred years ago, which had men wearing ruffles and satin breeches. But you're also thinking in terms of differences between the same recent flashy trends and the neutral colors and conservative styles of the fifties and sixties. Therefore, if you're going to talk of a "comeback," you will have to discuss the differences between the current fashion trends and those preceding it as well as the similarities between the current trends and those of, say, the Baroque period.

3. *Check your topic for the possibility of using comparison and contrast as* background. For example, the following thesis does not point to such a comparison: "Lobsters are expensive for a reason." Nevertheless, with a little imagination, you can easily see that there are actually two ways of corroborating and explaining your thesis: First, there is the obvious way, by discussing what it is that drives up the price of lobster; and, second, by comparing the growth and harvesting of an expensive seafood like lobster to that of a relatively inexpensive one like haddock.

4. *Check back in your secondary sources for ideas.* Say your thesis is that "icebergs can be used to meet the demands of drought-ridden nations for water." A search through your sources might produce some information on the cost of importing grain to stave off famine brought on by drought. Therefore, assuming your research has given you some idea of the cost of transporting and implementing icebergs as sources of water, you might compare the two different means of dealing with starvation in terms of cost. Should the comparison favor icebergs, you have an argument in support of your thesis; should it not favor icebergs, you should rethink your thesis and perhaps modify it.

Introducing Comparison

Remember to introduce your discussion of differences or similarities with a statement. For example: "Lobsters are more expensive to harvest than haddock."

Organizing Comparison

Writing a formal, full-scale comparison is a lot like juggling; it means keeping two or more things going at the same time. It also means that order and balance are crucial. Therefore, in a comparison, the writer must follow a special pattern to keep the subjects of comparison from getting lost, crashing into one another, in short, from turning into chaos.

In organizing a comparison, you will have two separate decisions to make before you can begin:

1. You have to decide whether your comparison is to be informational or judgmental.
2. You have to decide whether your discussion will follow subject by subject or point by point.

An *informational* comparison can cover either similarities (primarily) or differences (primarily) or both. If it does both, it can do so in either order.

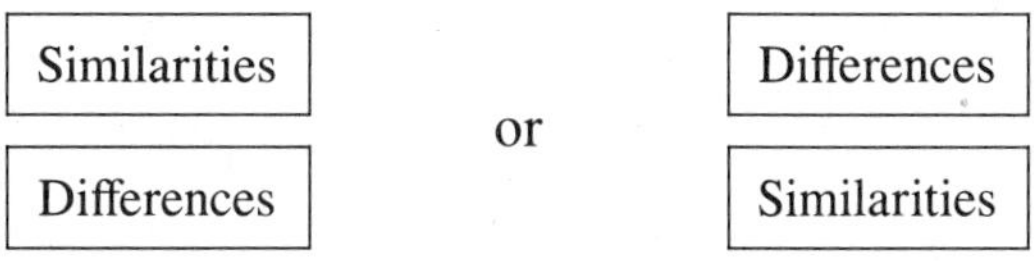

On the other hand, if similarities have an edge in importance over differences, place the similarities last and vice versa. (Take that as a general rule, namely, that whatever you want your reader to remember best, place last.)

A *judgmental* comparison always stresses differences; therefore, any discussion of similarities has to be covered and gotten out of the way first:

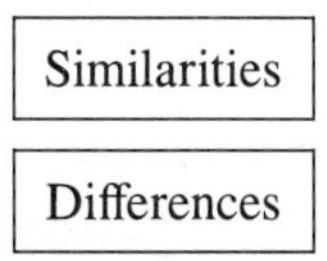

Then, as a rule, you would discuss differences in the order of emphasis: that is, whatever gets emphasized gets discussed last. Or think of it this way: if you're comparing A to B, you have to discuss B, first, in order to have something to compare A to. Thus in a comparison of two friends, for example, if you're comparing David (A) to Michael (B), *first,* describe Michael (B), *then* David (A):

When it comes to going out of his way for a friend, David (A) is better than Michael (B). Michael (B) will give you a ride to school on the days when you both have the same schedule of classes and will drop you off at work, which is on his way home. But it's David (A) who will pick you up at work when you haven't got a ride home and offer to run some of your errands on a Saturday morning in the summer so you can both get to the beach earlier.

Another example:

Harvey Leonard is the most specific and informative of the weeknight T.V. meteorologists.

Meteorologist 1
Meteorologist 2
Harvey Leonard

Once you have decided on the nature of your comparison (informational or judgmental), you must decide on how you intend to organize the comparison—subject by subject or point by point.

Subject by subject is easiest. It means saying everything you have to say about A in one continuous block of information and then moving on to B and discussing that in the following block of information. Within each block of information, the points discussed for one subject are then also discussed for the other subject and usually in the same order. Suppose, for example, you wanted to make the following judgment regarding electric motors and gas engines: "The electric motor is more desirable and more practical than a gas engine." You might arrange your discussion thus:

A. Gas engine
   1. Cost
   2. Efficiency
   3. Pollution
B. Electric motor
   1. Cost
   2. Efficiency
   3. Pollution

A subject-by-subject arrangement is just as possible if you're discussing similarities: "Although built with different purposes in mind, St. Anthony's Shrine and the South Shore Cinema both cater to universal human needs."

A. St. Anthony's Shrine
  1. Social contact/interaction
  2. Self-expression

B. South Shore Cinema
  1. Social contact
  2. Self-expression

Point by point is the more demanding of the two methods of organization. It means organizing your discussion according to idea (1, 2, 3) rather than topic and discussing each topic (A, B) in relation to each idea.

1. Cost
   A. Gas engine
   B. Electric motor
2. Efficiency
   A. Gas engine
   B. Electric motor
3. Pollution
   A. Gas engine
   B. Electric motor

1. Same kinds of patrons
   A. St. Anthony's Shrine
   B. South Shore Cinema
2. Same need for social contact
   A. St. Anthony's Shrine
   B. South Shore Cinema
3. Same reliance on rituals
   A. St. Anthony's Shrine
   B. South Shore Cinema

When it comes to the two methods of organization, bear in mind that neither method is preferable to the other. Length and complexity of subject are the usual criteria by which you decide to do one rather than the other. Obviously, the one that is the easier of the two to write (subject by subject) is also the one that is the more difficult for the reader to retain. If the discussion is a long one, by the time the reader has gotten to the end of B, he or she may well have forgotten what comparable things you said about A and be forced to flip back and forth between A and B. In the end the reader may find himself/herself doing more work reading your paper than you did writing it. In such a case, a point-by-point arrangement may be the more desirable of the two.

Yet it's possible for the comparison to be so long and so intricate (perhaps even an essay in length) as to make the point-by-point discussion unmanageable. In that case, subject-by-subject is the natural choice.

Short comparisons, on the other hand, lend themselves well to the point-by-point approach. But in the case of extreme brevity, the alternating patterns of the point by point can sound very mechanical.

In other words, there are no clear guidelines here. Sometimes it actually means trying it both ways and discovering which sounds better.

Finding Location for Comparison

1. If the comparison is expressed in your thesis, it's either the most essential component of your essay or it *is* your essay. In the first instance, the comparison needs a key location: the end of the essay, whether it's the last two or three or four pages or whatever. Everything else in the essay must build up to it. In the case of the latter, organize your entire essay by comparison or contrast.

2. If the comparison is not expressed in your thesis and constitutes background information, place it early in the essay. Background is what you get out of the way first.

3. If the comparison is not expressed in your thesis and does not constitute background, use it to develop some localized section of your essay.

EXERCISE 4

Write an outline that shows how you would organize the following comparisons if you were doing them subject by subject; point by point. Before you begin, however, establish the point of your comparison in a sentence.

1. High school and college
2. Flying and driving

EXERCISE 5

Read the following essay written by James R. Dickenson of the prestigious but now defunct *National Observer.* First, decide whether it is an informational comparison or a judgmental one and underline the thesis sentence. Second, starting with paragraph 4, identify each paragraph as a discussion of either similarities or differences by writing "sim." or "diff." in the right margin. Third, rearrange the paragraphs, starting with 4, according to the guidelines given for the organization of a comparison. In other words, exercise your judgment regarding where to put all the similarities and all the differences *and* in what order. Reread the section on organizing the comparison if necessary.

MUD ON THE WHITE HOUSE STEPS

In 1876 one of the ways the U.S. Senate celebrated the centennial 1
of American independence was in trying the impeachment of W. W.

Belknap, Secretary of War in the Grant Administration, for selling the favors of his office.

In 1926, the 150th anniversary of the Declaration of Independence, the first criminal trial of the Harding Administration's Teapot Dome oil scandal began. Will 1976, the bicentennial year, feature the apparently endless Watergate scandal, which is to Richard Nixon what the Credit Mobilier was to Ulysses S. Grant and Teapot Dome was to Warren G. Harding? 2

The obverse of the great American experiment in democracy is the cupidity, stupidity, and rascality of some of the leading players in the drama. Credit Mobilier, Teapot Dome, and Watergate are code words for the three most lurid scandals involving the Presidency in American history, and of them all Watergate may turn out to be the worst. 3

For one thing Watergate has not yet run its course, and the question of Nixon's possible complicity in it is still dangling; in the other scandals there was no evidence that either Grant or Harding was directly implicated in activities that led to talk of impeachment. For another, the state of the U.S. Presidency is a more crucial matter in the age of nuclear superpowers than in the relatively simple times of Reconstruction and the Roaring Twenties. Today the stakes are survival itself. 4

There are certain similarities in the three scandals, however. Each was a complex of illegalities and corruption in high office. They are similar in scale and size, involving Cabinet officers and other Presidential intimates. Harding's Secretary of the Interior, for example, is the only Cabinet officer to date to be imprisoned, and his Attorney General was forced to resign after standing trial for bribery. 5

Credit Mobilier tarred both of Grant's Vice Presidents and eight members of Congress, including James Garfield, later to be President. Events of the Watergate era have resulted in the indictment of Attorney General John Mitchell and Commerce Secretary Maurice Stans and have implicated Nixon's top White House staff. 6

All three scandals appear to have been the result of the President's bad judgment in placing high trust in men who, for differing reasons, abused their power and offices. All three happened after a landslide Republican Presidential victory and at a time when the nation had been gravely disrupted by war. 7

There are important differences, however. Watergate differs from the others because it is primarily a pattern of official lawbreaking and abuse of Presidential powers for political ends, specifically to manipulate the 1972 election (although Nixon contends that it was a result partly of his concern over high policy). There is no evidence that anyone high up in the scandal made a dime off it, although some enterprising little bag man somewhere down the line may have ripped off a few of those $100 bills. 8

Teapot Dome and Credit Mobilier, on the other hand, were exam- 9
ples of good old run-of-the-mill, garden-variety thievery of the sort everyone instantly recognizes and appreciates, although on a breathtaking scale. Even so, there was a difference here; Harding's Ohio Gang probably had some idea that they were going to be in trouble if they got caught, while the Spoilsmen of the Reconstruction viewed their depradations as no more than their rightful share of the Great Barbecue that followed the Civil War.

These differences, of course, reflect the differences in the personal- 10
ities of the Presidents involved as well as the variations in their historical circumstances. Grant was the great general who was honored and revered for leading the Union to victory over the rebellion and was a personally honest man (in these respects the Eisenhower of his day).

James R. Dickenson, *The National Observer,* June 9, 1973

WRITING ASSIGNMENT

Using Comparison and Contrast

Write one solid paragraph or more in which you compare and/or contrast two or more things or ideas that are relevant to your thesis or the subject of your research paper.

After you've written your first draft, check out your organization by circling the subjects (the "A" and the "B") of your comparison and numbering the points that you make about each. Be sure that you cover the same points in B that you cover in A, and, in the case of a contrast, be sure that A and B alternate according to the guidelines regarding emphasis discussed earlier in this chapter.

If your thesis statement expresses a comparison and/or contrast, you are not expected to submit the entire essay now. Instead write an outline of the similarities and/or differences, first; then take one self-contained segment of the outline and write it up for this particular assignment. For example, say that your thesis is that "the medieval Chinese had a different attitude to battle, death, and personal honor than did the Europeans of the Middle Ages." First, you would submit an outline:

A. Battle
   1. Europeans
   2. Chinese

B. Death
   1. Europeans
   2. Chinese

C. Personal honor
   1. Europeans
   2. Chinese

Then you would choose one of the categories (for example, Bl and B2) to contrast and submit that.

Prose Models

THE BRIGHT CHILD AND THE DULL CHILD

When we talk about intelligence, we do not mean the ability to get a 1
good score on a certain kind of test, or even the ability to do well in school; these are at best only indicators of something larger, deeper, and far more important. By intelligence we mean a style of life, a way of behaving in various situations, and particularly in new, strange, and perplexing situations. The true test of intelligence is not how much we know how to do, but how we behave when we don't know what to do.

The intelligent person, young or old, meeting a new situation or 2
problem, opens himself up to it; he tries to take in with mind and senses everything he can about it; he thinks about *it,* instead of about himself or what it might cause to happen to him; he grapples with it boldly, imaginatively, resourcefully, and if not confidently at least hopefully; if he fails to master it, he looks without shame or fear at his mistakes and learns what he can from them. This is intelligence. Clearly its roots lie in a certain feeling about life, and one's self with respect to life. Just as clearly, unintelligence is not what most psychologists seem to suppose, the same thing as intelligence only less of it. It is an entirely different style of behavior, arising out of an entirely different set of attitudes.

Years of watching and comparing bright children and the not-bright, 3
or less bright, have shown that they are very different kinds of people. The bright child is curious about life and reality, eager to get in touch with it, embrace it, unite himself with it. There is no wall, no barrier between him and life. The dull child is far less curious, far less interested in what goes on and what is real, more inclined to live in worlds of fantasy. The bright child likes to experiment, to try things out. He lives by the maxim that there is more than one way to skin a cat. If he can't do something one way, he'll try another. The dull child is usually afraid to try at all. It takes a good deal of urging to get him to try even once; if that try fails, he is through.

The bright child is patient. He can tolerate uncertainty and failure, 4
and will keep trying until he gets an answer. When all his experiments fail, he can even admit to himself and others that for the time being he is not going to get an answer. This may annoy him, but he can wait. Very often, he does not want to be told how to do the problem or solve the

puzzle he has struggled with, because he does not want to be cheated out of the chance to figure it out for himself in the future. Not so the dull child. He cannot stand uncertainty or failure. To him, an unanswered question is not a challenge or an opportunity, but a threat. If he can't find the answer quickly, it must be given to him, and quickly; and he must have answers for everything. Such are the children of whom a second-grade teacher once said, "But my children *like* to have questions for which there is only one answer." They did; and by a mysterious coincidence, so did she.

5 The bright child is willing to go ahead on the basis of incomplete understanding and information. He will take risks, sail uncharted seas, explore when the landscape is dim, the landmarks few, the light poor. To give only one example, he will often read books he does not understand in the hope that after a while enough understanding will emerge to make it worth while to go on. In this spirit some of my fifth graders tried to read *Moby Dick.* But the dull child will go ahead only when he thinks he knows exactly where he stands and exactly what is ahead of him. If he does not feel he knows exactly what an experience will be like, and if it will not be exactly like other experiences he already knows, he wants no part of it. For while the bright child feels that the universe is, on the whole, a sensible, reasonable, and trustworthy place, the dull child feels that it is senseless, unpredictable, and treacherous. He feels that he can never tell what may happen, particularly in a new situation, except that it will probably be bad.

John Holt, *How Children Fail,* 1964

DISCUSSION QUESTIONS

1. What is Holt comparing? Underline the words "bright child" and "dull child" each time they are used. Now indicate whether the comparison is subject by subject or point by point. Exactly what points does Holt cover in his comparison? How does he paragraph them?
2. How does Holt keep his "ping-pong" approach (the bright child . . . the dull child . . . the bright child . . . the dull child) from becoming monotonous? Does he spend the same number of sentences on each? Look at the sentences that introduce each discussion of A and each discussion of B. Does Holt vary the sentence pattern at all? Explain.
3. Does he use any signal words as he moves from A to B? Why so few?
4. Is Holt's contrast informational or judgmental? Look at the sentence that introduces the contrast. Does that tell you? What is the point of his comparison?

THE BLACK AND WHITE TRUTH ABOUT BASKETBALL

1 The dominance of black athletes over professional basketball is beyond dispute. Two thirds of the players are black, and the number

would be greater were it not for the continuing practice of picking white bench warmers for the sake of balance. The Most Valuable Player award of the National Basketball Association has gone to blacks for sixteen of the last twenty years, and in the newer American Basketball Association, blacks have won it all but once in the league's eight years. In the 1974–75 season, four of the top five All-Stars and seven of the top ten were black. The N.B.A. was the first pro sports league of any stature to hire a black coach (Bill Russell of the Celtics) and the first black general manager (Wayne Embry of the Bucks). What discrimination remains—lack of opportunity for lucrative benefits such as speaking engagements and product endorsements—has more to do with society than with basketball.

This dominance reflects a natural inheritance; basketball is a pastime of the urban poor. The current generation of black athletes are heirs to a tradition half a century old: in a neighborhood without the money for bats, gloves, hockey sticks, tennis rackets, or shoulder pads, basketball is accessible. "Once it was the game of the Irish and Italian Catholics in Rockaway and the Jews on Fordham Road in the Bronx," writes David Wolf in his brilliant book, *Foul!* "It was recreation, status, and a way out." But now the ethnic names are changed; instead of Red Holzmans, Red Auerbachs, and McGuire brothers, there are Earl Monroes and Connie Hawkins and Nate Archibalds. And professional basketball is a sport with a national television contract and million-dollar salaries. 2

But the mark on basketball of today's players can be measured by more than money or visibility. It is a question of style. For there is a clear difference between "black" and "white" styles of play that is as clear as the difference between 155th Street at Eighth Avenue and Crystal City, Missouri. Most simply (remembering we are talking about culture, not chromosomes), "black" basketball is the use of superb athletic skill to adapt to the limits of space imposed by the game. "White" ball is the pulverization of that space by sheer intensity. 3

It takes a conscious effort to realize how constricted the space is on a basketball court. Place a regulation court (ninety-four by fifty feet) on a football field, and it will reach from the back of the end zone to the twenty-one-yard line; its width will cover less than a third of the field. On a baseball diamond, a basketball court will reach from home plate to just beyond first base. Compared to its principal indoor rival, ice hockey, basketball covers about one fourth the playing area. And during the normal flow of the game, most of the action takes place on about the third of the court nearest the basket. It is in this dollhouse space that ten men, each of them half a foot taller than the average man, come together to battle each other. 4

There is, thus, no room; basketball is a struggle for the edge: the half step with which to cut around the defender for a lay-up, the half second of freedom with which to release a jump shot, the instant a head turns allowing a pass to a teammate breaking for the basket. It is an arena for the subtlest of skills: the head fake, the shoulder fake, the shift of body weight to the right and the sudden cut to the left. Deception is crucial to success; and to young men who have learned early and painfully that life is a battle for survival, basketball is one of the few games in which the weapon of deception is a legitimate rule and not the source of trouble. 5

If there is, then, the need to compete in a crowd, to battle for the edge, then the surest strategy is to develop the *unexpected;* to develop a shot that is simply and fundamentally different from the usual methods of putting the ball in the basket. Drive to the hoop, but go under it and come up the other side; hold the ball at waist level and shoot from there instead of bringing the ball up to eye level; leap into the air and fall away from the basket instead of toward it. All these tactics take maximum advantage of the crowding on a court; they also stamp uniqueness on young men who may feel it nowhere else. 6

"For many young men in the slums," David Wolf writes, "the school yard is the only place they can feel true pride in what they do, where they can move free of inhibitions and where they can, by being spectacular, rise for the moment against the drabness and anonymity of their lives. Thus, when a player develops extraordinary 'school yard' moves and shots . . . [they] become his measure as a man." 7

So the moves that begin as tactics for scoring soon become calling cards. You don't just lay the ball in for an uncontested basket; you take the ball in both hands, leap as high as you can, and slam the ball through the hoop. When you jump in the air, fake a shot, bring the ball back to your body, and throw up a shot, all without coming back down, you have proven your worth in uncontestable fashion. 8

This liquid grace is an integral part of "black" ball, almost exclusively the province of the playground player. Some white stars like Richie Guerin, Bob Cousy, and Billy Cunningham have it: the body control, the moves to the basket, the free-ranging mobility. They also have the surface ease that is integral to the "black" style; an incorporation of the ethic of mean streets – to "make it" is not just to have wealth, but to have it without strain. Whatever the muscles and organs are doing, the face of the "black" star almost never shows it. Bob McAdoo of the Buffalo Braves can drive to the basket with two men on him, pull up, turn around, and hit a basket without the least flicker of emotion. The Knicks' Walt Frazier, flamboyant in dress, cars, and companions, displays nothing but a quickly raised fist after scoring a particularly 9 important basket. (Interestingly, the black coaches in the N.B.A. exhibit far less emotion on the bench than their white counterparts; Washington's K. C. Jones and Seattle's Bill Russell are statuelike compared with Tommy Heinsohn, Jack Ramsey, or Dick Motta.)

If there is a single trait that characterizes "black" ball it is leaping 10
agility. Bob Cousy, ex-Celtic great and former pro coach, says that "when coaches get together, one is sure to say, 'I've got the one black kid in the country who can't jump.' When coaches see a white boy who can jump or who moves with extraordinary quickness, they say, 'He should have been born black, he's that good.' "

Don Nelson of the Celtics recalls that in 1970, Dave Cowens, then a 11
relatively unknown Florida State graduate, prepared for his rookie season by playing in the Rucker League, an outdoor Harlem competition that pits pros against playground stars and college kids. So ferocious was Cowens' leaping power, Nelson says, that "when the summer was over, everyone wanted to know who the white son of a bitch was who could jump so high." That's another way to overcome a crowd around the basket—just go over it.

Speed, mobility, quickness, acceleration, "the moves"—all of these 12
are catch-phrases that surround the "black" playground style of play. So does the most racially tinged of attributes, "rhythm." Yet rhythm is what the black stars themselves talk about; feeling the flow of the game, finding the tempo of the dribble, the step, the shot. It is an instinctive quality, one that has led to difficulty between systematic coaches and free-form players. "Cats from the street have their own rhythm when they play," said college dropout Bill Spivey, onetime New York high-school star. "It's not a matter of somebody setting you up and you shooting. You *feel* the shot. When a coach holds you back, you lose the feel and it isn't fun anymore."

Connie Hawkins, the legendary Brooklyn playground star, said of 13
Laker coach Bill Sharman's methodical style of teaching, "He's systematic to the point where it begins to be a little too much. It's such an action-reaction type of game that when you have to do everything the same way, I think you lose something."

There is another kind of basketball that has grown up in America. It 14
is not played on asphalt playgrounds with a crowd of kids competing for the court; it is played on macadam driveways by one boy with a ball and a backboard nailed over the garage; it is played in Midwestern gyms and on Southern dirt courts. It is a mechanical, precise development of skills (when Don Nelson was an Iowa farm boy his incentive to make his shots was that an errant rebound would land in the middle of chicken droppings), without frills, without flow, but with effectiveness. It is "white" basketball: jagged, sweaty, stumbling, intense. A "black" player

overcomes an obstacle with finesse and body control; a "white" player reacts by outrunning or outpowering the obstacle.

By this definition, the Boston Celtics and the Chicago Bulls are classically "white" teams. The Celtics almost never use a player with dazzling moves; that would probably make Red Auerbach swallow his cigar. Instead, the Celtics wear you down with execution, with constant running, with the same play run again and again. The rebound triggers the fast break, with everyone racing downcourt; the ball goes to John Havlicek, who pulls up and takes the jump shot, or who fakes the shot and passes off to the man following, the "trailer," who has the momentum to go inside for a relatively easy shot. 15

The Bulls wear you down with punishing intensity, hustling, and defensive tactics which are either aggressive or illegal, depending on what side you're on. The Bulls—particularly Jerry Sloan and Norm Van Lier (one white, one black for the quota-minded)—seem to reject the concept of an out-of-bounds line. They are as likely to be found under the press table or wrapped around the ushers as on the court. 16

Perhaps the most classically "white" position is that of the quick forward, one without great moves to the basket, without highly developed shots, without the height and mobility for rebounding effectiveness. What does he do? He runs. He runs from the opening jump to the last horn. He runs up and down the court, from base line to base line, back and forth under the basket, looking for the opening, for the pass, for the chance to take a quick step and the high-percentage shot. To watch Boston's Don Nelson, a player without speed or moves, is to wonder what this thirty-five-year-old is doing in the N.B.A.—until you see him swing free and throw up a shot that, without demanding any apparent skill, somehow goes in the basket more frequently than the shots of any of his teammates. And to watch his teammate John Havlicek, also thirty-five, is to see "white" ball at its best. 17

Havlicek stands in dramatic contrast to Julius Erving of the New York Nets. Erving has the capacity to make legends come true; leaping from the foul line and slam-dunking the ball on his way down; going up for a lay-up, pulling the ball to his body and throwing under and up the other side of the rim, defying gravity and probability with moves and jumps. Havlicek looks like the living embodiment of his small-town Ohio background. He brings the ball downcourt, weaving left, then right, looking for the path. He swings the ball to a teammate, cuts behind a pick, takes the pass and releases the shot in a flicker of time. It looks plain, unvarnished. But there are not half a dozen players in the league who can see such possibilities for a free shot, then get that shot off as quickly and efficiently as Havlicek. 18

To Jim McMillian of Buffalo, a black with "white" attributes, himself a quick forward, "it's a matter of environment. Julius Erving grew up in a different environment from Havlicek—John came from a very small town in Ohio. There everything was done the easy way, the shortest distance between two points. It's nothing fancy, very few times will he go one-on-one; he hits the lay-up, hits the jump shot, makes the free throw, and after the game you look up and you say, 'How did he hurt us that much?' " 19

"White" ball, then, is the basketball of patience and method. "Black" ball is the basketball of electric self-expression. One player has all the time in the world to perfect his skills, the other a need to prove himself. These are slippery categories, because a poor boy who is black can play "white" and a white boy of middle-class parents can play "black." K. C. Jones and Pete Maravich are athletes who seem to defy these categories. And what makes basketball the most intriguing of sports is how these styles do not necessarily clash; how the punishing intensity of "white" players and the dazzling moves of the "blacks" can fit together, a fusion of cultures that seems more and more difficult in the world beyond the out-of-bounds line. 20

Jeff Greenfield, *Esquire Magazine,* October 1975

DISCUSSION QUESTIONS

1. As you can see, Greenfield uses the comparison to organize his entire essay (thus using the rhetorical strategy in its organizational capacity, which you have not yet seen illustrated in any of the prose models). Therefore, there are paragraphs that don't actually compare or contrast but are important to the essay in other ways. Which paragraphs do not specifically compare "black" and "white" basketball? What is their function?
2. Where in the essay does Greenfield introduce the *entire* comparison and, therefore, the entire essay? In short, what is the thesis?
3. Which does Greenfield discuss first? Black (A) or white (B) ball? Where does his discussion of A begin? B? Does he have a sentence introducing A? Introducing B?
4. What points does he discuss with regard to black ball? Does he discuss the same points with regard to white ball? In the same order? Go back to the essay and number the points.
5. Look at paragraph 18. Is this a discussion of black or white ball? Why is Julius Erving brought into the discussion? Does the paragraph emphasize either Havlicek or Erving? Explain.
6. What does Greenfield do in the last paragraph besides summarize the difference between black and white ball?
7. Has Greenfield approached the comparison subject by subject or point by point? And is it informational or judgmental? Explain.

TRIGGER CONTROL

Donna Brugnoli (Student)

The main reason that a gun acts as such a powerful stimulant to violence is the ease with which a gun can be used as opposed to any other weapon. It takes less effort to use a gun than a knife on a person. Using a knife involves muscle, force, and physical contact with the victim. It requires confronting the victim in person and, therefore, risking counterattack, since the victim isn't guaranteed to stand still, if he can help it. A gun, on the other hand, can be fired from a distance; by making the killer "invisible," it protects him from any counterviolence by the victim. One quick, light pull of the trigger and the damage is done. 1

The same restraining principle that applies to the knife also applies to any other object that can be used as a weapon, such as a club or even bare fists. The aggressor cannot detach himself from his actions. He has to make bodily, auditory, and eye contact with the victim. As he approaches him, he has time for second thoughts. A gun is impersonal. It can shoot its victim as mechanically as it would an object on a practice range. The offender does not have to see, hear, or feel the victim's suffering; he can sever himself totally after pulling the trigger. In fact, he may even feel that it wasn't he that has killed, but the bullet. 2

DISCUSSION QUESTIONS

The thesis of Brugnoli's research paper: The mere presence of a gun can have an aggressive effect on behavior because of a phenomenon called "the weapons effect."

1. You will probably remember this as the sample causal analysis. You can see that it's also a comparison. It's a good example of how interrelated rhetorical devices can be. Brugnoli has, in effect, used comparison to explain cause.
2. What is being contrasted? Does Brugnoli attend to similarities at all? Why not?
3. Which gets the emphasis—guns or other weapons? Does the order of discussion reflect the emphasis? Explain.
4. Underline the A (guns) and B (other weapons) in the discussion. Is the comparison organized subject by subject? Or point by point? Explain.
5. Is this an informational or judgmental comparison? What sentence introduces it?

6. Explain the relationship between the comparison and the thesis. Is the comparison expressed or implied by the thesis statement or does it serve as background?

Note: The comparison is found on page 251 of the research paper.

CALIFORNIA WINES ARE ALIVE AND WELL

Ned Hawkins (Student)

Wines can differ from one another. French and California wines have two things in common. They are both grown from the same grapes and in the same dry soil, which, Leon D. Adams points out, "can be found almost anywhere" (4). These two similarities ought to make the wine they produce rather similar (assuming similar winegrowing techniques as well). But then there is the matter of climate. Unlike France, California has "long rainless growing seasons and . . . mild winters" (Adams 5); "more reliable [weather] than Europe's from day to day" (Thompson and Johnson 19); and a bigger range of "microclimates" (Asher 84). Therefore, California can produce more consistently fine wine than France (Hannum and Blumberg 55), and it has so many types of climates (microclimates) that it has one suitable for every kind of wine grape (Hannum and Blumberg 36). Adams writes that it is "easier to raise Vinifera grapes in the fabulous climates of California than in any other part of the globe" (222). Therefore, "In the average quality of its wines, [California] ranks first" (Adams 1). What that means in everyday terms is that the gallon jugs that the average American picks up in his local package store are superior to the wine the average Frenchman drinks and serves to his family every day.

DISCUSSION QUESTIONS

The thesis of Hawkins' research paper: The finest California wines are now challenging the finest French wines and sometimes winning.

1. Does Hawkins discuss both similarities and differences? Give equal treatment to each? Does the order—similarities first, then differences—reflect weightier treatment of one over the other? Explain.
2. Is his contrast informational or judgmental? Explain.
3. Look at the contrast that begins with sentence 6. Has Hawkins weakened his discussion by *not* discussing France's climate before he discusses California's?

Has he short-changed the reader by using just two words—"Unlike France"—to suggest certain facts about France's climate that are opposite from comparable facts about California's climate?

4. Turn to pages 271 (last paragraph) through 273 in Hawkins' research paper. Would you say that the rest of the essay is a comparison and contrast as well? Explain.
5. Did the thesis suggest a comparison to Hawkins? Does it express one? Why didn't he begin with a comparison right at the beginning of his essay?

13
Writing the Research Paper

By now you have spent a number of weeks researching your topic, thinking about it, and writing about it. You have long since taken the chill off your subject and should feel fairly comfortable with it. More importantly, you should feel you've developed control over your material and a sense of direction. You are now ready to bring it all together. The final stretch consists of six stages: (1) organizing ideas by writing another summary of the essay, as you see it *now*; (2) writing the research paper, which is to say, filling in the summary with data from your notes and the five prewrites; (3) revising and polishing the essay; (4) inserting the formal documentation of your sources; (5) preparing the final draft for typing; and (6) typing it.

Organizing Ideas and Writing a Summary

Back in Chapter 5, you wrote a brief summary in order to establish the main points of your discussion and their general order. What you're going to do now is not very different from that, except that the summary will be somewhat more elaborate—without being any more detailed. Since you have compared, defined, and so on, in the preceding weeks, you have introduced dimensions into your essay it originally did not have. Needless to say, your thesis may also have undergone modification, your subject narrowed, your focus sharpened. As a result, you need a new summary (or an elaboration of the previous one) to use as a guide.

Preparing this final summary (or blueprint) is a crucial stage in the composition of your research paper. Unless you can see your paper whole *right now,* you are in danger of producing a fragmented essay. Instead of an essay flowing in a single direction, it will puddle up; none of the ideas, to use one more metaphor, will mesh like interlocking gears. Actually, metaphors come to mind in describing the compositional process because composition is like a lot of other creative endeavors in which order and unity are paramount. You can also think of your summary as the framing of a house or the sketching of a picture in pencil. The next stage in all three cases is going to be the filling in: windows, doors, siding in the case of the house; colors, shading in the painting; facts, expert opinions, details in the case of your essay.

In other words, the purpose of the summary is to help you establish a logical sequence for the ideas you'll be using to support your thesis. Since a summary by definition excludes the details, data, and discussion that will eventually fill your essay, it serves to highlight its organization. If there are any weaknesses in organization, they will stand out in a summary; any lack of connection between ideas or absence of progression can, therefore, be corrected before you become engaged in other concerns of writing.

To be sure, there is no simple formula for arranging ideas or finding an ideal sequence of discussion. Nevertheless, the following guidelines might help you organize your material:

1. Those ideas that are crucial to the verification of your thesis should be saved for *last* (which could mean the last two pages or the last seven; "last" is a flexible word, its meaning to be determined by the needs of your thesis and length of your essay). What "last" does mean, however, is that you *build up* to the point of the essay rather than away from it. And when it comes to arranging the corroborating ideas themselves, arrange in the order of *increasing* importance, placing the ideas that "clinch" your argument last.

2. Those ideas that constitute background or general development of the topic, in short, anything that you want to get out of the way before getting down to the business (thesis) at hand, place first. What's more, move from the general to the specific—like a camera closing in on its subject.

3. Locate the thesis sentence early in the essay—even though you may not actually verify it until relatively late in the paper. The reason for stating the thesis somewhere in the initial segments of the essay should be obvious: The reader needs more than a topic to engage his or her continued attention; the reader needs a sense of what the essay is building up to. Then once you've stated the thesis, you can always back away from it, discuss more general matters, then return to it in the "home stretch," where the corroboration of the thesis gets sole attention.

Remember to regard the above only as guidelines not as inflexible formulas. Let the demands of your topic and thesis control the arrangement of ideas. For an illustration of how these guidelines apply to the two sample research essays, look at the formal outlines in Chapter 15. They have been attached to the student papers to reveal some of the basic principles of organization at a glance. (They can also be used as models should your instructor require a formal outline with your research paper. Note: the outline accompanying the "wine" paper is a **topic outline**, consisting of concise phrases; the one accompanying the "gun" paper is a **sentence outline**, which consists of just that, sentences, making it the more explicit of the two outlines. The topic outline, however, has the advantage of brevity.)

Annotating the Summary

Once you have written your summary, treat it like an informal or preliminary outline.

1. In the *right* margin label the subjects of discussion found in your summary.

2. Examine your subjects and your summary for logical progression; see to it that the ideas hinge on one another. The subjects you treat in your summary should not materialize out of nowhere. Each must link up with the idea that precedes it.

3. Assemble your prewrites. Examine the summary for use of the five rhetorical modes. Without having even been conscious of it, you may already have incorporated one or more of them in your summary. Therefore, locate the rhetorical modes and label them in the *left* margin. If you have any modes left unmentioned in the summary, use an arrow to locate a logical spot for them. If you still have any mode that resists incorporation into your paper, see Chapter 14 for an explanation of the content note, which can be used to accommodate it.

An Annotated Summary of the Research Paper on Wine

Here's the summary written by Ned Hawkins, the student whose five rhetorical modes you've been reading in the last five chapters.

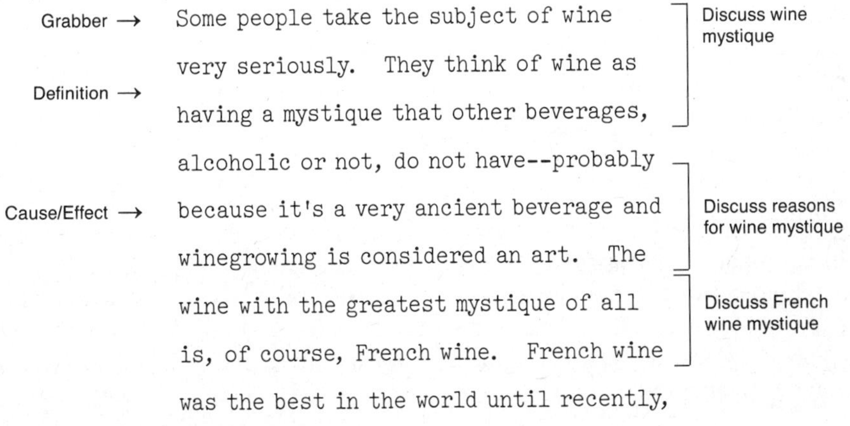
Grabber →
Some people take the subject of wine
very seriously. They think of wine as
Definition →
having a mystique that other beverages,
Discuss wine mystique
alcoholic or not, do not have--probably
Cause/Effect →
because it's a very ancient beverage and
winegrowing is considered an art. The
Discuss reasons for wine mystique
wine with the greatest mystique of all
is, of course, French wine. French wine
Discuss French wine mystique
was the best in the world until recently,

when American wines finally caught up in quality and began challenging French wines and sometimes winning. For a long time, American wines tried to overcome the setback they had suffered during the years of the Prohibition. But today American wines are no longer inferior to French wines. To understand just what makes a wine great, it is important to understand what it takes to make one different from the other. The secret is in the grape, soil, and climate. Those American wines that are on a par with French wines come from California and are called premier wines, the only type of wine used in the competition. When premier California wines are compared with premier French wines, California wines are sometimes rated higher. There are three indicators that are used to prove the occasional superiority of California wines: they sometimes sell for more than French wines; they sometimes win first place over French wines in blind wine tastings; and foreign investors are investing in California vineyards like mad.

Discuss problems of American wines

Discuss secret of winegrowing

Comparison/Contrast →

Division/Classification →

Discuss similarities and differences between French and California wines

Discuss superiority of California wines:

prices,

wine tastings

foreign investments

To complete your examination of this summary, look in Chapter 15 at the research paper (and *formal* outline) that Hawkins wrote using his summary as a guide. Notice how closely he was able to follow the order of the summary and how he used some of the sentences in the summary as topic sentences in his essay—just changing the wording here and there to accommodate the final version.

WRITING ASSIGNMENT

Write a one-paragraph summary of what you perceive your essay is going to say. Do it in one sitting; do not look at any notes; and do not worry about inserting any details or corroborating ideas. Concentrate your full attention on only one thing: getting each sentence to relate to the other and getting each idea to flow smoothly out of the preceding one and into the following. After you have written your summary, annotate it according to the sample above.

Writing the Research Paper

1. Assemble your notes and arrange them according to the subjects of discussion you identified in the *right* margin of your summary; or, if you cover more than one topic on a page of notes, color code them. For example, circle each topic in the margin of the summary with a differently colored ink, and then use a corresponding color to bracket material relevant to the topic in your notes.

2. Assemble your prewrites in the order in which you identified them in the *left* margin of your summary.

3. Write your research essay. To maintain momentum, eliminate the temptation to quote excessively and keep the essay from reading like a patchwork of notes; write as much of the first draft as possible without consulting any notes at all. Refrain, furthermore, from concentrating at all on your prose. If you sit there struggling with the phrasing of a sentence, you're likely to lose your train of thought. "Getting it together" is your only concern at this stage (just leave ample space between lines and generous margins for later additions and revisions). You will also want to work in the prewrites as you go along, modifying them only if you can do so effortlessly. Once again, do not stop to fiddle with sentences and ideas in an effort to link the prewrites with the rest of the essay. Just slip them in whole wherever they fit logically; you can supply the connecting phrases or sentences later along with the corrections in grammar and style and everything else involved in revising. Remember that this stage of your writing is one of several in the composition process. Therefore, concentrate on the large picture only; there will be time later for word-by-word and sentence-by-sentence improvements.

4. The next stage involves two separate activities. (a) Fill in the gaps you've reserved for borrowed material. Refer to your notes for the expert opinions, data, details, and examples your essay still needs to explain and corroborate its thesis. Say, in a paper on hurricanes, you wrote the following from memory: "Hurricanes also produce uncontrolled flooding, and drowning accounts for most deaths associated with hurricanes." The statement is fine for a first time around. Now add specifics: some authoritative explanation for the uncontrolled flooding; data, or, at least, expert opinion, to corroborate your observation regarding drowning; and possibly examples of actual hurricanes, places, and people that would illustrate your observations regarding the flooding and drowning.

Some of the corroborating material you will want to quote; the rest paraphrase. Resist the temptation to work in as many of your notes as possible. Remember, you're not writing an essay just to accommodate your notes. Use only those that serve the essay; the rest set aside and forget. At this point you should identify all borrowed words and ideas that have not yet been so identified. (See Chapters 7 and 14 for acknowledging and documenting your sources.) (b) Smoothe out the transitions linking the prewritten matter with the surrounding text. If necessary, that is, if the evolution of ideas in your paper suggests the need, rework the prewrite by expanding, condensing, or deleting parts of it. If, however, the prewrite disrupts the flow of ideas, relegate it to a content note. (See Chapter 14.)

5. Then go on to reread your entire essay for smoothness. Ideas should progress logically; all sentences should fit together—as smoothly as boards joined in tongue-and-groove fashion. Wherever you find gaps, especially between paragraphs, insert transitional statements. For example, notice the absence of continuity between the following two paragraphs:

In other words, Presley spent money lavishly and lived flamboyantly.

Elvis "consistently declined as a creative force in music. Clearly, he was a victim of his own success" (Goldman 201).

The student rereading his essay above for smoothness would be immediately struck by the sudden shift—completely unannounced—from Elvis' generosity to his decline. Clearly, a transition is in order. Notice the enormous improvement as a result of just one additional sentence that both covers what has been said and introduces what is to follow:

In other words, Presley spent money lavishly and lived flamboyantly.

Unfortunately, his spending habits and lifestyle had far-reaching consequences for his career. He "consistently declined as a creative force in music. Clearly, he was a victim of his own success" (Goldman 201).

Sometimes all that is needed to link two sentences is one word:

Before the transition

Presley became an international success in about two years. According to Sobran, "he became an institution in record time" (85). For the first time in his life, this small-town boy could buy anything he wanted.

After the transition

```
"he became an institution in record time" (85). Thus
for the first time in his life, this small-town boy
could buy anything he wanted.
```

At other times, a student may need an entire paragraph (or two) to serve as a transition. Take a look at the transitional paragraphs on page 5 of the sample research paper, "California Wines Are Alive and Well." Notice how the student uses two paragraphs, like locks in a canal, to move the essay from one level of discussion to another: in the first transitional paragraph he maneuvers the essay away from the problems of the American wine industry to the competition between California and French wines; in the second, he shifts again—this time from the competition to the variables that create differences and make competition possible. Thus a transitional paragraph can bring a discussion closer to the thesis after a brief foray into background (first paragraph) or retard the headlong sweep into the home stretch (second paragraph).

6. Finally, there's the matter of introducing and concluding your essay. Both the introduction and conclusion should be strong. The former should make your reader want to continue; the latter should leave a good impression on a reader who may already have forgotten what you said on page 2 but will definitely remember what you said last. If you used a lead example (grabber), your introduction is all set; if you didn't, consider writing one. Or consider introducing your essay in some other fashion. An introduction should be informative (establish the topic) and engaging (attract the reader). The student who began his essay with a flat statement of his thesis—"Migrating birds encounter many obstacles"—met only the first requirement. When asked to inject a little appeal into it, he came up with two possibilities, both an improvement over the first: (a) "What most people do not realize about bird migration is that the obstacles a bird encounters are enormous." (b) "When most people look up at a solitary bird or a V-formation flying south, they think how effortless flight is. But it isn't. Migrating birds encounter enormous obstacles. For every ten migrating birds, four don't make it." An arresting fact, a striking quotation, an intriguing anecdote, an erroneous opinion about to be challenged by the thesis are just several of the strategies that can be employed to bait the reader. Take time to explore some of the possibilities for a forceful introduction.

Your conclusion should be equally strong. It should "feel" like an ending. A summation of what you've said in the essay is a conventional approach. But merely restating your thesis in a single sentence is going to sound too abrupt, as though your energy had fizzled out just short of the final paragraph. Elaborate on your summary, if that's how you've decided to end, by restating your major points. Use one of the following phrases to introduce the summation: "in short," "in brief," "in other words" *not* "in conclusion" or "in summary."

Another possibility is to end on the most dramatic or most convincing example of your most important idea. The example, however, must be presented in language that explicitly states its significance to your thesis. Look at the concluding paragraphs in the sample essays in Chapter 15.

Revising

Between the time you write your summary and the time you type the final version of your essay for submission to your instructor, you should devote considerable time and energy to revising it—more than once. Go over the essay for organization, transitional ideas, and logical progression of ideas. Then go over it again for further discussion of undeveloped ideas or deletion of superfluous material; and again for accuracy of documentation and possible plagiarism of poorly paraphrased material; and once more with a fine-tooth comb for diction, grammar, spelling, and punctuation. Polish your essay to a high gloss. If at all possible, try to type even the first draft; a typed copy is much easier to proofread for problems than a handwritten one. In any case, all your drafts should be written on one side of the paper only: nothing is more distracting to concentration than having to flip pages front to back.

Revision Checklist

1. Have you included a statement of your thesis in the essay?

2. Does the phrasing of your thesis accurately reflect the essence of your paper?

3. Does the essay explain and corroborate the thesis?

4. When you scan each paragraph, are you satisfied that each has a topic idea and that each idea is adequately developed?

5. When you scan each paragraph in sequence, can you see an obvious progression of ideas?

6. Does this progression of ideas reveal a clear relation to the thesis?

7. Does each rhetorical mode in your prewrites proceed out of the ideas of the preceding paragraph and lead into the ones that follow?

8. Is your essay a well-proportioned blend of your own ideas in your own words (usually to be found introducing and concluding a paragraph), borrowed ideas in your own words, and borrowed ideas in borrowed words?

9. When you scan the sentences that introduce the borrowed material, especially the quotations, do you see enough variety? Have you made a point to introduce some of the borrowings with the author's name or names of the author and title?

10. Have you documented the ideas/facts that you've paraphrased as well as those you've quoted?

11. Have you rewritten the paraphrased material several times without looking at the original to eliminate any resemblance to the diction, style, and order of the original?

12. Is your tone appropriate to your subject and audience?

13. Have you avoided overly specialized words (jargon)?

14. Do you have an effective introduction? conclusion? appropriate title?

Formal Documentation

Just before you type your final version, check all your documentary references in parentheses for accuracy—not only of content but also of format. Then add an additional page(s) called "Works Cited." For a complete explanation of the procedure and format that your parenthetical references and bibliographical citations must follow see Chapter 14.

Preparing the Final Draft for Typing

If your instructor expresses no particular preference for the format of your research paper, use the following standard manuscript form. Any questions or difficulties that arise, which are not covered by the following guidelines below, can usually be answered simply by looking at the sample research papers in Chapter 15.

Typing

Research papers should be typed (not handwritten) on one side only. Use white bond paper (8½″ × 11″); do not use onion-skin.

Margins and Spacing

Leave ample margins, about one inch—top, bottom, and sides. The exceptions to the rule are the first page of the paper, the first page of content notes (if any), and the first page of "Works Cited." In these three instances, allow for a deeper margin at the top—about two inches—then quadruple-space below the title. Double-space the entire text, including long quotations, content note entries, and list of works cited. Indent five spaces for paragraphs and ten spaces for long quotations.

Title Page

The title page should consist of the title you've chosen for your paper, your name, the name and number of the course, the name of the instructor, and the date the paper is due. All that information should appear centered on the page. If you need more than one line for your title, double-space between lines. Do not underline your title or put it in quotation marks. Capitalize all the words in the title except for articles, conjunctions, and prepositions. Include the word "By" two spaces above your name. Include the title on page 1 of your text.

Page Numbering

Use Arabic numerals (1, 2, 3, etc.). Do not number the title page or the first page of your text. But count the first page of the text when numbering the others. Type the page number in the upper right-hand corner, about a half-inch from the top and more or less in line with the right margin.

Tables and Other Illustrations

Tables, graphs, charts, maps, drawings, photographs, and any other illustrations you use are to be placed on separate pages and as close as possible to the part of your paper they are illustrating. Tables that consist of information listed in columns should be identified as "Table," captioned two spaces below, and numbered. The captioning should be double-spaced. All other illustrative material should be labeled as "Figure" and numbered. The source of *all* illustrative material should be acknowledged unless the source is yourself.

Proofreading

Do not hand in any paper after you've typed it without proofreading it first. Typographical errors are bound to crop up; and unless they're corrected, they will be looked upon as spelling errors by the instructor. If there are too many corrected typographical errors and the page begins to look sloppy, retype the whole page. As you know, appearance counts, and while a paper isn't going to get you an "A" on the strength of its looks, image helps. A messy paper has to work twice as hard as a neat one to overcome the prejudice its appearance arouses in a reader. Even if it's first-rate inside, an instructor is not likely to overlook the insult that a careless appearance implies when grading the paper.

14
Documenting Your Sources

In the Text and at the End of the Text

Parenthetical documentation is a brief identification of borrowed material by author, sometimes short title, and page within the text of the paper. *List of works cited* is a single alphabetized list of sources used in the research and preparation of the essay; it corresponds with all the sources cited parenthetically within the text; it provides all the information necessary to identify and retrieve each source; and it is placed at the end of the paper. Together they document your work; provide a record of your research; inform the reader of the types of sources that have been used; lend authority to a paper; and enable the reader to locate the sources in the library. There is no single format that is universally accepted by all the academic disciplines, but the one taught below for both parenthetical documentation and list of works cited is widely accepted by college departments, graduate schools, and journal editors. It follows the revised style recommended by the *MLA Handbook for Writers of Research Papers* (1984), a publication of the Modern Language Association. Unless your instructor indicates otherwise, use the format presented here. Be assured that it is consistent with current trends in scholarship and publishing. If you ever have to modify it to accord with the preferences of your instructor or your discipline, use that modification consistently throughout the paper.

Parenthetical Documentation Within the Text

Parenthetical documentation has replaced footnotes and endnotes as a method of citing sources. The essence of it is economy and clarity—giving the reader just enough information to identify a work and locate the complete citation in the list of works cited at the end of the paper. A set of guidelines with examples is provided below. If you have a source for which you cannot find an exact model, improvise according to the general principles of parenthetical documentation explained above and in the remainder of this section.

Insert the following information in parentheses each time you refer to borrowed material: author, short title, and page, in that order. *Omit* any or all of these items *if* you mention them in the text. *Omit* the title *if* only one work by the author in question is cited. Use a comma to separate author from title, but no punctuation between title and page (nor, if the title is omitted, between author and page).

1. *Author.* Use surname only. If two or more authors with identical surnames are cited, add title. If more than one work by an author is cited, add title. If there are two or three authors, give all their surnames; if more than three, give the surname of just the first author and add "and others." If you are referring to material (musical recording, film, etc.) that has no author, use the author position to identify whatever name (composer's, performer's, director's, etc.) appears first in the corresponding entry in the list of works cited.

2. *Title.* Use a shortened version by giving a key word or two that appear *together.* Thus for "Leisure Time Activities," you might give "Activities" or "Leisure Time" but *not* "Leisure Activities." If the source is an article or a work (essay, play, short story, poem) within a volume of other writings, the title used must be that of the article or individual work (rather than the title of the periodical or volume of writings). If your source has no author (in the case of a news article, for example), cite the *first* few significant words of the entry in the list of works cited (usually those of the title). Note that key words alone, when there is no author, would not be much help in locating the complete citation. Use double quotation marks around the short title of an article or individual work within a volume of writings, and underline the short title of a book.

3. *Page.* Give the page number or numbers *without* the abbreviations "p." and "pp.," except where confusion might result. Write the number in Arabic numerals. Use Roman numerals only for citing pages that are so numbered (for example, the Preface or Introduction of a book). In the case of a lecture, film, theatrical performance, musical composition, work of art, radio or television program, recording, and interview, no pagination is involved and, therefore, none required.

Models of Parenthetical Documentation

WHEN NEITHER *AUTHOR* NOR *TITLE APPEARS IN THE TEXT*

```
"poetry is a ritual of resurrection and rebirth" (Cope 174)
```

The parenthetical documentation above refers the reader to the following entry in the list of works cited:

Cope, Jackson I. The Theater and the Dream: From Metaphor to Form in Renaissance Drama. Baltimore: Johns Hopkins UP, 1973.

If more than one work by an author is cited in the paper, include a shortened version of the title:

to promote the sale of diamonds (Epstein, "Tried" 23)

The parenthetical documentation above refers the reader to the following citations in the list of works cited:

Epstein, Edward Jay. "Have You Ever Tried to Sell a Diamond?" The Atlantic Monthly Feb. 1982: 23-24.

---. The Rise and Fall of Diamonds: The Shattering of a Brilliant Illusion. New York: Simon & Schuster, 1982.

Notice how the short title, "Tried," distinguishes between two works with the same author.

If a work has two or three authors, cite all of them:

(Moro, Flagg, and Keefe 58)

If more than three, cite the first author and add "and others":

(Emond and others 73)

There is no comma separating author's name from "and others."

WHEN EITHER *AUTHOR* OR *TITLE APPEARS IN THE TEXT*

Argenzio writes that De Beers also buys up Australian diamonds (95).

The library is described in A History of Education During the Middle Ages as the most distinctive feature of the monastic community (Graves 10-11).

Since the author appears as part of the narrative in the first example and only one work by Argenzio is being cited in the paper, no short title is given; the page is enough. In the second reference, where only the title is mentioned in the text, the author is included in parentheses since the citation could not be located without it.

WHEN BOTH *AUTHOR* AND *TITLE APPEAR IN THE TEXT*

In Essentials of Advertising Kaufman lists Ayer as one of the largest advertising agencies in 1938 (12).

WHEN CITING THE BIBLE

(Genesis 42.10)

(Matt. 20.1-15)

Cite only book, chapter, and verse. Do *not* underline, and do *not* space the numbers. You may use abbreviations.

WHEN CITING THE CLASSICS

(Othello 1.1.4)

(Odyssey 21.5)

The *MLA Handbook* recommends Arabic numerals for acts and scenes of plays; and cantos and stanzas of poems. If the title is mentioned in the text, omit it from the parentheses. Abbreviations are permitted.

List of Works Cited at the End of the Text

The list of works cited, which appears at the end of the paper, provides the information a reader needs to retrieve the sources mentioned parenthetically in the narrative. Only those works that were actually used in the writing of your paper should be listed. In this regard, a list of works cited differs from a bibliography; the latter aims either to include all the works written on a particular subject or to add works useful to the reader as "background" but not actually cited in the essay. In short, the references you give parenthetically in your text must be the only ones to appear in the list of works cited at the end and conversely: each citation at the end must appear parenthetically in the text.

The models given below cover the most frequently used kinds of sources. They do not, however, exhaust all the possibilities. Should you have a source for which you can find no exact model, use the one that comes closest and improvise. Be guided by documentation logic: providing the bibliographic information necessary in the retrieval of sources.

Do not bother memorizing formats: simply keep this reference guide handy and pull it out whenever you have to write a research paper. Finally, be sure to allow ample time to compile your list of works cited. Even though documentation is only a matter of transferring information from your working bibliography to a formal reference list, because of the detail and precision involved, it is a fussy and tedious process. So give yourself time!

1. List all the sources you used in preparing your research paper on a separate page, labeled "Works Cited." Type as many pages of citations as you need. Place your list at the very end. It should be the *last* segment of your paper.
2. Arrange the entries in alphabetical order according to the first word, usually a surname; if there is no author, alphabetize according to the first word of the title other than "A" or "The."
3. Double-space the lines within the citations and between citations.
4. Indent the second and subsequent lines of each entry five spaces.
5. Separate units of information with periods and begin each new unit with a capital letter.

Citing Books

The following are the key elements that are usually found in citations of books.

1. *Author.* Give the full name of the author as it appears on the title page, not the cover. Invert the author's name so that the surname comes first. If there is more than one author, invert only the first name and list the authors in the order in which they appear on the title page. If you cite more than one work by a particular author, type the name only once the first time you list it. For subsequent entries with the same author, type *three* hyphens followed by a period. If the name of the author isn't given, begin the citation without it.

2. *Title.* Give the complete title as it appears on the title page not the cover. Capitalize the first letter of each word—excluding articles, conjunctions, and prepositions. Exception: Capitalize the first word of the subtitle even if it is an article, conjunction, or preposition. Separate the subtitle from the main title with a colon. Underline the complete title of a book; place quotation marks around the title of an individual work found within a volume of other writings.

3. *Place of publication.* Copy it from the title or copyright page (reverse side of title page). If several cities are given, list one, usually the major city. Include the state or country (abbreviated) only if the place is not a major city, or there is more than one city of that name. If no place of publication is given, write "n.p." for "no place" in the place of publication position.

4. *Publisher.* Copy it from the title or copyright page. Shorten or abbreviate it whenever appropriate (for example, Pergamon, instead of Pergamon Press). If the publisher is not given, write "n.p." for "no publisher" in the publisher position.

5. *Date.* Copy it from the title or copyright page. It's the date that follows the copyright symbol ©. If more than one date is listed (© 1937, 1938,

1939), give the most recent. If the book has gone through several impressions or reprintings by the same publisher:

- © 1959
- First printing 1959
- Second printing 1966

use the original date (1959). If the date is not given, write "n.d." for "no date" in the date position.

Reference Models for Books

BOOK WITH ONE AUTHOR

Argenzio, Victor. <u>Diamonds Eternal</u>. New York: David McKay, 1974.

The end of a unit is marked by a period. A colon separates city from publisher, and a comma separates publisher from date.

BOOK WITH TWO OR THREE AUTHORS

Taylor, John, and Frederick Swanborough. <u>Military Aircraft of the World</u>. New York: Scribner's, 1971.

Only the first author's name is inverted, and the authors are separated by a comma.

BOOK WITH MORE THAN THREE AUTHORS

Oster, Sharon M., and others. <u>The Definition and Measurement of Poverty</u>. Boulder, CO: Westview, 1978.

The first author is separated from the phrase "and others" with a comma.

WORK OF SEVERAL VOLUMES

Manchester, William. <u>The Glory and the Dream: A Narrative History of America 1932-1972</u>. 2 vols. Boston: Little, Brown, 1974. Vol. 2.

When citing only one of the volumes, place the volume you are using after the date and give the total number of volumes after the title. Use Arabic numerals for the volume numbers and periods to separate the information from the rest of the entry.

If the volumes are published in different years, use this form:

Rawlinson, George. The History of Herodotus. Vol. 4. New York: D. Appleton, 1864.

If each volume of a multivolume work has individual titles, use this form:

Dunham, Dows. Royal Tombs at Meroe and Barkal. Vol. 4 of Royal Cemeteries of Kush. 5 vols. Cambridge, MA: Harvard UP, 1950.

If you are citing the entire set of volumes, use this form:

Dunham, Dows. Royal Cemeteries of Kush. 5 vols. Cambridge, MA: Harvard UP, 1950.

ESSAY, PLAY, SHORT STORY, POEM IN A VOLUME OF WRITINGS BY THE SAME AUTHOR

Chomsky, Noam. "The Remaking of History." Towards a New Cold War: Essays on the Current Crisis and How We Got There. By Chomsky. New York: Pantheon, 1982. 134-53.

The page numbers cover the whole essay, are separated from the date by a period, and no abbreviation for pages is used.

ESSAY, PLAY, SHORT STORY, POEM IN A VOLUME OF WRITINGS BY DIFFERENT AUTHORS

Chase, Richard. "The Broken Circuit." Theories of American Literature. Eds. Donald M. Kartiganer and Malcolm A. Griffith. New York: Macmillan, 1972. 41-59.

The abbreviation for editor is "Ed." ("Eds." for editors).

BOOK THAT IS PART OF A SERIES

Campbell, Joseph. The Hero with a Thousand Faces. Bollingen Series 17. Princeton, NJ: Princeton UP, 1949.

SECOND OR LATER EDITIONS OF A BOOK

Paterson, John Harris. North America: A Geography of Canada and the United States. 4th ed. London: Oxford UP, 1970.

There is no period after "4th."

REPRINT OF A BOOK

Rand, Edward Kennard. Founders of the Middle Ages. Boston, 1928; rpt. New York: Dover, 1957.

BOOK WITH AN EDITOR

Adams, Joseph Quincy, ed. Chief Pre-Shakespearean Dramas. Boston: Houghton Mifflin, 1924.

INTRODUCTION, PREFACE, FOREWORD, OR AFTERWORD TO A BOOK

Cole, John. Introduction. Ulster at the Crossroads. By Terence O'Neill. London: Faber, 1969.

BOOK WITH A TRANSLATOR

Flaubert, Gustave. Madame Bovary. Trans. Mildred Marmur. New York: New American Library, 1964.

ARTICLE IN AN ENCYCLOPEDIA

"Aran Islands." Encyclopedia Americana. 1982 ed.

Page numbers are omitted for encyclopedia articles arranged alphabetically.

GOVERNMENT PUBLICATION

United States. Environmental Protection Agency. Effects of Noise on People. Washington: GPO, 1971.

"GPO" is the abbreviation for "Government Printing Office."

BIBLE

The Bible

No other information is necessary unless you used a version other than the King James.

The Jerusalem Bible

The Bible. Revised Standard Edition.

CLASSICS

Shakespeare, William. Macbeth. The Riverside Shakespeare. Ed. G. Blakemore Evans. Boston: Houghton Mifflin, 1974. 1312-39.

PAMPHLET OR BOOK WITH A CORPORATE AUTHOR

International Center for the Disabled. Pity and Fear: Myths and Images of the Disabled in Literature Old and New. New York: ICD, 1981.

Citing Periodicals

The following are the key elements that are usually found in references to periodicals.

1. *Author.* Give the complete name. If the article is unsigned, move the title into the author position and begin the citation without the author's name.

2. *Title of article.* Place the complete title in quotation marks.

3. *Title of periodical.* Underline the complete title.

4. *Date.* For magazines and newspapers, give the complete date, as it appears on the cover of the issue. For journals, give only volume number and year if the issues are paginated consecutively throughout the volume: 21 (1981). Give the month (or season) along with the year and volume if each issue begins with page 1: 6 (Spring 1973). If the month (or season) isn't known, give the issue number along with the volume (separated by a period) and year: 13.2 (1975).

5. *Page.* Give the inclusive page numbers for the *entire* article, unless they're discontinuous (7–8, 17), in which case you would use a plus sign to indicate the article continues on a later page (7–8+). Omit the abbreviations "p." and "pp." and use a colon to separate page from date.

Reference Models for Periodicals

ARTICLE IN A JOURNAL THAT PAGES CONSECUTIVELY FROM ISSUE TO ISSUE

Rudick, Sara. "Pacifying the Forces: Drafting Women in the Interests of Peace." Signs 8 (1983): 471-89.

The period at the end of the article is placed *within* quotation marks. The volume number precedes the date, and a colon separates the date from the inclusive page numbers. No punctuation separates periodical from numerical information.

ARTICLE IN A JOURNAL THAT PAGES EACH ISSUE SEPARATELY

Gilder, George. "Making It." The Wilson Quarterly 9 (Winter 1985): 70-75.

Frey, John R. "America and Her Literature Reviewed by Postwar Germany." American-German Review 20.5 (1984): 5-15.

For a journal that pages each issue separately but does not designate a season or month, add the issue number and separate it from the volume with a period: 20.5.

ARTICLE IN A MONTHLY MAGAZINE

Laycock, George. "The Darkest Frontier." Audubon May 1983: 86-91.

No punctuation is used to separate the month (or season) from the year.

ARTICLE IN A WEEKLY MAGAZINE OR WEEKLY NEWSPAPER

"Trouble at Stanford." Newsweek 6 June 1983: 92.

The date is written without a comma because month and day are inverted.

ARTICLE IN A DAILY NEWSPAPER

"Ships May Tie Up at 2 Ice 'Islands.' " New York Times 23 Feb. 1969, late ed., sec. 1: 13.

Whenever an edition is given on the masthead and a newspaper is divided into sections, include this information after the date.

EDITORIAL IN A NEWSPAPER

"The $3,000 License to Kill." Editorial. Washington Post 30 April 1983, sec. A: 18.

LETTER TO THE EDITOR

Echikson, William. Letter. Christian Science Monitor 7 June 1983: 22.

BOOK REVIEW

Stade, George. "The Duluth We Deserve?" Rev. of Duluth, by Gore Vidal. New York Times Book Review 5 June 1983: 3+.

Discontinuous page numbers are indicated by a plus sign.

Reference Models for Other Sources

UNPUBLISHED DOCTORAL DISSERTATION

Heath, Jim Frank. "John F. Kennedy and the Business Community." Diss. Stanford U, 1967.

SUMMARY ARTICLE OF DOCTORAL DISSERTATION IN DISSERTATION ABSTRACTS *(OR* DISSERTATION ABSTRACTS INTERNATIONAL*)*

Ribordy, Sheila C. "The Behavioral Treatment of Insomnia." DAI 37 (1975): 477B. U of Kansas.

LECTURE

Barglow, Peter. "Psychological Reactions to Job Loss." MLA Convention. Chicago, 28 Dec. 1977.

FILM

Truffaut, François, dir. Stolen Kisses. With Jean-Pierre Leaud and Delphine Seyrig. Lopert Pictures, 1969.

THEATRICAL PERFORMANCE

Hall, Peter, dir. Amadeus. By Peter Shaffer. With John Wood and John Pankow. Shubert Theatre, Boston. 14 May 1983.

MUSICAL COMPOSITION

Bach, Johann Sebastian. Sonata in B Minor for Flute and Harpsichord.

WORK OF ART

Botticelli, Sandro. The Birth of Venus. Uffizzi Gallery, Florence.

RADIO OR TELEVISION PROGRAM

The Russians Are Here. Writ. and Prod. Ofra Bikel. Narr. Jessica Savitch. GBH Frontline. 13 June 1983.

RECORDING

Brubeck, Dave. The Dave Brubeck Quartet: Gone with the Wind and Time Out. Columbia, CG 33666, 1983.

INTERVIEW

Welty, Eudora. Personal interview. 27 April 1983.

COMPUTER SOFTWARE

Light, Charles U. Malthusian Population Growth. Computer software. Reading, MA: Addison-Wesley, 1982.

Content Notes

Notes are frequently used to supplement or amplify information in the text. Occasionally, you will have ideas or data that, you believe, strengthen the discussion in your paper but, unfortunately, interrupt the flow of thought. Perhaps a "prewrite" that you have not been able to accommodate in your essay presents such a problem. The content note is the place for this sort of material:

[1]Autry was also charged with the murder of one potential eyewitness and the crippling injury of another. The cases were never brought to trial.

Use it also to indicate the *original* source of an indirect quote:

[2]M. G. Field, Doctor and Patient in Russia (Cambridge, MA: Harvard UP, 1957) 76, qtd. in Block and Reddaway 151.

The complete citation for Block and Reddaway would be found in your list of works cited.

Finally, you can use it in combination with parenthetical documentation:

[3]For a more detailed discussion of man's paradoxical nature, see Becker (25-30).

The rest of the bibliographical information on Becker would be found in your list of works cited.

Observe the following directions for typing your content notes:

1. Place an Arabic numeral slightly elevated above the line and as close as possible to the material in the text that the note is explaining.
2. Arrange the notes in chronological order on a separate page labeled "Notes" at the end of the paper, immediately preceding the list of works cited.
3. Attach an Arabic numeral to each note in your list of notes, also slightly elevated above the line, to correspond with the numbers in the text. (See the use of content notes in the sample research papers, pages 255, 258, 267, and 275.)

The Footnote/Endnote Style of Documentation

If your instructor prefers the earlier MLA style of citing sources using footnotes or endnotes, follow the guidelines below, which reflect the minor changes recommended by the second edition of the *MLA Handbook* (1984).

Footnotes are references that appear at the *foot* of the page:

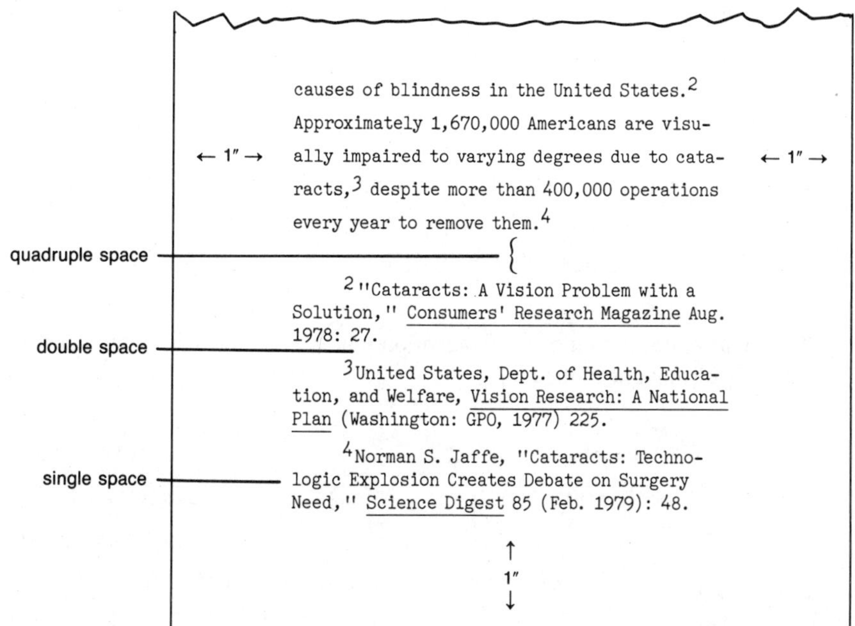

Endnotes are references gathered together on a separate page at the *end* of the paper:

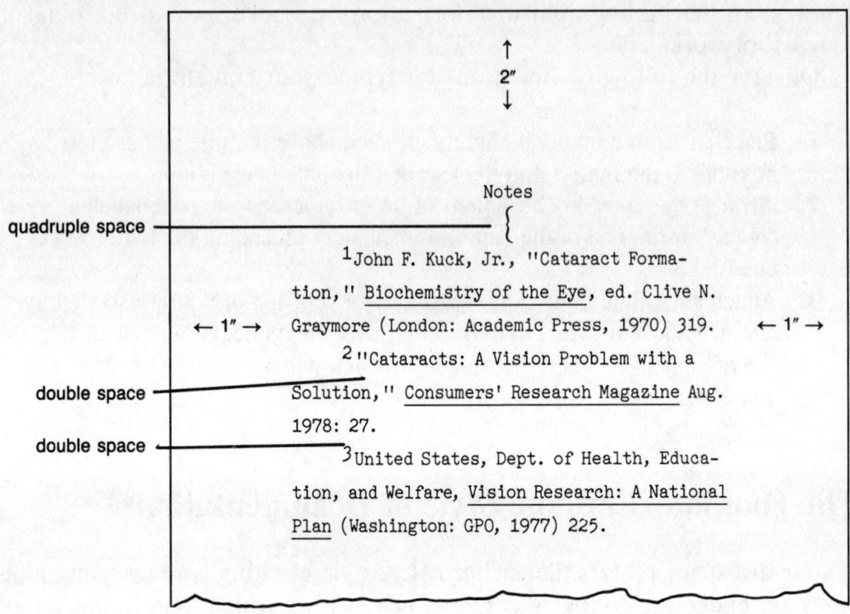
2"
Notes
quadruple space
[1]John F. Kuck, Jr., "Cataract Formation," Biochemistry of the Eye, ed. Clive N. Graymore (London: Academic Press, 1970) 319.
← 1" →
← 1" →
[2] "Cataracts: A Vision Problem with a Solution," Consumers' Research Magazine Aug. 1978: 27.
double space
double space
[3]United States, Dept. of Health, Education, and Welfare, Vision Research: A National Plan (Washington: GPO, 1977) 225.

When to Use Notes

Notes (whether footnotes or endnotes) have three uses:

1. To document a source for borrowed material.

[1]Peter Burra, Van Gogh (London: Duckworth, 1934) 97.

2. To add information or an explanation that would otherwise interrupt the flow of thought in the text.

[2]Unlike the urban child, the country child acquires knowledge of both birth and death gradually--and naturally. By witnessing the birth and death of plants and animals at close range, the child has an easier time understanding the life cycle.

3. To direct the reader to another source of information.

> [3]For more information on the disadvantages of the electric car, see Harris E. Dark, Auto Engines of Tomorrow (Bloomington: Indiana UP, 1975).

How to Write Notes

Notes making a *first* reference to a source of information will have the following characteristics:

1. An elevated number, corresponding to an identical number in the text, precedes each note.
2. Note numbers follow in consecutive order within the essay.
3. First line is indented five spaces.
4. Footnotes are single-spaced within the note and double-spaced between notes. Endnotes are double-spaced throughout.
5. Authors' names are not inverted.
6. Commas separate units of information.
7. Parentheses enclose city of publication, publisher, and date.
8. Exact page reference is listed.

Once you have provided complete bibliographical information for a particular source, give only author and page number(s) for all *subsequent references* to it:

> [3]Jaffe 46.

If there is no author, give title and page number(s):

> [4]"Cataracts: A Vision Problem with a Solution" 27.

If you are citing more than one work by the same author, provide title as well as author and page number(s):

> [5]Clark, Vision of the Future 319-20.

No punctuation or abbreviation for "page" precedes the page number.

Reference Models

The following notes illustrate the correct format for both *footnotes* and *endnotes.* They do not, however, cover all the possibilities, only the most common. If you have a source for which you cannot find a model, use the one closest to it and improvise the rest, observing the general principles of footnote/endnote logic.

BOOK WITH ONE AUTHOR

[1]Victor Argenzio, Diamonds Eternal (New York: David McKay, 1974) 34.

BOOK WITH TWO OR THREE AUTHORS

[2]John Taylor and Frederick Swanborough, Military Aircraft of the World (New York: Scribner's, 1971) 115.

BOOK WITH MORE THAN THREE AUTHORS

[3]Sharon M. Oster and others, The Definition and Measurement of Poverty (Boulder, CO: Westview, 1978) 78-79.

WORK OF SEVERAL VOLUMES

[4]William Manchester, The Glory and the Dream: A Narrative History of America 1932-1972, 2 vols. (Boston: Little, Brown, 1974) 2: 251.

ESSAY, PLAY, SHORT STORY, POEM IN A VOLUME OF WRITINGS BY THE SAME AUTHOR

[5]Noam Chomsky, "The Remaking of History," Towards a New Cold War: Essays on the Current Crisis and How We Got There by Chomsky (New York: Pantheon, 1982) 134-36.

ESSAY, PLAY, SHORT STORY, POEM IN A VOLUME OF WRITINGS BY DIFFERENT AUTHORS

[6]Richard Chase, "The Broken Circuit," Theories of American Literature, ed. Donald M. Kartiganer and Malcolm A. Griffith (New York: Macmillan, 1972) 45.

SECOND OR LATER EDITIONS OF A BOOK

[7]John Harris Paterson, North America: A Geography of Canada and the United States, 4th ed. (London: Oxford UP, 1970) 107.

BOOK WITH AN EDITOR

[8]Joseph Quincy Adams, ed., Chief Pre-Shakespearean Dramas (Boston: Houghton Mifflin, 1924) 17.

ARTICLE IN AN ENCYCLOPEDIA

[9]"Aran Islands," Encyclopedia Americana, 1982 ed.

GOVERNMENT PUBLICATION

[10]United States, Environmental Protection Agency, Effects of Noise on People (Washington: GPO, 1971) 2.

PAMPHLET OR BOOK WITH A CORPORATE AUTHOR

[11]International Center for the Disabled, Pity and Fear: Myths and Images of the Disabled in Literature Old and New (New York: ICD, 1981) 2.

ARTICLE IN A JOURNAL THAT PAGES CONSECUTIVELY FROM ISSUE TO ISSUE

[12]Sara Rudick, "Pacifying the Forces: Drafting Women in the Interests of Peace," Signs 8 (1983): 472.

ARTICLE IN A JOURNAL THAT PAGES EACH ISSUE SEPARATELY

[13]George Gilder, "Making It," The Wilson Quarterly 9 (Winter 1985): 71.

[14]John R. Frey, "America and Her Literature Reviewed by Postwar Germany," American-German Review 20.5 (1984): 5.

ARTICLE IN A MONTHLY MAGAZINE

[15]George Laycock, "The Darkest Frontier," Audubon May 1983: 90.

ARTICLE IN A WEEKLY MAGAZINE OR WEEKLY NEWSPAPER

[16]"Trouble at Stanford," Newsweek 6 June 1983: 92.

ARTICLE IN A DAILY NEWSPAPER

[17]"Ships May Tie Up at 2 Ice 'Islands,' " New York Times 23 Feb. 1969, late ed., sec. 1: 13.

UNPUBLISHED DOCTORAL DISSERTATION

[18]Jim Frank Heath, "John F. Kennedy and the Business Community," diss. (Stanford U, 1967), 55.

LECTURE

[19]Peter Barglow, "Psychological Reactions to Job Loss," MLA Convention, Chicago, 28 Dec. 1977.

FILM

[20]François Truffaut, dir., Stolen Kisses, with Jean-Pierre Leaud and Delphine Seyrig, Lopert Pictures, 1969.

RADIO OR TELEVISION PROGRAM

[21]The Russians Are Here, writ. and prod. Ofra Bikel, GBH Frontline, 13 June 1983.

RECORDING

[22]Dave Brubeck, The Dave Brubeck Quartet: Gone with the Wind and Time Out, Columbia, CG 33666, 1983.

INTERVIEW

[23]Eudora Welty, personal interview, 27 April 1983.

Other Forms of Documentation Style

For all other systems of documentation (that is, those recommended by learned societies in the natural and social sciences as well as in other disciplines within the humanities), consult the style manual of the appropriate discipline. You will find that despite the diversity, most have adopted a system of documentation that, like the revised MLA format, omits footnotes and endnotes in favor of brief identification of the source parenthetically in the body of the paper and gives complete documentation only once in a list of works cited at the end. Various styles are used for identifying the source parenthetically, many of them falling into one of the following three categories: author-title, author-date, or number system. In the first two, the author and a short title (or date) and page number appear in parentheses. In the last case, numbers are assigned to all the citations in the list of works cited, and whenever a reference is made to one of them, its corresponding number and page are cited in the text.

APA (Author-Date) Style

The following models will give you an idea of what one such system of documentation (author-date) is like. The APA format below is recommended by the *Publication Manual of the American Psychological Association* (1983). Author and date of publication are cited in parentheses within the text to identify the source of borrowed material, and a complete citation is provided in the reference list at the end.

Models of Text Citations Following the APA Style

WHEN NEITHER AUTHOR NOR DATE APPEARS IN THE TEXT

a recent study (Gardner, 1981)

Use a comma to separate author from date.

WHEN EITHER AUTHOR OR DATE APPEARS IN THE TEXT

demonstrated by Gardner (1981)

study in 1981 (Gardner)

Omit author or date from parentheses when either is mentioned in the narrative.

WHEN BOTH AUTHOR AND DATE APPEAR IN THE TEXT

In 1981, Gardner undertook

No parenthetical documentation is given.

WORK BY TWO AUTHORS

(Diener & Kerber, 1979)

Cite both names each time the reference is made. Join the names by an ampersand (&). (When the names appear in the text, however, they are joined by an "and.")

WORK BY THREE TO FIVE AUTHORS

(McClelland, Davis, Kalin, & Wanner, 1972)

Cite all the authors the first time the reference is made. In all subsequent citations, however, give the surname of the first author followed by the abbreviation "et al.," unless the abbreviated reference can be confused with another abbreviated reference. For example, McClelland, Davis, Kalin, & Wanner, 1972 and McClelland, Kalin, Wanner, & Roberts, 1972 would both abbreviate to McClelland et al., 1972. In that case, cite all the names each time the reference is made.

WORK BY MORE THAN FIVE AUTHORS

`(Rybakowski et al., 1977)`

Cite only the name of the first author, unless confusion (such as that described above) results. In that case, cite as many of the names each time as are necessary to differentiate between the sources. Do not underline anything and do not separate author from abbreviation "et al." with a comma. Note the period after "al." but none after "et" in the citation.

WORK BY A CORPORATE AUTHOR (ASSOCIATION, GOVERNMENT AGENCY, ETC.)

`(Alexander Hamilton Institute, 1962)`

If the name is awkwardly long, spell it out the first time and include an abbreviation in brackets. Thereafter, use the abbreviation without brackets. First citation:

`(Multiple Risk Factor Intervention Trial [MRFIT], 1976)`

Subsequent citations:

`(MRFIT, 1976)`

WORK WITHOUT AN AUTHOR

`("Firearms and Federal," 1975)`

Cite the first few significant words of the entry in the reference list (usually those of the title). Put double quotation marks around the title of an article or chapter; underline the title of a book or periodical. Place the comma *within* quotation marks.

WORKS BY AUTHORS WITH THE SAME LAST NAME

(E. R. Smith, 1980)

(W. H. Smith, 1981)

Add initials even if the dates are different.

TWO OR MORE WORKS BY THE SAME AUTHOR WITHIN THE SAME PARENTHESES

(Danto, 1971, 1979, 1983)

Arrange by year of publication.

TWO OR MORE WORKS BY THE SAME AUTHOR WITH THE SAME PUBLICATION DATE WITHIN THE SAME PARENTHESES

(Krug, 1967, 1978a, 1978b)

Assign suffixes to the identical publication dates in parentheses, and then assign corresponding suffixes to the publication dates in the reference list citations.

TWO OR MORE WORKS BY DIFFERENT AUTHORS WITHIN THE SAME PARENTHESES

(Horowitz et al., 1977; Lester & Murrell, 1980; Massey, 1967)

Arrange the authors alphabetically. Separate the units by semicolons.

SPECIFIC PARTS OF A SOURCE (PAGE, CHAPTER, FIGURE, TABLE, OR EQUATION)

(Wood, 1980, p. 460)

(Brown, 1979, pp. 1120-1121)

(Choron, 1972, chap. 3)

(Boor, 1981, table 1)

Always cite page numbers when quoting and give the complete page number (1120–1121 *not* 1120–21). Use abbreviations “p.” and “pp.” for page and pages, respectively, and “chap.” for chapter.

Models of Reference List Citations Following the APA Style

BOOK WITH ONE AUTHOR

French, A. P. (1977). Disturbed children and their families: Innovations in evaluation and treatment. New York: Human Sciences Press.

Cite only the initials of the author's first name. Capitalize only the first word of the title and of the subtitle. Place year of publication in parentheses immediately following the author's name.

BOOK WITH TWO AUTHORS

Jenkins, G. M., & Watts, D. G. (1967). Spectral analysis and its applications. San Francisco: Holden-Day.

Invert the surnames of both authors. Separate the authors with a comma and an ampersand (&). If you are citing other works by the *same first author,* type out the first author each time and arrange each entry according to the following guidelines: single author precedes multiple authors; multiple author entries are arranged alphabetically by the surname of the second and following authors; identical author entries are arranged by year of publication in chronological order; identical author and year entries are arranged alphabetically by title, excluding "A" and "The," and suffixes are added to the identical years of publication.

Howells, R. G. (1978)

Howells, R. G., Coller, C. M., & Bruggen, P. (1977)

Howells, R. G., & Dix, A. L. (1978)

Howells, R. G., & Dix, A. L. (1980a). Death in the addict family

Howells, R. G., & Dix, A. L. (1980b). Family psychiatry

BOOK WITH MORE THAN TWO AUTHORS

Katz, J., Goldstein, J., & Dershowitz, A. M. (1967). Psychoanalysis, psychiatry and the law. New York: Free Press.

Invert all names and spell out regardless of the number.

BOOK WITH AN EDITOR

Miller, J. (Ed.). (1972). Freud: The man, his world, his influence. Boston: Little, Brown.

The abbreviation for editors would be "Eds." Use a period to separate editor from date and date from title.

SECOND OR LATER EDITIONS OF A BOOK

Poole, L., & Borchers, M. (1978). Some common basic programs (2nd ed.). Berkeley, CA: Adam Osborne and Assoc.

Do not use any punctuation to separate the title from the edition in parentheses. Place a period after the closing parenthesis. Use the postal abbreviation for state (without periods) to identify nonmajor cities of publication or to avoid confusing the city with another one of the same name.

BOOK WITH A CORPORATE AUTHOR AND AUTHOR AS PUBLISHER

American Psychiatric Association. (1969). A psychiatric glossary: The meaning of terms frequently used in psychiatry (3rd ed.). Washington, DC: Author.

Place a period after the corporate author and after the date. If the author is also the publisher, use the word "Author" in the publisher position.

WORK OF SEVERAL VOLUMES AND PUBLICATION PERIOD COVERS MORE THAN ONE YEAR

Jones, E. (1953-1957). The life and work of Sigmund Freud (Vols. 1-3). New York: Basic Books.

Since volume 1 was published in 1953, volume 2 in 1955, and volume 3 in 1957, the five-year span is indicated in parentheses.

CHAPTER OR ARTICLE IN AN EDITED BOOK

Stickney, S. B. (1967). Hunting. In R. Slovenko & J. A. Knights (Eds.), Motivations in play, games, and sports (pp. 202-245). Springfield, IL: Thomas.

Do not enclose the title of the chapter or article in quotation marks, but underline the title of the book. Do not invert the names of editors. If there are only two, use an ampersand (&); if there are more than two, separate *all* the names with commas, and add an ampersand before the last one. Cite inclusive page numbers and use the abbreviations "p." or "pp." for page and pages, respectively.

ARTICLE IN A JOURNAL THAT PAGES CONSECUTIVELY FROM ISSUE TO ISSUE

Lawson, B. R. (1979). Cognitive strategies in architectural design. Ergonomics, 22, 59-68.

Use Arabic numerals for the volume number without an abbreviation for volume, and underline it. Give the inclusive page numbers of the article. Omit abbreviation for pages. Use commas to separate journal from volume and volume from pages.

ARTICLE IN A JOURNAL THAT PAGES EACH ISSUE SEPARATELY

Escalona, S. K. (1981). Infant day care: A social and psychological perspective on mental health implications. Infant Mental Health Journal, 2(1), 4-17.

Give the issue number in parentheses—only if each issue begins on page 1—and underline the volume.

ARTICLE IN A MAGAZINE

Weinberg, R. A. (1983, October). The search for the origins of cancer. Technology Review, pp. 46-55.

Give the date as year, month, and day (if any), in that order. Use the abbreviations for page and pages.

ARTICLE IN A NEWSPAPER

PPG, aided by pruning campaign, has record net in sight for '84. (1983, December 5). Barron's, pp. 63, 66.

When no author is given, place the title in the author position and then give the date. Otherwise, use the standard order: author, date, title. The abbreviation for page and pages is used. Separate noncontinuous pages with a comma.

LETTER TO THE EDITOR

Simpson, C. (1983, December 5). Bargaining for health [Letter to the editor]. Washington Post, p. 10.

TECHNICAL AND RESEARCH REPORTS

Turem, J. S. (1975). Report of the comprehensive service needs study (Contract No. HEW 100-74-0309). Washington, DC: Department of Health, Education and Welfare.

If a number (of a report, contract, monograph) has been assigned to the report, give the number in parentheses after the title.

DOCTORAL DISSERTATION ABSTRACTED IN DISSERTATION ABSTRACTS INTERNATIONAL *AND OBTAINED ON UNIVERSITY MICROFILM*

Weber, W. M. (1980). A comparison of media for public participation in national environmental planning. Dissertation Abstracts International, 41, 2345A. (University Microfilms No. 8025798)

The order number for the microfilm is placed in parentheses *outside* of the period at the end of the citation.

DOCTORAL DISSERTATION ABSTRACTED IN DISSERTATION ABSTRACTS INTERNATIONAL *AND OBTAINED FROM THE UNIVERSITY*

Coppersmith, E. (1978). Intergenerational relatedness and attitudes toward aging: A case study in family therapy (Doctoral dissertation, University of Pittsburgh). Dissertation Abstracts International, 38, 5244A.

UNPUBLISHED RAW DATA FROM STUDY, UNTITLED

Huntress, E. L. (1983). [Assessing developmental differences in children's estimation skills.] Unpublished raw data.

Place the topic of the study in brackets to indicate that it is not a title. Do not underline it.

PUBLISHED INTERVIEW

Troy, T. (1984, February-March). Contemporary American Indian art. [Interview with G. Peter Jemison.] Art and Artists, pp. 5-6.

Follow the format appropriate for the published source of the interview, in this case a newspaper. Use brackets to describe content whether the interview is titled or not.

FILM, VIDEOTAPE, AUDIOTAPE, SLIDE, CHART, ARTWORK

Loeb, J., & Levitt, W. (Producers), & Myers, S. (Director). (1970). The quiet one [Film]. New York: McGraw-Hill.

Give name(s) of primary contributor(s) and identify in parentheses. Specify medium in brackets after the title. Name the location and distributor at the end.

COMPUTER PROGRAM

Light, C. U. (1982). Malthusian population growth [Computer program]. Reading, MA: Addison-Wesley.

Place the main contributor in the author position. Use brackets to specify the source as a computer program. If you have any additional information that would help in retrieving the source, place it in parentheses at the end of the citation (*after* the period).

15 Model Research Papers

Two student research essays with formal outlines have been provided as models. Each essay and outline have been annotated to illustrate a different principle:

1. The outline of "Trigger Control"* to illustrate the integration of the *rhetorical modes* (as developed in the prewrites).
2. The essay "Trigger Control" to illustrate the use of *documented* material (other people's ideas).
3. The outline of "California Wines Are Alive and Well" to illustrate *organization* and location of *thesis.*
4. The essay "California Wines Are Alive and Well" to illustrate the use of *undocumented* material (your own ideas).

*For the purpose of illustrating a system of documentation other than the MLA, sources in this essay have been identified by means of the APA style (author/year system). Annotations, however, apply to *both* the MLA and APA styles.

TRIGGER CONTROL

By

Donna Brugnoli

EN 101-15 English Composition

Prof. Hughes

May 9, 1986

TRIGGER CONTROL

Thesis: The mere presence of a gun can have an aggressive effect on behavior because of a phenomenon called "the weapons effect."

I. A gun is a weapon whose sole purpose is to destroy.
   A. It is used to kill animals.
   B. It is used to kill people.

Lead example (grabber)

II. Gun owners can be divided into two categories.
   A. Ordinary citizens include hunters, collectors, and individuals who purchase guns for protection.
   B. Criminals acquire guns for the purpose of committing illegal actions.

Division

III. Studies show gun control laws will not save ordinary citizens from criminals, but they will save "ordinary citizens from other ordinary citizens" because of a phenomenon called "the weapons effect."
   A. The gun itself can provoke violence.
   B. Other weapons do not have the same effect.

Unfamiliar term, definition

Question *why*, causal analysis

Express comparison

IV. The weapons effect has been linked with various kinds of ordinary citizens.
   A. Guns exert the weapons effect on suicidal individuals.
      1. Peter Gregg is a case in point.
   B. They exert it on people who are not angry nor emotionally aroused in any way.

Examples illustrate and corroborate the thesis

1. Researchers used a college campus to test the effect.

C. They exert it on people who are already angry.
   1. Frederick W. Cowan is a case in point.

D. They exert it on frustrated individuals.
   1. Researchers conducted an experiment at a busy intersection to test the effect.
   2. Kay Marion Beach is a case in point.

E. They exert it on children.
   1. Two uncontrolled studies of nursery school children were conducted to test the effect.
   2. David is a case in point.

Trigger Control

The 1861 Shiloh, a .177-cal. CO_2-powered single-action revolver, popular with youngsters, topples tin cans and easily dispatches field mice, fox squirrels, and Texas scrub jays. The Perazzi can pick out a grouse that is flying incredibly fast over the brow of a hill and with a single pull of the trigger slam it against a rock wall. The Weatherby Mark V Magnum is designed to drop a magnificently antlered buck, its matted coat steaming in the morning air, with one shot at 100 yards. And Saturday night specials maim and kill human victims daily in the living rooms, stores, parks, highways, and streets of America.

A gun is a weapon whose sole purpose is to destroy. Whether he is shooting at animals, tin cans in a junkyard, clay pigeons, or people, the marksman's goal is to hit and destroy or maim that object. In the United States today there are an estimated 90 million guns in private hands; in fact, about half of America's families admit to owning at least one firearm (Diener & Kerber, 1979).

Documents statistics

Gun owners can be divided into two main categories--ordinary citizens and criminals. Ordinary citizens include hunters, sportsmen, security personnel, collectors, and individuals who purchase guns for protection against antisocial elements. These people register their weapons and customarily abide by the law. Criminals buy or steal firearms with the express purpose of committing illegal actions. Numerous statistics and

2

Documentary reference acknowledges an expert opinion. Documentation is crucial since opinion is controversial

Student consolidates documentation by enclosing borrowed material with the author's name at the beginning and a page number at the end

Quotation marks call attention to a key word/phrase

studies prove that strict gun control laws will not save ordinary citizens from criminals because they do not deter criminals from obtaining weapons (Murray, 1975), but, as Leonard Berkowitz (1981) explains, gun control laws may "save some ordinary citizens from other ordinary citizens" because of a phenomenon called "the weapons effect." Research in recent years suggests that "the mere presence of guns can have an aggressive effect on behavior. . . . [The] weapon itself is a stimulant to violence" (p. 11). This one factor is the strongest argument for strict gun control.

The weapons effect is an unconscious aggressive reaction to the sight of a weapon. The weapon itself, writes Berkowitz (1981), functions as a "conditioned stimulus," provoking violent behavior (p. 12). People associate guns with violence and behave accordingly. Wanting to kill somebody, getting a gun, and shooting isn't necessarily the usual sequence of events. In the case of "ordinary citizens," the following is the more likely sequence: having a gun, getting depressed, angry, or frustrated, then shooting. This kind of killing isn't planned; it's triggered by the gun; it's "impulsive" violence (Berkowitz, 1968, p. 19). Nor can the weapons effect be related to other instruments of aggression such as knives, clubs, or axes, because these weapons have other uses. The link between the weapon and aggression is strongest when the weapon's only purpose is killing.

3

The main reason that a gun acts as such a powerful stimulant is the ease with which a gun can be used as opposed to any other weapon. It takes less effort to use a gun than a knife on a person. Using a knife involves muscle, force, and physical contact with the victim. It requires confronting the victim in person and, therefore, risking counterattack. A gun, on the other hand, can be fired from a distance; by making the killer "invisible," it protects him from the victim's reaction. One quick, light pull of the trigger and the damage is done.

The same restraining principle that applies to the knife also applies to any other object that can be used as a weapon, such as a club or even bare fists. The aggressor cannot detach himself from his actions. He has to make bodily, auditory, and eye contact with the victim. As he approaches him, he has time for second thoughts. A gun is impersonal. It can shoot its victim as mechanically as it would a bull's eye on a practice range. The offender does not have to see, hear, or feel the victim's suffering; he can sever himself totally from the victim after pulling the trigger. In fact, he may even get the distorted impression that it wasn't he that did the killing but the bullet.

In various recent studies the weapons effect has been linked with suicide victims, angry as well as non-angry people, frustrated individuals, and most tragic of all, children. These investigations show how ordinary

4

people's aggressions are aroused when they are in the presence of a gun and how they react in accordance with their aggressions.

Sometimes more effective to introduce data, a quotation, or paraphrased material with bibliographical information other than the author's name

Behavioral scientists frequently study the relation between the availability of guns and suicidal behavior. In 1980, a report in the American Journal of Psychiatry documented the results of an investigation that reveals a correlation between suicide rates and gun control laws: the stricter the laws, the lower the suicide rates (Lester & Murrell). The following year, after examining suicide methods and rates in the United States over a thirteen-year period, Myron Boor (1981) of the Western Psychiatric Institute and Clinic (University of Pittsburgh) confirmed the conclusion that the easy availability of guns influences suicidal behavior:

Blocked quotation is introduced with the author's name, a complete sentence, and a colon

> Virtually all of the increases in the suicide rates of each of the four sex-ethnic groups--white males, white females, nonwhite males, nonwhite females--between 1962 and 1975 can be attributed to increases in the rates of suicides by firearms. These increases in suicide rates accompanied marked increases in the availability of firearms. . . . The suicide rates by other methods remained quite stable during the 1962-1975 time period. . . . (p. 73)

5

In other words, it seems that if a gun could not be easily purchased, were not already in the individual's possession, nor readily available in the individual's home, some individuals would not kill themselves. Because of the weapons effect, therefore, the gun becomes more than just an instrument for killing oneself; it sometimes acts as a "reason" to kill oneself.

Case in point: Peter Gregg was a race car driver, who was forced off the track because of injuries he'd sustained during a racing accident. For over a year, he was depressed over the loss of his career and even sought psychiatric help. One day on a Florida beach, he shot himself in the head with a newly purchased .38-caliber gun. A briefcase with a sales slip inside was found next to his body ("Driver's Suicide," 1980). He'd apparently been carrying the pistol in his briefcase for days. His original resolve to kill himself had not been strong enough to make him go through with it as soon as he bought the gun. But having the gun around for a while finally raised his aggression to the point of suicide.

Each sentence of news story is not footnoted because as news item it cannot be mistaken for writer's ideas

The presence of a gun also has an effect on people who are not despondent nor even upset. An experiment was conducted by researchers to prove that a person does not have to be in any particular state of mind to succumb to the weapons effect. In identical experiments on two separate college campuses, they had students throw wet sponges at a clown in a carnival booth.

6

In order to test the weapons effect, they exposed some of the sponge throwers to a rifle placed "conspicuously near the front of the booth." Then to arouse anger, they subjected some of these throwers to insults from the clown. The rest of the throwers saw no rifle nor heard any insults. The results supported the weapons effect. The insulted students did not throw any more sponges than did the uninsulted students. But the students exposed to the rifle threw more sponges than the unexposed students (Berkowitz, 1981, p. 12). In other words, a person does not necessarily have to be depressed or angry for the weapons effect to take place.

However, if a person is already enraged, the presence of the gun will make him even more belligerent (Page & O'Neal, 1977). Case in point: when the police arrived at the Neptune Worldwide Moving Company, Frederick W. Cowan had already killed four co-workers in a shooting rampage. By the time it ended, six people would be dead (including Cowan) and five wounded. After a probe into the circumstances surrounding the incident, the police discovered that Cowan had been suspended from the moving company for two weeks "for refusing an order to move a refrigerator" and had sworn "to 'get even' " with the supervisor, who had disciplined him. He had returned to the company armed with a semi-automatic rifle, four handguns, and belts of ammunition, shooting everyone in sight while he stalked the building for his supervisor (McFadden, 1977, pp. 1, 28).

Single quotations indicate the student is quoting a phrase quoted in the original

Documentation at beginning and end of paragraph indicates Page/O'Neal as source of the topic idea but McFadden as source of the corroborating example

7

Then there was the study that was done to show the correlation between the weapons effect and frustration; it was conducted at an intersection. The researchers created several frustrating situations to determine the effect seeing a gun would have on drivers who had suddenly become frustrated. They put a rifle in the rear window of a pickup truck and then stalled it on a green light. As a control, they also stalled the truck on another occasion without a rifle in the window. Again, the results confirmed the theory of the weapons effect. There was more honking at the truck with the rifle than at the one without (Berkowitz, 1981).

Case in point: Kay Marion Beach was 70 years old and didn't fit anybody's picture of a killer; yet frustrated by a man's refusal to move his car, which was blocking her driveway, she shot him ("Woman," 1980). If she had not had a gun, the only immediate outlet for her frustration might have been a kick at the offending car--not murder. It was the gun that had provoked the killing.

The weapons effect is also apparent in children. In two uncontrolled studies of four- and five-year-olds in a nursery school, it was observed over a several week period that even playing with guns causes aggression. Those children who were given toy guns to play with did more hitting and pushing and used nastier language than the children given other kinds of toys (Berkowitz, 1981).[1] Needless to say, when the guns are real, playing with them can be fatal.

Superscript number refers to a content note

8

Case in point: Robin, Sharon, and Julia Ann, all aged 15, were enjoying a swim in Julia Ann's backyard pool. Meanwhile, Julia Ann's two brothers, Robert, 14, and David, 16, were fighting in front of the TV set; the tussle had broken out because of David's persistence in hitting his brother with a yo-yo. Suddenly, David stopped fighting, walked into his bedroom, picked up his .22-caliber semi-automatic rifle, went outside, and began shooting. Result: three girls dead ("Youth Kills," 1977). What really demonstrates the weapons effect in this story is that David did not return from the bedroom to shoot his brother, with whom he'd been fighting. Apparently, David had no quarrel with Robert; he had just been playing--out of boredom maybe or nervousness. Each game, however, had produced a different level of aggression. The yo-yo game had led only to a scuffle; the game with the gun, however, raised David's aggression to a murderous level, which he then worked off on his sister and her girlfriends.

In short, guns aren't just another weapon in the history of violence. They're a very unique weapon. They trigger aggression in ordinary people who aren't criminals. Studies prove that people can get aggressive just by seeing a gun; and real life proves that when "plain folk" kill, it is because a gun just happened to be around when they were in an emotionally receptive state. Therefore, the slogan of the National Rifle Association ("Guns don't kill people. People kill people.") is a naive oversimplification (Berkowitz, 1981). Guns _do_ kill people because without them, ordinary people would settle arguments and cope with depression, anger, and frustration in less fatal ways.

This content note is a combination of information and documentation

10

Notes

[1]Other experiments involving guns and children have yielded similar results. For an experiment conducted by the University of Indiana, see Berkowitz (1968).

11

References

Sources used in essay are listed

Berkowitz, L. (1968, September). Impulse, aggression and the gun. Psychology Today, pp. 19-20, 22.

Berkowitz, L. (1981, June). How guns control us. Psychology Today, pp. 11-12.

Boor, M. (1981). Methods of suicide and implications for suicide prevention. Journal of Clinical Psychology, 37(1), 70-75.

Diener, E., & Kerber, K. W. (1979). Personality characteristics of American gun-owners. The Journal of Social Psychology, 107, 227-238.

Driver's suicide is laid to post-accident worry. (1980, December 17). New York Times, Sec. B, p. 6.

Lester, D., & Murrell, M. E. (1980). The influence of gun control laws on suicidal behavior. American Journal of Psychiatry, 137(1), 121-122.

McFadden, R. D. (1977, February 15). Nazi admirer also wounds 5 in wild attack followed by a siege at moving company. New York Times, pp. 1, 28.

Murray, D. R. (1975). Handguns, gun control laws and firearm violence. Social Problems, 23(1), 81-93.

Page, D., & O'Neal, E. (1977). 'Weapons effect' without demand characteristics. Psychological Reports, 41(1), 29-30.

Woman, 70, is held in shooting. (1980, December 29). New York Times, Sec. A., p. 16.

Youth kills three after yo-yo fight. (1977, August 3). Brockton Enterprise, p. 2.

While Berkowitz's titles suggest the student has adopted his thesis, the remaining citations indicate she's done more than summarize him: she's introduced additional sources to corroborate his thesis

CALIFORNIA WINES ARE ALIVE AND WELL

By

Ned Hawkins

ENG 21.001 Writing I

Dr. Lindsay

December 5, 1986

CALIFORNIA WINES ARE ALIVE AND WELL

Thesis sentence: The finest California wines are now challenging the finest French wines and sometimes winning.

I. Mystique of wine
   A. Uniqueness of the beverage
   B. Historical associations
   C. Artistry of wine making

II. Mystique of French wine
   A. Standard for other wines

III. Problems of American wine
   A. Failure of European wine grape to thrive in the East
   B. Unpalatable flavor of native grapes
   C. Prohibition

IV. Variables that determine quality of wine
   A. Grape
   B. Soil
   C. Climate

V. Basic types of grapes/wines
   A. Premier
   B. All the rest

VI. General comparison of French and California premier wines
   A. Chardonnays
   B. Cabernets

Background information

Thesis suggested

Thesis stated outright

General development of topic

Thesis implied; corroborating data and ideas introduced

Specific corroboration of thesis

VII. Superiority of California Chardonnays and Cabernets

A. Based on price

B. Based on wine tastings

C. Based on foreign investments

California Wines Are Alive and Well

Terry Robards, wine critic for the New York Times, chooses the five wines he serves at a Thanksgiving dinner with the care of an artist blending his colors (Robards, "Thanks" 148).

In preparation for a wine-tasting ceremony in New York, the Barons Elie and Eric de Rothschild ship their wines from France three months ahead of the event to "give them time to rest" and then turn them upside down for three weeks prior to the tasting to give the sediment a chance to settle (Prial, "Tasting" 22).

Gerald Asher writes in what sounds like poetry of a 1951 Cabernet Sauvignon from the Louis M. Martini Vineyard of California: "But as we talked, sniffing, sipping, and wondering aloud, the wine changed, its strangeness clearing like morning fog to reveal a youthful berrylike bouquet that contradicts its 28 years" (6).

These are people who take their wine seriously and believe, like Edward VII, that " 'Not only does one drink wine, but one inhales it, one looks at it, one tastes it, one swallows it . . . and one talks about it' " (Quoted by Lichine and Massee 11). For the wine connoisseur, wine isn't simply another beverage. It's not like a bottle of Coke or a glass of Scotch on the rocks. It's not something to guzzle when you're thirsty after a football game or hold onto for hours at a cocktail party. It's certainly not something to get drunk

Undocumented: topic sentence (of grabber above) to be explained or supported by either borrowed material or personal observations or both

Undocumented: topic sentence; personal observation

2

on. It's the aristocrat of alcoholic beverages to be served in crystal goblets and golden chalices. Everything associated with it is regal. The vineyards that grow the wine have mansions and chateaus as their centerpieces. Their visitors include "heads of state, Hollywood celebrities, [and] corporate moguls" (Robards, "Premium Red" 54), who wouldn't think of visiting a Coca-Cola plant or the Scotch distilleries in Scotland. Notables like Prince Charles, Henry Kissinger, Gen. Douglas MacArthur, and ten American presidents, who wouldn't dream of phoning Seagram's for a case of whiskey, find it perfectly respectable to call the Beaulieu Vineyard in California's Napa Valley, so the story goes, to order a Private Reserve Cabernet (Robards, "Premium Red" 54). Clearly, wine is in a class by itself.

Undocumented: personal observation

Undocumented: restatement of topic sentence

Undocumented: topic sentence

There are two reasons for the wine mystique: its history and the skill and knowledge (even love) that it takes to make it. Alec Waugh points out that archaeologists have determined that making wine from grapes goes back 10,000 years, and the historians have learned from Middle Eastern writings that Sennacherib and Nebuchadnezzar were drinking wine from their own vineyards some 2000 years before Christ (39). In the popular mind wine is associated with aristocratic wine drinkers, who live in moated castles, own wine cellars, and serve wine after first dusting it of cobwebs. It is also associated with wine festivals in which sultry

Undocumented: personal observation

3

Italian girls crush the grapes with their bare feet to the rhythms of the tarantella.

But it's not only the ancient and colorful history of wine that gives it a special aura; it's also the artistry it takes to create it. Even today when practically nobody uses their feet to crush grapes anymore (Waugh 37) and modern technology has introduced temperature-controlled stainless steel storage tanks and mechanical harvesters (Langway 59), winegrowing in most places is still a craft with an artisan. It is still "a matter of judgment, not only as to the time when the grapes should be harvested, but as to how long the wine should ferment, how long it should stay in the barrel, how it should be treated if it gets sick, when it should be bottled" (Lichine and Massee 10). If a cellar-master begins the harvest even a day too late, for example, the sugar-acid ratio will be out of balance in the wine (Lichine and Massee 49). A good example of just how important a role the winegrower plays is Clos de Vougeot, a vineyard in Burgundy, France, "where fifty owners divide forty acres, to produce an astonishing range of character and quality in wines called Clos de Vougeot" (Thompson and Johnson 165). No two winemakers end up producing identical wines; each wine is stamped with the personality of the winemaker (Thompson and Johnson 166).

Undocumented: topic sentence

The wines with the greatest mystique attached to them and the ones usually considered superior to all other wines have always been French. "The greatest

Undocumented: topic sentence

4

wines on earth come from France" is the opening sentence of Lichine and Massee's guide to French wines published in 1951 (3). Even as recently as ten years ago, however, the superiority of French wines was still uncontested (Robards, "Thanks" 146). They have always been the standard against which all other wines have been measured. So it's understandable that people should ask the inevitable question: How do American wines compare with French wines? The answer has been astonishing questioners on both sides of the Atlantic.

Undocumented: personal observation

Undocumented: reference to thesis

Undocumented: topic sentence

As already pointed out, a mere decade ago American wines weren't even in the running. For one thing, writes André L. Simon, the European wine grape (the species botanically known as Vitis vinifera as opposed to Vitis labrusca, which is the common table grape) did not thrive in the eastern United States. As for native grapes, they have a "low sugar content . . . which results in a low alcoholic content causing the wine to spoil easily" (49). The wine also has a strange flavor wine lovers used to European wines consider "foxy" and, according to one California winegrower, "can't stand" (Adams 8). As a result, the eastern wine industry produces mainly table (inexpensive) wines, sparkling wines in which the "foxy" flavor isn't objectionable, and very sweet (kosher-type) wines to which sugar has been added (Simon 50).

Unlike the eastern United States, California has the perfect climate for the European wine grape, and so,

5

when it was first introduced in the 1800s, it thrived very well (Simon 49). But then Prohibition came along (1918-1932) and all but wiped out the wine industry. Hannum and Blumberg list the problems that it caused. The vineyards lost their trained personnel and their skilled winegrowers. They were replanted with mediocre grapes. The wine casks sat unused for thirteen years; and the industry lost a "knowledgeable clientele" (25-26). By the late sixties and early seventies, it had revived, but leading wine experts like Amerine and Joslyn still called American table wine defective in Table Wine, a basic text on the subject: " 'The most common defect of California wines is their lack of distinctive aroma or bouquet. . . .' "[1]

Undocumented: topic sentence and common knowledge

Undocumented: introduction of borrowed material

But times have changed. California wines have arrived. No one is apologizing for American wines any longer. The finest California wines are now challenging the finest French wines and sometimes winning. When a wine expert wants to be diplomatic about the question of which is the better wine, he answers like John De Luca, president of the California Wine Institute: " 'We make great California wines and they make great French wines' " (Quoted by Prial, "Quality" 93). But apparently the polite answer hasn't satisfied either the French or the Americans because the competition continues.

Undocumented: transitional paragraph

Undocumented: reference to thesis

The question of the superiority of one wine over another will always get asked because wines are never

Undocumented: transitional paragraph

6

identical, unless all the conditions under which the grapes are grown and the wines are made are identical. In other words, some people might think that looking for differences between wines is just a matter of snobbishness. But that is not the case. Wines are different because of the many variables that go into the making of wine. Even a slight change in one will affect the taste and quality of wine. The <u>main</u> variables are the grape, the soil, and the climate.

Undocumented: topic sentence

First, the grape. While only one species of wine grape (though many varieties) is used both in France and in California, the berry itself must have the proper balance between sugar and acid (Hannum and Blumberg 31); the vine must also be free of defects, because they show up, first, in the berry and then in the wine (Asher 84).

Topic sentence implied: Soil is second variable

The soil must have "the ideal chemical properties for the wine grape" (Lichine and Massee 9), and it must be gravelly and well drained, "a key factor in nearly every other superior vineyard anywhere in the world" (Robards, "Premium Red" 54). Lichine and Massee explain, "The earth is what gives wine its character" (9).

Undocumented: topic sentence

The climate is the biggest variable of all, since it's the one thing that the winegrower cannot control. The ideal climate for growing wine grapes is dry and warm during the day but cool at night (Robards, "Humming" 130). Hannum and Blumberg describe the effect of climate on the wine:

7

> If the climate is too cold, the wine will be high in acid and low in alcohol due to the sugar deficiency. If the climate is too hot, wines high in alcohol may result, but the acid content will be so low as to lead to flat-tasting, poorly colored wines. (31)

What might seem minor, like a "day or two of spring freeze or an early autumn rainy spell may . . . be enough to impair quality" (Hannum and Blumberg 56). In other words, when wine buffs speak of a "great year," they're referring to grapes that ripened to perfection under ideal weather conditions. The partial list of ratings below, adapted by the Atlas World Press Review from the Paris L'Express, illustrates the effects weather has on wine grapes:

Undocumented: personal observation

Undocumented: introduction of borrowed material

> Bordeaux
>
> 1975
>
> A great year, comparable to 1961 and 1928. Many warm, sunny days with little rain gave the wine a rich, concentrated, well-formed quality. . . .
>
> 1976
>
> Strong rains during the grape-gathering spoiled the chances for this to be a great year. . . . The grapes that had been very sugary became swollen and diluted. . . .

Beaujolais

1975

A wine that will leave few memories. Storms and fog disturbed the late harvest. The wines are diluted and less alcoholic, lacking both acidity and character. . . .

1976

Great vintage. The year was hot and dry, the grapes were gathered under ideal conditions. Sugary, rich in tannin, the grape reached maximum maturity, giving a strong aromatic wine.

("French Experts' " 54-55)

Undocumented: topic sentence

Even wine casks make a difference. For years no one understood why European wines had a more "complex bouquet" (fragrance) until an amateur California wine-grower stumbled on the answer: Americans use a different species of oak to make wine casks than do the French. He discovered that the aroma comes from the wood and not the grape (Adams 12).

Undocumented: transitional paragraph and general knowledge

Because of these variables, wines can differ sharply from one another.[2] In fact, it's the difference between grapes that is responsible for the primary difference between wines. There are basically two kinds of grapes: those that produce the premier wines (dinner wines stacked on their sides in liquor stores) and those that produce all the remaining wines (bulk wines often sold by the gallon). Any comparison of French and California wines in international competitions always involves the premier wines--the best of California vying against the best of France.

Two of the grapes that produce premier wines are the chardonnay grape and the cabernet sauvignon grape. The chardonnay grape is a famous white grape that yields a white wine; it is responsible for some of the best and most expensive wines, called Burgundy in France and Chardonnay in America. The cabernet sauvignon is the grape that yields a dry red wine, which is called Bordeaux in France and Cabernet Sauvignon in the United States and is considered one of the finest in the world. Such French wines as Chateau Lafite-Rothschild, Chateau Mouton Rothschild, Chateau Latour, Chateau Margaux, and Chateau Haut-Brion are the most celebrated examples of it. The intriguing question, of course, is how these two sets of wines, produced from the same two grapes but on different sides of the Atlantic, compare with each other.

Undocumented: general knowledge not derived from any one source

Undocumented: reference to thesis

Wine experts seem to agree that as far as taste and quality go, the California Chardonnays today are similar to the French Burgundies (Prial, "Quality" 93). In the early seventies, Hannum and Blumberg had written that "it is not often that a California Chardonnay measures up to the greatness of its name" (45). Since then, however, the Chardonnay, according to Robards, has improved more than any other California varietal wine (a wine derived from, at least, 51 percent of a particular grape); today there are California Chardonnays, like those of the Sonoma Vineyards, River West, Firestone, Robert Mondavi, and Belle Terre, that are the equal of the great French Burgundies ("Thanks" 148).

Unlike the Chardonnays, the California Cabernets are showing indications that they "will develop along different lines" from the Bordeaux of France (Prial, "Quality" 93). In fact, some California Cabernets, like the Private Reserve Cabernet of the Beaulieu Vineyard, are already competing with the best premium Bordeaux of France--the Lafites and the Haut-Brions (Robards, "Premium Red" 54). To quote Hugh Johnson, the internationally renowned British authority on wine, " 'The best of California's wines today are among the world's best' " (Quoted by Adams 11).

Undocumented: topic sentence

Undocumented: introduction of borrowed material

Some California wines are even better than the best, if price is any indicator. California wines are now commanding record prices. A 1970 Heitz Martha's Vineyard Cabernet sells for $40 a bottle (Prial, "Quality" 93); a 1972 California Cabernet outpriced a celebrated Bordeaux at a London auction (Langway 56); and a 12-bottle case of a 1979 Cabernet Sauvignon (which had never been tasted and was so new it hadn't been named yet) sold for a record price for any American wine to date--$24,000. That made it just $7000 short of a world record for any bottle of wine--$31,000 for a Chateau Lafite 1822 ("Wine Talk" 15).

11

California Cabernets are also competing in blind tasting tests with French wines and winning. California winemaker Robert Mondavi finds his Cabernets "often" doing "as well or better than the French" (Prial, "Quality" 93). In 1976, French experts chose a California Cabernet over four French grand cru (meaning "outstanding") Bordeaux (Adams 12); and in 1981, in Ottawa tasters gave the first five places to five California Cabernets, which defeated such famous Bordeaux as Chateau Lafite-Rothschild, Chateau Latour, and Chateau Margaux (Robards, "Talk" 12).

Undocumented: topic sentence

Appropriately enough, Americans, like the French, have become wine drinkers. In 1981, wine outsold liquor in the United States for the first time in its history (Robards, "Outsells" 70). What's more, 80 percent of all the wine Americans drink is domestic (Langway 56). But the most obvious sign of the wine boom in the United States and America's having finally made it as a wine country is the rest of the world's interest in California's wine industry. Wine producers and investors from all over the world are seeing a future in California wines. According to Nika Hazelton, a number of French winegrowers are making California champagnes, Cabernets, and Zinfandels; the Swiss company Nestlé is co-owner of vineyards in Napa Valley; a German bought Buena Vista, the oldest winery in California; the Japanese own one-third of the Firestone Vineyard; and the Thai have investments in the Cambiasco winery (305).

Undocumented: introduction of borrowed material

Undocumented: topic sentence

Undocumented: introduction of borrowed material

12

Undocumented: topic sentence

Undocumented: introduction of borrowed material

But the most flattering proof of all is that the French themselves, whose vineyards have been producing wine for millennia (as compared to 100 years or so in America) and whose country is synonymous with wine the way America's is with Mom and apple pie, think highly enough of the New World to join Californians in making wine. The best example is the Baron Philippe de Rothschild himself, producer of one of the five most celebrated of all red wines, Chateau Mouton Rothschild. He has joined California producer Robert Mondavi in a unique venture to try to create "one of the best American wines ever made" ("Wine Talk" 15).

13

Notes

[1]M. A. Amerine and M. A. Joslyn, Table Wines: The Technology of Their Products, 2nd ed. (Berkeley: U of California P, 1970) 30, qtd. in Asher 83.

Comparison in a content note

[2]Generally speaking, the French and California wines have two things in common. They are grown from the same grapes and in the same kind of dry soil (Adams 4). These similarities ought to make the wine produced rather similar (assuming similar winegrowing techniques as well). But then there is the matter of climate. Unlike France, California has "long rainless growing seasons and . . . mild winters" (Adams 5); much "more reliable weather than Europe's from day to day" (Thompson and Johnson 19); and a bigger range of "microclimates" (Asher 84). Therefore, California can produce more consistently fine wines than France (Hannum and Blumberg 55). It has so many microclimates that it has one suitable for every possible variety of grape (Hannum and Blumberg 36). Adams claims that it is "easier to raise Vinifera grapes in the fabulous climates of California than in any other part of the globe" (222). Therefore, "In the average quality of its wines, California ranks first" (Adams 1). What that means in everyday terms is that the gallon jugs that the average American picks up in his local package store are superior to the wine the average Frenchman drinks and serves to his family every day.

14

Works Cited

Adams, Leon D. The Wines of America. 2nd ed. New York: McGraw-Hill, 1978.

Asher, Gerald. "Wine Journal." Gourmet Feb. 1981: 6+.

"French Experts' Favorite Wines." Atlas: World Press Review Jan. 1978: 54-55.

Hannum, Hurst, and Robert S. Blumberg. The Fine Wines of California. Garden City, NY: Doubleday, 1971.

Hazelton, Nika. "California High." National Review 32 (1980): 305-06.

Langway, Lynn, and others. "Alors! American Wines Come of Age." Newsweek 1 Sept. 1980: 56-57+.

Lichine, Alexis, and William E. Massee. Wines of France. New York: Knopf, 1951.

Prial, Frank J. "Quality from California." New York Times Magazine 10 June 1979: 93.

---. "A Rare Tasting of Lafite-Rothschild Wines." New York Times 30 March 1979, late ed., sec. A: 22.

Robards, Terry. "Giving Thanks with American Vintages." New York Times Magazine 23 Nov. 1980: 148.

---. "Just Humming Along." New York Times 12 Sept. 1982, late ed., sec. 6: 130.

---. "A Premium Red from the West." New York Times Magazine 16 Aug. 1981: 54.

---. "Wine Outsells Spirits." New York Times 14 June 1981, late ed., sec. 1: 70.

15

---. "Wine Talk." New York Times 21 Jan. 1981, late ed., sec. 3: 12.

Simon, André L. The International Wine and Food Society's Encyclopedia of Wines. London: International Wine and Food Publishing, 1972.

Thompson, Bob, and Hugh Johnson. The California Wine Book. New York: William Morrow, 1976.

Waugh, Alec. In Praise of Wine and Certain Noble Spirits. New York: William Sloane, 1959.

"Wine Talk." New York Times 24 June 1981, late ed., sec. C: 15.

Appendix
Selected Reference Books

Generally speaking, most reference books fall into the following categories: **guides** to a particular subject field providing an overview of the subject as well as commentary on how to trace information and on the types of reference works available; **encyclopedias** containing information on all subjects or limited to a specific field and sometimes referred to as "dictionaries," in the secondary meaning of the word, as alphabetized lists of information on a subject; **dictionaries** explaining all the words of a language or the specialized terms of a specific subject field; **biographical dictionaries** containing the lives of people arranged in alphabetical order; **bibliographies** containing lists of books and sometimes other material such as periodical articles, frequently arranged by subject; **indexes** containing lists usually of periodical articles, frequently arranged by subject; **abstracts** containing extracts or summaries of published reading material; **yearbooks** reviewing the events of the year and, therefore, published annually; **almanacs** containing miscellaneous information, including statistics and usually published annually; **gazetteers** containing geographical, historical, or statistical information; **atlases** containing maps of the world or a specific region; **directories** containing lists of names of residents, organizations, or businesses.

This appendix makes no attempt to be complete or cover all available types of reference sources on a given subject. The purpose of the citations is merely to provide you with some of the standard and indispensable references specializing in a particular subject area, while the purpose of the list above is to inform you of the types of works often available on a subject. Therefore, if you can't find what you're looking for in the appendix, consult your librarian for the type of reference you need.

Generally, the citations for each subject (and for each division within the subject in the case of broad fields like history, for instance, where reference coverage is very extensive) observe the order of categories in the preceding list. Thus guides (if any) will precede encyclopedias (if any), which will precede dictionaries, and so on. Any reference material that falls outside the categories indicated above is listed last in each subject field.

The appendix covers the following subject fields:

The Humanities	*The Sciences: Pure and Applied*	*The Social Sciences*
Architecture	Biology	Anthropology
Art	Chemistry	Business and Economics
Dance	Computer Science	Education
Film	Engineering	Folklore
Literature	Food and Agriculture	History
Music	Mathematics	Mythology
Philosophy	Physics	Political Science
Religion	Psychology	Sociology and Social Work
Theater	Space, Astronomy, and Earth Sciences	Women Studies

GENERAL

Sheehy, Eugene P. *Guide to Reference Books.* 9th ed. Chicago: American Library Assn., 1976. Supplements, 1980, 1982. An annotated guide, arranged by subject, to the identification of *all* the reference books in *all* the subject fields. Indispensable for reference material and subjects not covered below.

Bell, Marion V., and Eleanor A. Swidan. *Reference Books: A Brief Guide.* 8th ed. Baltimore: Enoch Pratt Library, 1978. A short but useful annotated guide to the principal and most indispensable reference books in the major subject fields.

Both of the reference guides above have been invaluable in the preparation of the list below.

THE HUMANITIES

ARCHITECTURE

Smith, Denison L. *How to Find Out in Architecture and Building: A Guide to Sources of Information.* Oxford: Pergamon, 1967.

Sturgis, Russell. *Dictionary of Architecture and Building: Biographical, Historical, and Descriptive.* 3 vols. New York: Macmillan, 1901; rpt. Detroit: Gale, 1966. Encyclopedic in content and a standard work in the field. Describes famous examples of architecture in various countries.

Encyclopedia of Modern Architecture. Ed. Wolfgang Fehnt. New York: Abrams, 1963.

American Association of Architectural Bibliographers. *Papers.* Charlottesville: UP of Virginia, 1965– . Lists bibliographies covering architects, specific eras, and architectures.

Ekistic Index, Jan. 1968– . Athens: Athens Technological Organization, 1968– . Ekistics is the science of urban planning. Index lists periodical articles of interest to urban planners, architects, social scientists, and so on.

ART

Carrick, Neville. *How to Find Out About the Arts: A Guide to Sources of Information.* Oxford: Pergamon, 1965.

Chamberlin, Mary W. *Guide to Art Reference Books.* Chicago: American Library Assn., 1959. A more comprehensive guide than the one above. Includes a bibliography.

Encyclopedia of World Art. 15 vols. New York: McGraw-Hill, 1959–1968.

Britannica Encyclopedia of American Art. Chicago: Encyclopedia Britannica, 1973.

Lucas, E. Louise. *Art Books: A Basic Bibliography on the Fine Arts.* Greenwich, CT: New York Graphic Soc., 1968.

Ryerson Library, The Art Institute of Chicago. *Index to Art Periodicals.* 11 vols. Boston: Hall, 1962.

DANCE

The Dance Encyclopedia. Comp. Anatole Chujoy and P. W. Manchester. Rev. and enl. ed. New York: Simon & Schuster, 1967.

Guide to Dance Periodicals, 1931–1962. 10 vols. Comp. S. Yancey Belknap. Gainesville: U of Florida P, 1948–1963.

FILM

Manchel, Frank. *Film Study: A Resource Guide.* Rutherford, NJ: Fairleigh Dickinson UP, 1973. Covers the approaches traditionally used to study film. Includes information on books and film rentals.

The Film Index: A Bibliography. New York: Museum of Modern Art Film Library, 1941. Lists books, periodical articles, and film reviews of various types of films including cartoons.

Film Literature Index. Vol. 1. Albany, NY: Filmdex, 1974. Lists articles from about 300 periodicals.

The New York Times Film Reviews, 1913–1968. 6 vols. New York: New York Times and Arno, 1970.

Halliwell, Leslie. *The Filmgoer's Companion.* 4th ed. New York: Hill, 1974. Lists films, performers, biographies of actors, producers, writers, and other valuable information on films.

LITERATURE

Atlick, Richard Daniel, and Andrew Wright. *Selective Bibliography for the Study of English and American Literature.* 4th ed. New York: Macmillan, 1971. A guide to important reference tools in the field.

Cassell's Encyclopedia of World Literature. Ed. J. Buchanan-Brown. 3 vols. New York: Morrow, 1973.

Holman, Clarence H. *A Handbook to Literature.* 3rd ed. Indianapolis: Odyssey, 1972. Explains terms, concepts, schools, and literary movements.

Literatures of the World in English Translation: A Bibliography. New York: Ungar, 1967–1970. Lists not only the translations of foreign literatures but also books on the background of each foreign literature.

Columbia Dictionary of Modern European Literature. Horatio Smith, gen. ed. New York: Columbia UP, 1947. A scholarly dictionary of major European literary works and authors of the twentieth century and the preceding decades. Includes bibliographies.

Harvey, Sir Paul. *The Oxford Companion to English Literature.* Rev. Dorothy Eagle. 4th ed. Oxford: Clarendon, 1967. Dictionary of English authors, works, literary characters, and so on. Includes synopses.

Hart, James David. *The Oxford Companion to American Literature.* 4th ed. New York: Oxford UP, 1965. A standard work. Dictionary of articles on American authors and their most important works. Includes discussions of their cultural and social background as well as synopses.

The New Cambridge Bibliography of English Literature. Vols. 1–3, ed. George Watson. Vol. 4, ed. I. R. Willison. New York: Cambridge UP, 1969–1974. Indispensable as a first bibliographical reference source. Covers English literature from 600 to 1950.

Howard-Hill, T. H. *Bibliography of British Literary Bibliographies.* Oxford: Clarendon, 1969– . Covers books and periodical articles published in the English-speaking countries after 1890.

Modern Humanities Research Association. *Annual Bibliography of the English Language and Literature, 1920–* . Cambridge: Cambridge UP, 1921– . Includes books, pamphlets, and periodical articles on both English and American literature.

Howard-Hill, T. H. *Shakespearean Bibliography and Textual Criticism: A Bibliography.* Oxford: Clarendon, 1971.

Rush, Theresa G., and others. *Black American Writers, Past and Present: A Biographical and Bibliographical Dictionary.* 2 vols. Metuchen, NJ: Scarecrow, 1975. Covers black American writers of the last 300 years.

MUSIC

Duckles, Vincent H. *Music Reference and Research Materials: An Annotated Bibliography.* 3rd ed. New York: Free Press, 1974. A guide to the reference works in the field.

Grove's Dictionary of Music and Musicians. 5th ed. 9 vols. Ed. Eric Blom. New York: St. Martin's, 1954. Supplement, 1961. Provides articles on the field beginning around 1450.

Fuld, James J. *The Book of World-Famous Music: Classical, Popular and Folk.* Rev. and enl. ed. New York: Crown, 1971. Provides articles on all varieties of songs for the last 500 years.

Stambler, Irwin. *Encyclopedia of Pop, Rock and Soul.* New York: St. Martin's, 1974. Covers popular music of past decade. Excludes country and western.

Kinkle, Roger D. *The Complete Encyclopedia of Popular Music and Jazz, 1900–1950.* 4 vols. New Rochelle, NY: Arlington House, 1974. Topics include Broadway musicals, country and western, and so on.

Feather, Leonard. *The Encyclopedia of Jazz in the Sixties/Seventies.* New York: Horizon, 1966. Covers more recent material than the preceding entry.

Ewen, David. *The New Encyclopedia of the Opera.* New York: Hill & Wang, 1971.

The Music Index: The Key to Current Music Periodical Literature, 1949– . Detroit: Information Coordinators, 1950– . Lists over 300 periodicals on all aspects of music (including retailing, for example) as well as reviews of musical performances and recordings.

Sears, Minnie Earl. *Song Index.* 2 vols. New York: Wilson, 1926. Supplement. New York: Wilson, 1934; rpt. 2 vols. in 1. Hamden, CT: Shoe String, 1966. A comprehensive index not of articles but of songs themselves—over 12,000. Used for locating and identifying titles, composers, lyrics, and music.

PHILOSOPHY

De George, Richard T. *A Guide to Philosophical Bibliography and Research.* New York: Appleton, 1971. Cites the encyclopedias, bibliographies, dictionaries, histories, and journals available on the subject.

The Encyclopedia of Philosophy. Ed. Paul Edwards. New York: Macmillan, 1967. Scholarly and thorough. Covers Eastern and Western philosophy of all periods. Includes bibliographies.

The Philosopher's Index: An International Index to Philosophical Periodicals. Bowling Green, OH: Bowling Green UP, 1967– . Covers primarily American and British periodicals.

RELIGION

A Dictionary of Comparative Religion. Ed. S. G. F. Brandon. New York: Scribner's, 1970. Encyclopedic in content. Contains articles on the world's major religions and cults from ancient times to the present. Includes articles on related topics such as anthropology and music as they pertain to religion.

Miller, Madeleine Sweeney, and J. L. Miller. *Encyclopedia of Bible Life.* Rev. ed. New York: Harper, 1955. Invaluable source of information on such topics as animals, flowers, clothes, homes, and so on of Biblical times.

Barrow, John G. *A Bibliography of Bibliographies in Religion.* Ann Arbor, MI: Edwards, 1955. Authoritative and comprehensive. Lists all the published bibliographies in religion.

Burr, Nelson R. *A Critical Bibliography of Religion in America.* Princeton, NJ: Princeton UP, 1961. Covers books, articles, and dissertations.

Wright, George, and Floyd V. Filson. *The Westminster Historical Atlas to the Bible.* Rev. ed. Philadelphia: Westminster, 1956. Features historical and archeological commentary, maps, photographs, and a table of dates placing Biblical events in a historical setting.

THEATER

Brockett, Oscar Gross, and others. *A Bibliographical Guide to Research in Speech and Dramatic Art.* Chicago: Scott, Foresman, 1963. Lists reference works useful to the study of theater arts.

Baker, Blanch M. *Theatre and Allied Arts: A Guide to Books Dealing with the History, Criticism, and Technic of the Drama and Theatre and Related Arts and Crafts.* New York: Wilson, 1952. A bibliography of about 6000 titles published between 1885 and 1948 on all aspects of the theater and related arts.

Annotated Bibliography of New Publications in the Performing Arts. New York: Drama Book Shop, 1970– .

Stratman, Carl Joseph. *American Theatrical Periodicals, 1789–1967: A Bibliographical Guide.* Durham, NC: Duke UP, 1970.

The New York Times Theater Reviews, 1920–1974. 10 vols. New York: New York Times and Arno, 1971–1975.

THE PHYSICAL SCIENCES

GENERAL

Malinowsky, Harold Robert. *Science and Engineering Reference Sources.* Rochester, NY: Libraries Unlimited, 1967. A guide to the most important reference works in science in general and in astronomy, biology, chemistry, engineering, geology, mathematics, medicine, and physics in particular.

McGraw-Hill Encyclopedia of Science and Technology. 3rd ed. 15 vols. New York: McGraw-Hill, 1971.

BIOLOGY

Bottle, R. T., and H. V. Wyatt, eds. *The Use of Biological Literature.* 2nd ed. Hamden, CT: Archon, 1971. A guide to the reference sources in the biological sciences, including such specialized areas as biochemistry, biophysics, ecology, genetics, microbiology, and so on.

Gray, Peter, ed. *The Encyclopedia of the Biological Sciences.* 2nd ed. New York: Van Nostrand Reinhold, 1970. Includes bibliographies.

Walker, Ernest P. *Mammals of the World.* 3rd ed. 2 vols. Baltimore: Johns Hopkins UP, 1975. Includes description and illustration of almost every known genus. Includes bibliography.

Blake, Sidney Fay, comp. *Geographical Guide to Floras of the World: An Annotated List with Special Reference to Useful Plants and Common Plant Names.* Washington: GPO, 1942, 1961. Lists books, monographs, and periodical articles on the world's plants. Arranged by geographical area.

CHEMISTRY

Woodburn, Henry M. *Using the Chemical Literature: A Practical Guide.* New York: Marcel Dekker, 1974.

Chemical Technology: An Encyclopedic Treatment. 8 vols. New York: Barnes & Noble, 1968–1975. Helpful to nonspecialists on topics of applied chemistry, including industrial processes and manufacturing.

Chemical Abstracts, 1907– . Columbus, OH: American Chemical Soc., 1907– . Indexes current articles in the field.

COMPUTER SCIENCE

Carter, Ciel. *Guide to Reference Sources in the Computer Sciences.* New York: Macmillan, 1974.

ENGINEERING

Mildren, K. W., ed. *Use of Engineering Literature.* Boston: Butterworths, 1976. A guide to the literature in the field, including such specific areas as automotive engineering, metallurgy, and so on.

Engineering Index, 1884– . New York: Engineering Index, 1934– . International in scope. Indexes over 3500 journals.

FOOD AND AGRICULTURE

Blanchard, Jay Richard, and Harald Ostvold. *Literature of Agricultural Research.* Berkeley: U of California P, 1958. Though somewhat dated, a useful guide to reference works in the field, which includes food and nutrition.

Johnson, Arnold, and Martin S. Peterson. *Encyclopedia of Food Technology and Food Science.* 2 vols. Westport, CT: AVI Publishing, 1974.

U.S. National Agricultural Library. *Bibliography of Agriculture, 1942–* . Phoenix, AZ: Oryz, 1975– . Gives international coverage to such areas as animal industry, fertilizers, forestry, rural sociology, and so on.

MATHEMATICS

Dick, Elie M. *Current Information Sources in Mathematics: An Annotated Guide to Books and Periodicals, 1960–1972.* Littleton, CO: Libraries Unlimited, 1973.

Mathematical Association of America. Committee on the Undergraduate Program in Mathematics. *A Basic Library List for Four-Year Colleges.* 2nd ed. Washington: Mathematical Assn. of America, 1976. A bibliography of books and periodicals arranged by subject.

PHYSICS

Besançon, Robert M. *The Encyclopedia of Physics.* 2nd ed. New York: Van Nostrand Reinhold, 1974. Accessible to nonspecialists as well as specialists. Includes a bibliography.

Current Physics Index, 1975– . New York: American Institute of Physics, 1975.

PSYCHOLOGY

Bell, James Edward. *A Guide to Library Research in Psychology.* Dubuque, IA: Brown, 1971. Intended for the undergraduate student.

Goldenson, Robert M. *The Encyclopedia of Human Behavior.* 2 vols. Garden City, NY: Doubleday, 1970. Provides both case histories and articles on various topics of psychology, psychiatry, and mental health.

Harvard University. *The Harvard List of Books in Psychology.* 4th ed. Cambridge, MA: Harvard UP, 1971. Lists over 700 books.

Bibliographic Guide to Psychology, 1975– . Boston: G. K. Hall, 1976. Annual list of publications.

Tompkins, Margaret, and Norma Shirley. *A Checklist of Serials in Psychology and Allied Fields.* 2nd ed. Troy, NY: Whitston, 1976. Lists over 400 periodicals.

SPACE, ASTRONOMY, AND EARTH SCIENCES

Fairbridge, Rhodes W., ed. *The Encyclopedia of Atmospheric Sciences and Astrogeology.* Vol. 2 of *Encyclopedia of Earth Sciences.* New York: Reinhold, 1967.

———. *The Encyclopedia of Oceanography.* Vol. 1 of *Encyclopedia of Earth Sciences.* New York: Reinhold, 1966. Both volumes 1 and 2 (above) are accessible to the nonspecialist and specialist alike. Includes bibliographies.

Bibliography and Index of Geology. Washington: Geological Society of America, 1924– .

THE SOCIAL SCIENCES

GENERAL

White, Carl M., and others. *Sources of Information in the Social Sciences: A Guide to the Literature.* 2nd ed. Chicago: American Library Assn., 1973. Covers anthropology, business administration, economics, education, geography, history, political science, psychology, and sociology.

Encyclopedia of the Social Sciences. 15 vols. New York: Macmillan, 1930–1935. Reissue, 8 vols., 1937. Comprehensive and authoritative. Emphasizes the historical aspects of the field. Includes bibliographies.

International Encyclopedia of the Social Sciences. Ed. David L. Sills. 17 vols. New York: Macmillan, 1968. Complements the encyclopedia above. Emphasizes the analytical and comparative aspects of the various disciplines. Includes bibliographies.

London Bibliography of the Social Sciences. London: London School of Economics, 1931–1932. Supplement, 1934–1975. International in scope and the most basic and extensive bibliography in the field.

Public Affairs Information Service (PAIS). Bulletin, 1915– . New York: Public Affairs Info. Service, 1915– . Indispensable index to books, periodicals, documents, pamphlets, reports of public/private agencies, and so on relating to public and economic affairs.

ANTHROPOLOGY

Frantz, Charles. *The Student Anthropologist's Handbook: A Guide to Research, Training, and Career.* Cambridge, MA: Schenkman, 1972. A guide to the use of libraries, museums, reference works in the field.

Winick, Charles. *Dictionary of Anthropology.* New York: Philosophical Library, 1956; rpt. Westport, CT: Greenwood, 1969. The brief entries are helpful in the absence of an encyclopedia on the subject.

International Bibliography of Social and Cultural Anthropology. Vol. 1, 1955– . Chicago: Aldine, 1958– .

The Human Relations Area Files. Collections of data available in hard copy or microform at numerous libraries throughout the country. The data consist of files, each on a different culture: primitive, historical, and contemporary. Each file contains information on source materials (books, articles, etc.) relevant to that culture.

BUSINESS AND ECONOMICS

Fletcher, John, ed. *The Use of Economics Literature.* London: Butterworths, 1971. Guide to reference materials in economics and its various subject areas.

Coman, Edwin T. *Sources of Business Information.* Rev. ed. Berkeley: U of California P, 1964. A guide to reference books in accounting, advertising, finance, foreign trade, insurance, marketing, management, public relations, real estate, statistics, and so on.

Heyel, Carl, ed. *The Encyclopedia of Management.* 2nd ed. New York: Van Nostrand Reinhold, 1973. Covers all aspects of industrial management such as retirement plans, work simplification, and so on. Includes bibliography.

Encyclopedia of Accounting Systems. Ed. Jerome K. Pescow. Rev. and enl. ed. 3 vols. Englewood Cliffs, NJ: Prentice-Hall, 1975. Articles arranged by specific type of business: meatpacking, department stores, and so on.

McGraw-Hill Dictionary of Modern Economics: A Handbook of Terms and Organizations. Ed. Douglas Greenwald. 2nd ed. New York: McGraw-Hill, 1973. For the nonspecialist.

Alexander Hamilton Institute. *2001 Business Terms and What They Mean.* New York: Institute, 1962.

Business Books in Print, 1973– . New York, 1973– . Lists all the business books published by author, title, and subject.

Fundaburk, Emma Lila. *Reference Materials and Periodicals in Economics: An International List.* Metuchen, NJ: Scarecrow, 1971–1972. Includes such related areas as agriculture, major manufacturing industries, and commerce.

International Bibliography of Economics. Vol. 1, 1952– . Chicago: Aldine, 1955– .

Index of Economic Articles in Journals and Collective Volumes, 1886/1924– . Homewood, IL: R. D. Irwin, 1961– . Lists articles in the periodicals of various countries.

Accountants' Index. New York: American Institute of Accountants, 1921– . Lists books, periodical articles, and pamphlets.

Statistics Sources. Ed. Paul Wasserman. 4th ed. Detroit: Gale, 1974. Covers American and international statistics in very specific subject areas such as soil conservation, Swedish advertising, and so on.

Consumers Index to Product Evaluations and Information Sources, 1973– . Ann Arbor, MI: Pierian, 1974– . Lists books, periodical articles, and pamphlets evaluating consumer goods and services.

EDUCATION

Burke, Arvid J., and Mary A. Burke. *Documentation in Education.* New York: Teachers College, 1967. A guide to the use of the library by students of education with helpful information on pertinent reference books.

Monroe, Paul, ed. *Cyclopedia of Education.* 5 vols. in 3. New York: Macmillan, 1911–1913; rpt. 5 vols. Detroit: Gale, 1968. Covers world education in all historical periods. Excellent for historical and comparative purposes but out of date for recent trends. Includes bibliographies.

World Survey of Education. 5 vols. Paris: UNESCO, 1955–1971. Separate volumes devoted to primary, secondary, and higher education of many countries.

Harris, Chester W. *Encyclopedia of Educational Research.* 4th ed. New York: Macmillan, 1969. Useful for summaries of studies in the field on diverse topics like attendance, grades, and so on. Selected bibliography included.

The Encyclopedia of Education. Ed. Lee C. Deighton. 10 vols. New York: Macmillan and Free Press, 1971. Focuses on American education with most entries citing books and journal articles on the subject.

Education Index, 1929– : A Cumulative Subject Index to a Selected List of Educational Periodicals, Proceedings, and Yearbooks. New York: Wilson, 1932– .

Current Index to Journals in Education, 1969– . New York: Macmillan Information, 1969– .

FOLKLORE

Thompson, Stith. *The Folktale.* New York: Dryden, 1946. A guide to the field: folktales, methods, and bibliographies.

Funk and Wagnalls Standard Dictionary of Folklore, Mythology and Legend. Eds. Maria Leach and Jerome Fried. New York: Funk & Wagnalls, 1973. Covers not only the mythologies of the world but also customs, dances, fairytales, songs, dances, games, and proverbs. Includes bibliographies.

Frazer, Sir James George. *The Golden Bough: A Study in Magic and Religion.* 3rd ed. London: Macmillan, 1907–1915. 12 vols.; rpt. London: Macmillan, 1955. Not a reference work but a study of primitive religions that has become a classic in its field. Covers such matters as taboos, myths of the dying god, the scapegoat motif, fire festivals, and so on. Includes bibliography. For an updating of Frazer's original work see *Aftermath: A Supplement to the Golden Bough.* London: Macmillan, 1936, and *The New Golden Bough: A New Abridgment of the Classic Work.* Ed. Theodor H. Gaster. New York: Criterion, 1959.

Robbins, Russell Hope. *The Encyclopedia of Witchcraft and Demonology.* New York: Crown, 1959. Covers primarily the period 1450–1750. Includes a bibliography.

Haywood, Charles. *A Bibliography of North American Folklore and Folksong.* 2nd ed. New York: Dover, 1961.

HISTORY

American Historical Association. *Guide to Historical Literature.* Ed. G. F. Howe and others. New York: Macmillan, 1961. A standard guide to the historical writings and reference works on the subject and related topics such as anthropology.

Langer, William Leonard. *An Encyclopedia of World History, Ancient, Medieval, and Modern: Chronologically Arranged.* 5th ed. Boston: Houghton Mifflin, 1972. Emphasis primarily on diplomatic, political, and military history.

Freeman-Grenville, G. S. P. *Chronology of World History: A Calendar of Principal Events from 3000 B.C. to A.D. 1973.* Totowa, NJ: Rowman and Littlefield, 1975. Covers the same ground as Langer above, but also includes cultural, artistic, and scientific events in its chronological table.

Cambridge Ancient History. 12 vols. Cambridge: University Press; New York: Macmillan, 1923–1939.

Cambridge Medieval History. 8 vols. Cambridge: University Press; New York: Macmillan, 1911–1936.

Cambridge Modern History. Ed. A. W. Ward and others. 13 vols. Cambridge: University Press; New York: Macmillan, 1902–1926. The three excellent histories above, written by specialists, are frequently used for reference. Extensive bibliographies included at the end of each volume.

New Cambridge Modern History. 12 vols. Cambridge: University Press, 1957–1970. Does not include bibliographies.

American Universities Field Staff. *A Select Bibliography: Asia, Africa, Eastern Europe, Latin America.* New York, 1960. Supplement, 1961–1971. New York, 1973. Nearly 7000 books and periodical articles arranged by geographical area and subject.

Harvard Guide to American History. Ed. Frank Freidel. Rev. ed. 2 vols. Cambridge, MA: Harvard UP, 1974. A guide to the reference materials on all aspects and periods of American history.

Dictionary of American History. Ed. Louise B. Ketz. 7 vols. New York: Scribner's, 1976. Encyclopedic in content. Covers topics related to American history and life, including that of Indians and blacks.

U.S. Library of Congress. General Reference and Bibliography Division. *A Guide to the Study of the United States of America.* Washington: GPO, 1960. Supplement, 1956–1965. Washington: GPO, 1976. A supplement covering 1966–1975 is in preparation. A bibliography covering all aspects of American civilization: government, law, medicine, military, religion, and so on.

Writings on American History, 1902– . 1902, Princeton, NJ: Library Book Store; 1903, Washington: Carnegie Institution; 1906–1908, New York: Macmillan; 1912–1917, New Haven, CT: Yale; 1909–1911, 1918–1961, Washington: GPO; 1962– , Washington/Millwood, NY: American Historical Assn./Kraus-Thomson (1962–1973 in 4 vols.). Index 1902–1940. Washington: American Historical Assn., 1956. Annually lists books and periodical articles dealing with U.S. history conceived in the broadest sense to include cultural, political, and economic history.

Carruth, Gorton, ed. *The Encyclopedia of American Facts and Dates.* 6th ed. New York: Crowell, 1972. A chronological table of events in American history, including events in such related areas as American literature, art, education, sports, science, and so on.

Hodge, F. W. *Handbook of American Indians North of Mexico.* 2 vols. Washington: GPO, 1907–1910; rpt. Westport, CT: Greenwood, 1969. Provides articles on various aspects of the subject: Indian history, manners, tribes, institutions, and so on.

Klein, Barry T., and Daniel Icolari, eds. *Reference Encyclopedia of the American Indian.* 2nd ed. Rye, NY: Todd Publications, 1973. Includes a bibliography as well as a directory of addresses (government agencies, etc.) pertinent to the subject.

Smythe, Mabel M., ed. *The Black American Reference Book.* Englewood Cliffs, NJ: Prentice-Hall, 1976. Covers a wide variety of topics: Afro-American music, family life, relations with Africa, and so on.

Smith, Dwight L. *Afro-American History: A Bibliography.* Santa Barbara, CA: ABC-Clio, 1974. Lists periodical articles as well as books and gives nearly 3000 summaries of articles.

MYTHOLOGY

Mythologies of the World: A Concise Encyclopedia. Ed. Max S. Shapiro. Garden City, NY: Doubleday, 1979. Brief discussions of deities, place names, terms, and so on.

Mythology of All Races. Louis Herbert Gray, ed., vols. 1, 3, 6, 9–12; John Arnott Macculloch and G. F. Moore, eds., vols. 2, 4–5, 7–8, 13. Boston: Archaeological Institute of America, Marshall Jones Co., 1916–1932. Each volume is devoted to the mythology of a separate race of people, including Eddic, Finno-Ugric, Siberian, and Oceanic. Valuable references to secondary sources made in the text.

Diehl, Katharine Smith. *Religions, Mythologies, Folklores: An Annotated Bibliography.* 2nd ed. New York: Scarecrow, 1962.

POLITICAL SCIENCE

Brock, Clifton. *The Literature of Political Science.* New York: Bowker, 1969. A guide to the reference works in the field including the publications of the U.S. government, the United Nations, and other international organizations.

Foreign Affairs Bibliography: A Selected and Annotated List of Books on International Relations, 1919– . New York: Bowker, 1933– .

International Bibliography of Political Science, 1953– . Chicago: Aldine, 1954– . Covers periodical articles as well as books published in many countries and languages.

United Nations Documents Index. January, 1950– . Lists publications of the United Nations arranged by subject and country.

Treaties and Alliances of the World: An International Survey Covering Treaties in Force and Communities of States. New York: Scribner's, 1974. A collection of significant treaties and international agreements in force as of 1968. Provides summaries of the provisions, and so on.

U.S. Congress. *Congressional Record, 1873–* . Washington: GPO, 1873– . Indispensable for tracing bills and legislation. Provides highlights and summaries of chamber and committee action for both houses.

Congressional Information Service/Index (CIS Index). Washington: CIS, 1970– . Indexes publications of the U.S. Congress and includes summaries of such publications as Congressional reports, papers, hearings, and documents.

SOCIOLOGY AND SOCIAL WORK

Encyclopedia of Social Work. New York: National Assn. of Social Workers, 1965– .

Mitchell, Geoffrey Duncan. *A Dictionary of Sociology.* London: Routledge & Kegan Paul, 1968. Lengthy articles intended for the beginning student.

International Bibliography of Sociology, 1951– . Chicago: Aldine, 1952– . Covers not only books, periodical articles, and pamphlets concerned with social conditions and social welfare but also government publications of many countries.

Handbook of Aging and the Social Sciences. Ed. Robert H. Binstock and Ethel Shanas. New York: Van Nostrand Reinhold, 1976. Provides articles written by specialists on the sociological aspects of aging. Bibliographies included in each chapter.

U.S. Dept. of Health, Education, and Welfare. *Words on Aging: A Bibliography of Selected Annotated References.* Washington: U.S. Administration on Aging, 1970. Supplement, 1971.

Gottlieb, David, and others. *The Emergence of Youth Societies: A Cross-Cultural Approach.* New York: Free, 1966. Lists publications about adolescents throughout the world.

Kalisch, Beatrice J. *Child Abuse and Neglect: An Annotated Bibliography.* Westport, CT: Greenwood, 1978.

Aldous, Joan, and Nancy Dahl. *International Bibliography of Research in Marriage and the Family.* Vol. 2, 1965–1972. Minneapolis: U of Minnesota P, 1974.

History of the Family and Kinship: A Select International Bibliography. Ed. Gerald L. Soliday and others. Millwood, NY: Kraus International, 1980. Arranged by geographical region. Includes chapters that go as far back as classical antiquity.

Poverty and Human Resources Abstracts, 1966– . Ann Arbor, MI: n.p., 1966– . Lists books and periodical articles. Title changed to *Human Resources Abstracts* beginning March 1975.

Bell, Gwen, and others. *Urban Environments and Human Behavior: An Annotated Bibliography.* Stroudsburg, PA: Dowden, Hutchinson & Ross, 1973. Lists books, essays, and periodical articles of many countries.

Abstracts on Criminology and Penology, 1961– . Amsterdam: Excerpta Criminologica Foundation, 1961– . Lists books and periodical articles of many countries.

Miller, Wayne C., and others. *Comprehensive Bibliography for the Study of American Minorities.* New York: New York UP, 1976.

Fisher, William H. *The Invisible Empire: A Bibliography of the Ku Klux Klan.* Metuchen, NJ: Scarecrow, 1980.

U.S. Dept. of Health and Human Services. Office of Refugee Resettlement. *Refugee Resettlement in the U.S.: An Annotated Bibliography on the Adjustment of Cuban, Soviet and Southeast Asian Refugees.* Washington: GPO, 1981. Covers the last twenty years.

U.S. Library of Congress. Congressional Research Service. *Illegal Aliens and Alien Labor: A Bibliography and Compilation of Background Materials, 1970–June 1977.* Washington: GPO, 1977.

SPORTS

Menke, Frank G. *The Encyclopedia of Sports.* 5th ed. Rev. Suzanne Treat. New York: Barnes, 1975. Provides articles as well as sports records, rules, and history.

Nunn, Marshall E. *Sports.* Littleton, CO: Libraries Unlimited, 1976. A bibliography of over 600 books and nearly 100 periodicals on American sports including such areas as martial arts and Olympics.

Turner, Pearl. *Index to Outdoor Sports, Games, and Activities.* Westwood, MA: Faxon, 1978.

WOMEN STUDIES

McKee, Kathleen Burke. *Women's Studies: A Guide to Reference Sources.* Storrs, CT: U of Connecticut Library, 1977.

Goodwater, Leanna. *Women in Antiquity: An Annotated Bibliography.* Metuchen, NJ: Scarecrow, 1975. Includes, among others, women of the Greek, Roman, Etruscan, and Minoan civilizations. Covers books by, as well as about, women.

Jacobs, Sue-Ellen. *Women in Perspective: A Guide for Cross-cultural Studies.* Urbana: U of Illinois P, 1974. A bibliography of books and articles arranged by geographical area as well as subject.

Rosenberg, Marie B., and Len V. Bergstrom. *Women and Society: A Critical Review of the Literature with a Selected Annotated Bibliography.* Beverly Hills, CA: Sage, 1975. Cites well over 3000 books, articles, and other readings.

Index

About the Author

Delija Valiukenas is Professor of English at Bridgewater State College in Bridgewater, Massachusetts, where she has taught since 1973. She received her A.B. from Hunter College of the City University of New York and her Ph.D. from Brown. She has published articles in bilingual studies (translation and comparative poetics) and on Lithuanian literature in both English and Lithuanian language journals.